# Miguel de Unamuno

# MIGUEL DE UNAMUNO

—✳—

*The Agony of Belief*

MARTIN NOZICK

Princeton University Press
Princeton, New Jersey

*To my mother*

"And as for my philosophy, let someone else write about it, some foolish Unamunist. . . ."

*Obras completas,* XI, 1015.

# Preface

ANYONE undertaking an analysis of Unamuno's life and work is bound to recall two of the many contradictions making up the skein of his thought: his enormous contempt for scholars and his equally great thirst for international fame. The first is a sobering thought, but the second lends courage. There is no doubt that Unamuno would have been extremely pleased by the plethora of books and articles on his personality and writings published in Spanish since his death, but depressed by the neglect he suffers in the histories of modern thought and especially in studies of contemporary existentialism done in English. And in the bulky literature readily available in many tongues on Soren Kierkegaard, he, Unamuno, among the first in our century to exalt the Dane's greatness and to assimilate him into his own philosophy, receives meager attention. "I have often observed," Gabriel Marcel states, "that this great Spanish writer is too often neglected when existential thinkers are discussed. . ."[1]

In Spain and Spanish America, despite disapproval by the orthodox and dire predictions to the contrary by such unorthodox but eminent figures as Pío Baroja[2] and Ramón Sender,[3] Unamuno has for some decades been incontestably a classic, his position best summed up by Antonio Machado: ". . . one day we shall have to dedicate Spain to the Archangel Michael, since Spain's Michaels (*Migueles*) have been so illustrious and representative: Miguel Servet, Miguel de Cervantes, Miguel de Molinos and Miguel de Unamuno."[4] Count Keyserling thought Unamuno to be probably the most important Spaniard since Goya;[5] already in 1926 Curtius placed him among the outstanding European writers;[6] and Miguel Cruz Hernández reports that when he visited Martin Heidegger, the latter pointed to the volumes of Unamuno in his library and remarked that Unamuno was the Spanish thinker who had most interested him.[7]

In France Unamuno has had such important admirers as Jean Cassou, Marcel Bataillon, and Pierre Emmanuel, but among the English-speaking intelligentsia his name is not yet one to be reckoned with. To be sure, he inspires awe among our Hispanists, and although this would have delighted Don Miguel, such interest manifests itself mainly in specialized studies and in rare, often unavailable translations, all of which helps his cause only minimally among the general enlightened reading public not especially interested in the Hispanic area.

It is frankly to redress such injustice that this book has been written. It cannot be denied that the sheer bulk of Unamuno's work is threatening, that his thought is meandering, incongruent, asystematic, as much the outcroppings of his irrepressible daemon as of ratiocination. Yet Unamuno's central concept of "the tragic sense of life" encompasses not only those religious doubts which have in recent years become especially harrowing, but extends to the other ideological crises of our times: the validity of philosophy and history, the question mark of identity, the dangers of both democracy and its opposing forces, the general obsession with politics, the bad faith of most allegiances.

These and other instabilities of the human condition are what Unamuno's work is about, and he disdains to treat them with the dispassionateness sometimes devoutly to be wished; instead, he acts them out in the various frameworks of essay, novel, poem, and play, with his own mercurial personality as protagonist, making us react with mind, emotions, and viscera. It is therefore impossible to separate his biography—chronological and spiritual—from his work, and while the first chapter of this study provides a more or less schematic outline of the subject's life, fuller treatment is left for subsequent chapters, particularly those concerned with his political actions and reactions.

If, in terms of Spanish literature, Unamuno is a major figure within a generation of major figures, he yet exceeds them in his relevance not only to the problems of his own country, but to the all-inclusive religious concern which, in Kierkegaardian terms, cannot be separated from any of life's activities. Politics, aesthetics, ethics, all of these are determined, Unamuno shows, by the degree of one's involvement with the ultimate question, and so thoroughly is he convinced of the validity of his convictions that he will not take the trouble to support them by orderly, sequential arguments. If, as Ortega y Gasset said, Unamuno's virtues are gigantic, so are his defects,[8] and it does not seem fair to follow the example of many an idolatrous "Unamunist" and present only the positive side of the author's performance, since in so outstanding a figure a frank discussion of weaknesses and limitations adds to the roundness and humanity of the portrait.

Most of the quotations in this book come from Unamuno's *Obras completas* or *Complete Works* in sixteen volumes, supplemented by others from essays and correspondence not included in the above collection. All translations are mine, including the verse which I have thought best to render into literal English. Since the primary and secondary bibliographies relating to Unamuno are without end, when any single work is being extensively analyzed, quotations from that work will bear no footnotes, while quotations from any other source will be documented.

# *Contents*

# *Chronology*

1864    September 29: Miguel de Unamuno y Jugo born in Bilbao.

1874    Witnesses the Carlist siege of Bilbao.

1875-   Secondary education in his native city.
1880

1880-   University of Madrid; doctorate in 1884.
1884

1884-   Gives private lessons and does other teaching in Bilbao;
1891    writes articles for local newspapers; prepares for permanent
        teaching position.

1891    Marries Concepción Lizárraga; wins chair of Greek at
        University of Salamanca where he will live for the rest of
        his life, except for the years of exile.

1895    The essays of *En torno al casticismo* (*On Authentic Tra-
        dition*) published separately; published as a book in 1902.

1897    Year of the religious crisis; starts writing the unpublished
        *Diario* or *Journal;* publishes first novel *Paz en la guerra*
        (*Peace in War*).

1898    Writes play *La esfinge* (*The Sphinx*).

1899    Publication of *Nicodemo el fariseo* (*Nicodemus the Phari-
        see*), and *De la enseñanza superior en España* (*On Uni-
        versity Teaching in Spain*); writes play *La venda* (*The
        Blindfold*).

1900    Named rector of the university; publishes *Tres Ensayos:
        "¡Adentro!" "La ideocracia" "La Fe"* (*Three Essays: "Go
        Within!" "Ideocracy" "Faith"*).

1902    The essays *En torno al casticismo* (*On Authentic Tradi-
        tion*) published in book form; the novel *Amor y pedagogía*
        (*Love and Education*); the travel sketches *Paisajes* (*Land-
        scapes*).

1903    *De mi país* (*From My Native Region*).

1905    *La vida de Don Quijote y Sancho* (*The Life of Don
        Quixote and Sancho*).

1907    *Poesías* (*Poems*).

1908    *Recuerdos de niñez y de mocedad* (*Memories of Childhood
        and Adolescence*).

1910   *Mi religión y otros ensayos breves* (*My Religion and Other Short Essays*).

1911   *Por tierras de Portugal y de España* (*Through Regions of Portugal and Spain*), travel book; *Soliloquios y conversaciones (Soliloquies and Conversations*), essays; *Rosario de sonetos líricos* (*Rosary of Lyrical Sonnets*).

1912   *Contra esto y aquello* (*Against This and That*), essays; his 1898 correspondence with Angel Ganivet published as *El porvenir de España* (*The Future of Spain*).

1913   Publication of Unamuno's central work *Del sentimiento trágico de la vida en los hombres y en los pueblos* (*On the Tragic Sense of Life in Men and Nations*); short stories, *El espejo de la muerte* (*The Mirror of Death*).

1914   Dismissed from rectorship; publication of *Niebla* (*Mist*), first novel to be dubbed *nivola*.

1917   *Abel Sánchez,* novel.

1920   Publication of the complete poem *El Cristo de Velázquez* (*The Christ of Velazquez*); *Tres novelas ejemplares y un prólogo* (*Three Exemplary Novels and a Prologue*).

1921   *La tía Tula* (*Aunt Gertrude*), novel; *Soledad* and *Raquel encadenada* (*Rachel in Chains*), both plays.

1922   *Andanzas y visiones españolas* (*Spanish Travels and Vistas*).

1923   *Rimas de dentro* (*Rhymes from Within*), poetry.

1924   February 21: Unamuno leaves Salamanca for exile to Fuerteventura, one of the Canary Islands, where he arrives March 10. Escapes from the island and arrives in Paris July 28. Publication of *Teresa,* poetry.

1925   Middle of August: Unamuno moves to Hendaye where he spends the remainder of his exile. Publication of *De Fuerteventura a París* (*From Fuerteventura to Paris*), sonnets of exile. *L'Agonie du christianisme* (*The Agony of Christianity*) published in the French translation of Jean Cassou; in 1931 it is published in Spanish as *La agonía del cristianismo.*

1926   *Sombras de sueño* (*Dream Shadows*), *El Otro* (*The Other One*), both plays.

1927   Publication in Spanish of *Cómo se hace una novela* (*How a Novel is Made*) which appeared in 1926 in Cassou's French translation as *Comment on fait un roman.*

1928   *Romancero del destierro* (*Ballads of Exile*).

1929   *El hermano Juan o el mundo es teatro* (*Brother John or The World is a Stage*), a play.

1930   February 9: Unamuno crosses the border back to Spain. Publication of *Dos artículos y dos discursos* (*Two Articles and Two Speeches*).

1931   April 14: Spain is declared a Republic; Unamuno reappointed rector of the University of Salamanca; publication in Spanish of *La agonía del cristianismo*.

1933   Publication of *San Manuel Bueno, mártir y tres historias más* (*St. Manuel Bueno, Martyr, and Three More Stories*). The other three stories are "La novela de Don Sandalio, jugador de ajedrez" ("The Novel of Don Sandalio, Chess-Player"), "Un pobre hombre rico o El sentimiento cómico de la vida" ("A Poor Rich Man, or The Comic Sense of Life"), and "Una historia de amor" ("A Love Story").

1934   May 15: Unamuno's wife dies, followed on July 14 by the death of his married daughter Salomé. In the Fall Unamuno is retired as professor and named lifetime rector of the university.

1936   Receives honorary doctorate from Oxford in late February. The Civil War breaks out on July 17. Unamuno reverses his pro-Franco stand on October 12. Dies December 31.

1937   *Soledad y otros cuentos* (*Soledad and Other Stories*).

1941   *La ciudad de Henoc* (*The City of Enoch*), articles written in 1933.

1943   *Cuenca ibérica* (*Iberian Watershed*), further essays from 1932-1933.

1944   *Paisajes del alma* (*Landscapes of the Soul*), essays.

1945   *La enormidad de España* (*The Enormity of Spain*), essays.

1949   *Visiones y comentarios* (*Vistas and Commentaries*), essays.

1953   *Cancionero* (*Book of Songs*).

1950-
1954   *De esto y de aquello* (*On This and That*), four volumes of essays.

1955   *España y los españoles* (*Spain and the Spaniards*), essays.

1956   *Inquietudes y meditaciones* (*Concerns and Meditations*), essays.

1957   *En el destierro* (*In Exile*), essays.

1959   *Mi vida y otros recuerdos personales* (*My Life and Other Personal Remembrances*), two volumes of essays.

CHAPTER 1

# Biography

WHEN, in the Fall of 1953 the University of Salamanca, the most ancient seat of higher learning in Spain, prepared to celebrate the seven-hundredth anniversary of its foundation, the authorities grew uneasy about the tribute their guests might pay to the memory of Miguel de Unamuno y Jugo, the most important figure closely associated with the university in more than three hundred years.

Throughout his lifetime, Unamuno's heterodox opinions had been sharply criticized as dangerous and heretical. However, after his death, with the unstaunched growth of his fame, books and articles flowed from orthodox pens to demonstrate that the author of *The Tragic Sense of Life* was the enemy of practically every basic dogma of the Church. On September 19 of the jubilee year, the Bishop of the Canary Islands, D. Antonio de Pildain y Zapiain, issued a pastoral letter condemning the writer as the greatest Spanish heretic of modern times; on October 6 the Cardinal Primate of Spain, Enrique Plá y Deniel, summoned the Minister of Education to his palace in Toledo, and an order was forthwith issued prohibiting any homage to the great "heretic" or even any reference to him in the program.

Despite the prohibition, scholars from many countries made their way in the rain to lay flowers at Unamuno's grave, and solemnly visited his house which had been converted into a museum containing his books and other effects. During the convocation in the Great Hall, as each speaker rose to congratulate the university, Unamuno's name cropped up again and again. The eminent scientist, historian, and man of letters Gregorio Marañón, delivered his eulogy and, with it, a rebuke aimed at those who did not appreciate Unamuno's significance, while at the end of the official ceremony, Pedro Laín Entralgo, then rector of the University of Madrid, launched into impassioned praise of "one

of the Spanish masters who will live forever, long after many
generations have died," which excited cheers and enthusiastic
applause, to the chagrin of State and Church.[1]

On January 31, 1957, the *Osservatore Romano* published the
decree of the Supreme Congregation of the Holy Office assigning
to the Index of Forbidden Books two of Unamuno's most contro-
versial and definitive books: *The Tragic Sense of Life* and *The
Agony of Christianity.* This decision was official Vatican confirmation of the previous denunciations by members of the Spanish
hierarchy, especially of the prohibition laid upon *The Tragic Sense
of Life* in 1942 by Plá y Deniel, then Bishop of Salamanca, by
virtue of canon 1309 of the Code of Canon Law, which condemns all books attempting to destroy the foundation of religion,
namely the truth of the existence of God and the immortality of
the soul known through natural reason.

In the same issue of the *Osservatore,* the errors of Unamuno's
works were itemized: he denied the possibility of rational demon-
stration of the existence of God, denied faith and the transcendental order in the name of reason, denied the spirituality and
immortality of the soul, the Trinity, the divinity of Jesus Christ,
original sin, eucharistic transubstantiation, the eternity of the
punishments of Hell. In addition to the ban laid on the two works,
warning was issued against the insidious errors contained in his
other writings, especially in the novella *St. Manuel Bueno, Martyr*
in which the protagonist, a priest who believes neither in the
divinity of Jesus Christ, the immortality of the soul, nor any of the
articles of faith, is delineated as saintly. The Vatican radio, com-
menting on the texts in the *Osservatore,* specified that the inclusion
of two of Unamuno's basic works on the Index was a measure
taken against the deleterious effects exercised by the growing fame
of those books on doctrine and morals, although the Church
expressed no opinion about the literary or philosophical value of
Unamuno's extensive work, nor even judged the author's sincerity.[2]

## I  *The Preparatory Years*

The "arch-heretic and master of heresies,"[3] Miguel de Unamuno
y Jugo, was born in the Basque city of Bilbao on September 29,
1864, the third of six children. His father, who as a young man

had left his native town of Vergara to seek his fortune in Mexico, had on his return to Spain married a niece considerably younger, had opened a bakery in Bilbao, and died when his son was only six. Although he had never received a university education, the elder Unamuno left a library of some four or five hundred volumes on history, philosophy, the social, political, and natural sciences.

In *Memories of Childhood and Adolescence* (*Recuerdos de niñez y de mocedad*) Unamuno recalls his early education at a *colegio* or paying institution sharply distinguished from the free schools, and his development in a conventional middle-class milieu governed by the strictest Catholic tradition. He was never to forget the processions of Holy Week, the first communion representing the culmination of childhood, and the bombardment of Bilbao in 1874 during the last Carlist War, to be later incorporated into his first novel *Peace in War* (*Paz en la guerra*).

In 1875 he entered secondary school, the *Instituto Vizcaíno,* with an enthusiasm that soon gave way to disappointment over the dullness of the subject matter. When the studious adolescent showed signs of faltering health, the doctors prescribed long walks, a habit the mature man was to follow assiduously. Vacations were spent at his grandmother's house in Deusto, near Bilbao, where he acquired that love of field, mountain, and river that enriched his life and work and provided the insights into the sub-historical rock on which all recorded vicissitude is played out.

Long nights of reading and participation in the Congregation of San Luis (St. Aloysius) Gonzaga brought on the first crisis of his soul entering puberty. Those were the days when he "wept without reason," when he gave himself up to periods of prayer, when he revelled in Ossian and "the fantastic creations of inconsistent Basque romanticism." He entered the labyrinth of books and ideas in the hope of finding solutions to eternal problems and read the Catholic apologists Jaime Balmes (1810-1848) and Juan Donoso Cortés (1809-1853), the only philosophers he could find in his father's library. It was in Balmes that he first came across the names of Kant, Fichte, Descartes, Hegel, philosophers Balmes knew only partially and indirectly through translations. Balmes' exact formulas nevertheless delighted the young student for it was only later that he was to understand and stress that "it is madness to try to enclose in equations the infinite complexity of the living world."

It was at this time that, imbued with religious fervor, he opened the Bible at random one day after communion, and came across the passage in Matthew (28:19): "Go ye therefore, and teach all nations . . ." which he interpreted as a command to become a priest. But since he was already in his early teens and in love with the bright-eyed Concha, he decided on another occasion to question the Scriptures in the same fashion and came upon the verse in John (9:27): "He answered them, I have told you already, and ye did not hear: wherefore would ye hear it again?" A sense of life as a series of unresolved contraries was already burgeoning in his brain as he grew aware that needs of the flesh could muffle the call to a virginal life just as pride and rivalry among his friends vitiated the religious spirit of the Congregation.

In 1880 Unamuno began his studies at the School of Philosophy and Letters of the University of Madrid, in a capital just awakening to a cosmopolitanism that had been the exclusive attribute of Barcelona. The introspective Basque youth, withdrawn and proud, aware of his rusticity and subject to religious transports, was swept up in the latest ideological currents; pedagogical innovations spearheaded by the Krausist Giner de los Ríos, the beginnings of national regenerationism, positivism, the Higher Biblical Criticism, Spencerian agnosticism, political radicalism, all pounding against the deeply ingrained orthodox training of his childhood.

Unamuno's state of mind and his intellectual adventures during the four years spent in Madrid may be reconstructed, on his own admission, from those of the young Francisco (Pachico) Zabalbide of the novel *Peace in War*. An orphan at seven and brought up by his uncle, Pachico was delicate and thin, yet devoured by a passion for knowledge. On the threshold of manhood, he passed through a period of mysticism and intellectual avidity; straining toward sainthood, he spent long painful hours on his knees, lost in vague dreams, and at the same time he devoured the books in his uncle's small library, especially Chateaubriand and other "ramblers of romantic Catholicism." At sixteen he went to Madrid where during the first year he attended mass every day and took communion every month, but the attempts to rationalize his faith resulted in a weakening of that very faith. He soon limited his attendance at church to feast days and then once, after Sunday mass, he abandoned the practice completely.

At the same time, his mind was humming with vague ideas, bits of Hegel and the positivists, and he began to arrange concepts symmetrically "like chess problems" in construction of his own theories. Swayed by his uncle's admonitions and memories of his pious mother, his faith described a "backward motion"; after a night of insomnia and spiritual torment, he went to confession, but the "retrocession" was short-lived and he attempted to direct his former faith, which was asleep but not dead, into new channels. He was, however, overcome by a sort of *acedia:* his studies seemed vain in comparison with his bottomless ignorance and the finality of death. "It was a mad terror of nothingness, at finding himself alone in empty time, a mad terror which sent his heart throbbing and made him dream how, lacking air and choking, he fell continuously and without end into eternal emptiness . . ." For Hell did not frighten him so much as unending nothingness.

Pachico was considered eccentric, tiresome, pedantic; those who listened to him discourse felt that he was not addressing them so much as carrying on a conversation with himself. This penchant for inner debate which later became highly-charged, confessional essays, was no doubt fostered by the loneliness the young antisocial Unamuno suffered during those university years when he did little else but study in the library and attend lectures at the *Ateneo,* the center of intellectual life in the capital. When he undertook to learn German he plunged into Hegel's *Logic* as a first text in that language.

As for his courses at the university, it was not so much what his teachers taught that mattered as the way their enthusiasm caught on. If his professor of metaphysics, Ortí y Lara, justified his ignorance of Kant by denouncing such philosophies as injurious and based on error and sin, his teacher of Greek, Lázaro Bardón, had a strong personal impact on the Unamuno who was to teach the same discipline. His initiation into the history of the Spanish language, an area he was also to teach later, came through courses of the erratic Sánchez Moguel, and the rousing way in which Menéndez y Pelayo read aloud in class from a minor national classic taught Unamuno how the effective reading of a text could point up its artistic values.

In June of 1883 Unamuno received the licentiate degree, and

after one more year was awarded the doctorate with a thesis called *Critical Study of the Problem of the Origins and Prehistory of the Basque Race* (*Crítica del problema sobre el origen y prehistoria de la raza vasca*) in which he destroyed the validity of all speculation on the origins of the Basque people and their tongue.

In 1884 Unamuno returned to his native city of Bilbao where for seven years he continued studying in preparation for the competitive teaching examinations known as the *oposiciones,* while supporting himself by giving private lessons and by part-time teaching in the Bilbao schools. He did work on the Basque language, published in regional newspapers, even translated a part of Wilhelm von Humboldt's *Reiseskizzen aus Biscaya* (*Basque Travel Sketches*) but resisted any pressure to put his knowledge at the service of the popular separatist sentiments of the Basque provinces or proving the superiority of Basque culture over the Latin.

Research into the Basque language and history was a proper academic pursuit, he would always maintain, but specious and unwholesome when directed towards political ends; therefore, despite the pertinent theme of his doctoral dissertation and subsequent related investigations, when he presented his candidacy in 1888 for the recently established chair of Basque at the *Instituto Vizcaíno* which he had attended as a boy, he was unsuccessful. He tried, also without success, for the chair of Logic, Psychology, and Ethics at the *Instituto,* then for the chair of Metaphysics. He failed, he claims, because of his independent opinions.[4] Although his primary interests lay in the field of thought, he tried twice again for a chair of Latin, and then, presenting himself as candidate before a committee presided over by his former teacher, Marcelino Menéndez y Pelayo, and including the noted novelist Juan Valera, he won the chair of Greek Language at the University of Salamanca. He had frightened all previous examiners, says Juan Arzadun, by his ebulliency and was probably awarded the post in Greek on the assumption that any wild statements made in an ancient language would pass over his students' heads.[5]

The Unamuno who took possession of his professorship on July 13, 1891, had on January 31 of that year married his childhood sweetheart Concepción Lizárraga. Although no other woman seems to have engaged his attention seriously either before or after his marriage to his "Concha," he wrote his friend Arzadun that he was cured of the romantic illusions of ardent, lasting love: "I consider marriage as a serious thing and my Quaker spirit accepts it as the least evil in the world . . ." [6] He was, above all, eager for children, and if he were denied children of his body, he would have "ideal" children born of his pen. Contrary to a Kierkegaard or a Kafka who felt that marriage meant defection from a higher way of life, Unamuno looked upon his Concha as a serene, healthy, warm spirit in a world of stupidity, selfishness, and routine, a mate who would exercise a civilizing influence on his unsociability and would provide a refuge from the nonsense all around him and refreshment from the arduous tasks that lay ahead. Although his wife remained always in the background, Unamuno's references to her provide ample testimony of her indispensable role in his life. Indeed, his greatest homage was to call her "Concha, my habit . . ." (*Concha, mi costumbre . . .*).

With the serenity that came of marriage, and the certainty of a secure position, Unamuno settled in Salamanca in the Fall of 1891 to become "the domesticated bear" (*oso casero*), brilliantly fertile and subversive, flinging paradoxes and thunderbolts over the Hispanic world in an uninterrupted output of novels, short stories, plays, poems, letters, and especially essays in the thousands. There his wife gave him nine children for his solace and the safety of a home or "military tent" (*tienda de campaña*) where he could sire, in addition, those endless children of his pen as assurance of an immortality which, in religious terms, he always questioned. Enjoying robust health despite attacks of hypochondria and depression ("I cannot digest my happiness"),[7] and enveloped by the quiet of the provincial university town that he soon dominated by his presence, he found plentiful time to teach, give public lectures, read, write, and keep in touch with most of the latest developments in the rest of Europe; in short, to forge for himself a position in Spanish intellectual life matched only by that of Croce in Italy.

## II  *Salamanca*

The University of Salamanca traces its beginnings back to the *Studium* established by Alfonso IX in 1218; favored by Alfonso the Wise (1220?-1284), it was placed by Pope Alexander IV on an equal footing with Paris, Oxford, and Bologna. The *Blütezeit* of the university coincided with the artistic, cultural, and political glories of the nation. Peter Martyr recounts that one could scarcely make one's way through the crowds that came in 1488 to hear him lecture on Juvenal; in 1492 Antonio Nebrija published the first Spanish grammar there; Salmantine bishops participated prominently in the Council of Trent, and in the last decades of the sixteenth century, the university boasted of seventy endowed professorial chairs.

There the incomparable religious poet and scholar Fray Luis de León studied, taught, and sought surcease from the din of city and classroom in the orchard of *La Flecha*. There St. John of the Cross studied from 1564 to 1567, and it was there also that the printing presses produced St. Teresa's *Dwellings of the Soul* (*Las Moradas*) and *The Way of Perfection* (*Camino de Perfección*). Góngora studied at the university; it is beyond doubt that Cervantes was well acquainted with both city and school; in 1618 the *Patio de Escuelas* saw the presentation of a religious play of Lope de Vega. Other outstanding literary figures associated with the name of Salamanca are Juan del Encina, one of the initiators of the Spanish Golden Age drama, Fernando de Rojas, author of *La Celestina,* the unknown author of the first picaresque novel *Lazarillo de Tormes,* the dramatists Juan Ruiz de Alarcón, Tirso de Molina, Rojas Zorrilla, Calderón.

By the beginnings of the eighteenth century, however, the tone of the university had fallen so low that when Diego de Torres Villarroel came to the chair of Mathematics in 1726, it had been vacant for thirty years, and when he struggled to establish the Academy of Mathematics, he was opposed on the grounds that "it would be the office of our dishonor." [8] Although towards the end of the eighteenth century Salamanca was the scene of a revival of neoclassical bucolic poetry and saw the presence of such figures as Cadalso and Meléndez Valdés, the university had become a museum of dead culture, an oddity in the European community of the learned. In the nineteenth century, the novelist Pedro de Alarcón noticed "a silence of death that serves as melancholy accompaniment to romantic solitude," [9] and Unamuno could not forget that Carlyle had called the university a "fortress of ignorance" and Remy de Gourmont had judged it a "ghost university." [10]

When the young professor of Greek arrived in Salamanca, it was a town of under 25,000 population, a place where one could idle one's time away or concentrate upon forging one's name and fame and imposing the strength and newness of one's concepts and images on a nation pathetically lacking in great intellectuals. Unamuno was entranced by the splendid ancient palaces, the two magnificent cathedrals, the lovely churches and convents, and especially the enormous, austere Plaza Mayor rimmed by shady arcades, shops, and cafés, where he could discourse at will on all topics, profane and divine, and where deferential friends and admirers could listen in silence to strange concatenations of ideas filtering through the soul of a man whose vocation was not only to arouse the dormant to cultural requirements but to urge them to dream of the immortality of the soul and the importance of each and every man on his way through life to a possible eternity.

### III   *Unamuno and His Generation*

It was in "his" Salamanca that Unamuno brought into focus a vigorous, belligerent faith in his "providential pedagogical or demagogical (the latter being understood in its etymological sense) mission in Spain . . ."[11] Within the tradition of his country, so beautifully if archaically contained in the microcosm of Salamanca, there were forces to be awakened, defined, or strengthened, for as Unamuno meditated on the beauties and virtues of his nation, he could not accept the stagnation of a peninsula that was not only peripheral in its geography but of small significance culturally.

In contradistinction to the growing empires of England, Germany, France, the Low Countries, the Spanish empire had been progressively shrinking in the nineteenth century, and in 1898 Spain was to lose its last important overseas possessions. In the dazzling history of Western scientific and technological advancement, Spain had a right to only the meagerest mention. The theater was flamboyantly romantic; in music a homegrown variety of operetta or *zarzuela* stood beside the awesome development of symphony and opera elsewhere; poetry could boast of the reduced Byronic figure of Espronceda, the picturesqueness of Zorrilla, or the exquisite yet small voice of Bécquer; the novel achieved great breadth in Benito Pérez Galdós, but was otherwise shackled by a regionalism accentuating provincial color and old-fashioned mores. Historical research expanded formidably in the hands of Marcelino Menéndez y Pelayo and his school, but philosophy was still Catholic apologetics.

With the growing consciousness of Spanish backwardness, many minds, aside from Unamuno's, were being roused from national solipsism to an attitude of questioning and a desire to catch up with the rest of Europe or at least select those clues from abroad which would be most useful to national regeneration. If they differed radically among themselves, they agreed on the vital need to create a fresh sense of national purpose and to reenergize thought and expression. Bold and uninhibited, they probed into the hidden riches of Spain while reaching out beyond its barriers: they extolled such early literary figures as Gonzalo de Berceo, the Archpriest of Hita, Jorge Manrique, "rediscovered" El Greco, paid homage to the early nineteenth-century satirist Larra, and were at the same time fascinated by Schopenhauer, Nietzsche, Tolstoy, Verlaine, and Bergson. If they read French eagerly, they also travelled to the sleepy corners of their country and were as impressed by their own landscape as they were by the literary and philosophical splendors of other European lands. In short, they so dramatically incarnated the "uneasy conscience" of their race that Azorín bracketed them under the collective heading of "The Generation of 1898," a name hotly debated but still widely used.

Of that generation, Unamuno must be chosen as *primus inter pares*. Azorín and Valle-Inclán are clearly more subtle stylists, Baroja may be conceded superiority as a novelist, Machado is certainly the more concentrated and "modern" poet, yet Unamuno's fecundity, his unflagging dynamism, the gigantic spectrum of his culture, the Protean variety of his interests, the swiftness of his intuitions, put him at the head of his contemporaries. If he spread himself thin, he also spread himself over the cosmos. Versed in many languages and in philology, in theology, and philosophy, he has with justification been called one of the most extensively "related" thinkers of Western culture.[12] Yet if his frame of reference is of astounding comprehensiveness, he mainly favored those writers and moralists who struck him as foreshadowings or duplications of himself and dubbed them "cardiac" writers since they composed as much with their hearts as with their pens: St. Paul, St. Augustine, Dante, Cervantes, the Spanish mystics, Pascal, Spinoza, Kant, Hegel, Leopardi, Sénancour, the English Lake poets, Kierkegaard, Flaubert, Carducci, the Portuguese end-of-the century poets. And so fiercely did he appropriate these favorites that he transubstantiated them into his own image or abstracted from them only what he could use.

Unlike his contemporaries, he keenly appreciated Portuguese and Catalan literature, wrote extensively on the literature and thought of Latin America, and even envisaged the development of a "Super Castilian" (*sobrecastellano*), a thriving, evolving idiom which would incorporate into itself not only the best of the non-Castilian tongues of the peninsula, but the variants prevalent in the former colonies. All his life he upheld the concept of Hispanic brotherhood based on a common language and without regard for ancestry, color, or creed; in a word, a spiritual imperialism in the highest sense.

His recognition of the Argentine epic *Martín Fierro* as early as 1894 places him in the forefront of that *Weltliteratur* which, still in our day, neglects the artistic productions of Ibero-America, and his interest in the output of the Spanish-speaking nations of the New World extended to such figures as Bolívar, Sarmiento, Zorrilla de San Martín, Martí, José Asunción Silva, Rodó, the Philippine patriot and author José Rizal, and a host of lesser names. He also felt impelled to turn the attention of Hispanic writers, too often entranced by the glitter of the latest artistic fashions in Paris, back to the literary and linguistic values of their heritage. If his *misogalism* or hatred of the *esprit français* did not blind him to those foreign impacts which would enrich Spain without hybridizing her, he was violently inimical to those influences which, in his mind, might weaken or vitiate the national genius. Early in life he had become convinced that Spain was endowed by national temperament and history to suggest to the world the highest degree of man's relationship to the unconditional, and such quasi-Spanish inclinations he found only in foreign writers like Pascal, Sénancour, Amiel, Kierkegaard, Ibsen, Renan.

Marking him off even further from his fellow writers is the fact that Unamuno was the only one of his generation to preach from the university professor's rostrum. He started his official teaching career in Salamanca by occupying one of the two chairs of Greek Language, later called Greek Language and Literature, and in 1900 inaugurated the course in Comparative Latin and Spanish Philology, later called History of the Spanish Language. But the subject matter he imparted to his students was to him the smallest portion of his work since he considered the pursuit of a small particle of knowledge to be a deplorable reduction of the teacher's mission to combat lethargy and to goad students' minds into fertile, independent thought. Objective scholarship required a suspension of judgment, an impersonality and a wariness of approach too alien to his explosive nature and to his uneasy, wide-ranging mind frequently at odds with itself.

Impatient with partial definitions of man as *homo faber* or *ens oeconomicus,* good citizen, professor, scientist, or less flatteringly as "word hunter, frog-dissector, mosquito-catcher or drop-counter," [13] he accused researchers of being so absorbed in paleontological curiosities that they could not hear the mastodon roar with pain or love down the centuries. The easiest way of avoiding the gaze of the Sphinx, he held, was to count the hairs of its tail. [14]

To counteract the divisive effect of compartmentalized interests, Unamuno engaged in constant dialogue to break down barriers and establish the basic community of all men subject to death. He took care, however, to emphasize that communication was not necessarily harmony since agreement is often a disinclination to courageous thinking, and that discord could pose questions to replace conclusive formulas which lead to self-righteousness, fanaticism, and a form of spiritual stoppage resembling death. Commonplaces were dangerous unless rethought and rearranged; petrified thought could be shocked into life through revaluation, through fresh juxtapositions, or downright opposition.

Irritated, frequently to the point of tantrum, by the criteria of common sense and the tendency of any body of knowledge toward fixedness, Unamuno played the game of paradox in order to pit life with its contradictions against the logic that struck him as a consensus of uninspired minds. He wielded his lance not so much against the technical contributions of science as against the hybris which looks upon scientific truth as an ultimate gauge rather than a collection of devices and methods subserving life and clearing the ground for the highest reaches of thought and desire. The methodological sciences observe man as he seems to be rather than as what he strives to be; to Unamuno there was no way of measuring man as the creature who sidesteps and transcends his observable limitations. To simplify the meanings of man in his relationship to himself, to others, and to the divine, to codify his refractory psyche and the supramundane exertions of his personality was dissecting to kill.

If man has any essence, Unamuno maintained, it is his problematicity, and rigorous classification or definition makes of him a laboratory specimen rather than a being whose urge is to an immortality that eludes all knowledge. Unamuno fixed his sights, therefore, on the metaproblem, on the effort to know rather than on a solidified corpus or system of knowledge. To contemplate Supreme Truth is like looking upon the face of God; it is consummation and therefore extermination, while learning, which is an endless extension of conscious activity, is the striving after, but not the acquisition of truth.

### IV  *Unamuno and the University*

Applying such a world-view to the technique of teaching a classical language, Unamuno ruled out the old method of grammatical rules and exercises as too dry and scholastic, although certainly the easiest way for the instructor. As soon as his students had grasped the Greek alphabet well enough to follow him, he translated and commented on a text in class while they learned the declensions and conjugations on their own. "Unamuno could not teach Greek except as a philosopher," [15] for he understood that Spain was in need of much more than trained Hellenists; national conditions required the universities to develop the *tête bien faite* rather than *bien garnie,* the wide-awake intelligence and not the specialist or *Fachmann,* locked in his own world of minutiae and perpetuated by professors lacking the sense of urgency.

Throughout his career, Unamuno was violently outspoken about the intellectual inadequacies of his colleagues, and even stressed the indispensability of government inspection which, despite its disadvantages, would eliminate such cases as that of the history teacher who, disregarding the unification of Italy, still referred to the Papal States and the various duchies. He himself advised students not to attend classes in which pre-Lavoisier chemistry was taught, or Ptolemaic astronomy, or eighth-century logic, or an ethos based on Hell.[16] Those involved in the life of the intellect must learn to feel aggrieved at the poverty of Spanish life on every level, and must with every instrument at their disposal spread dissatisfaction among the people who did not rebel because they had not been taught to think about their ills.

Since he conceived of teaching and learning in the broadest sense, he directed his broadsides at those powerful pedagogues, the Jesuits, who stressed appearances and eloquence, who turned knowledge into apologetics for their church and neglected the love of truth for itself. It was the Jesuit Father Astete whose popular Catechism encouraged seekers after knowledge to depend on others to think for them: "Do not ask that of me, for I am ignorant; the Holy Mother Church has doctors who can answer you." The Jesuits, Unamuno argued, encouraged the "holy ignorance" of the charcoal-burner's faith, the *fe del carbonero,* implicit belief rather than bold probing, and offered their students, not primary sources, but church-sanctioned commentaries. The wisdom of the Jesuits he summed up as "hollow pedantry, confused, useless erudition and feigned profundity . . ." [17]

Yet Unamuno did not oppose the study of religion as such, since along with the language, history, and legislation of the country, Catholicism had permeated every aspect of Spanish life and was one of the major keys to the understanding of the national spirit. The liberal view demanded that religion be taught in the schools lest it be left in the hands of mothers who convert it into fetishism, or in the hands of sectarians who convert it into pure dogma. Only when one has acquired an intimate knowledge of religion, its spirit, its power to console, along with its deformations, does one have the right to judge it. The catechism should not so much inculcate a strict adherence to form as a taste for spiritual things; and the fertile doubt that cuts through the deadening effect of ritual to a hunger for God unsupported by specious rationalizations can be built only on early religious instruction. "I could not live in a country entirely composed of absolute believers any more than in a country entirely composed of non-believers." [18] Education that is exclusively secular becomes as sectarian as education that is exclusively religious, and "Voltairean barbarism" was as deplorable to Unamuno as "traditional barbarism." [19]

Yet despite the animosity he earned with such outspoken criticism, Unamuno was named rector of the University in 1900 and kept the post until 1914. "Imagine," he wrote, "a conservative government appointing a Socialist, a dissenter, a propagator of dissolvent ideas, who is no more than 36 years of age, not a native of this city, and has been teaching here for only nine years . . ." [20]

Although this appointment involved extra duties, this time administrative, Unamuno scarcely altered his Spartan way of life. He taught each of his two courses one hour daily, in the morning, after which he repaired to the rector's office where he dispatched official business and answered his own growing correspondence faithfully in his own hand, or wrote some of the newspaper articles which supplemented the income he needed for a large family and kept his name in the limelight. After lunch, the hours from about three to five were given over to long walks, usually along the Zamora road going north, and to conversations with friends. The café and club also provided listeners for those long monologues in which he assayed the subtle convolutions of ideas that were to find their way into essays, poetry, fiction, and public oratory, or which had already been used but were subject to constant refinements and variations.

To accredit his right to be the leading ideological non-conformist of his country, he had to prove beyond a doubt, through constant asseveration of his "Spanishness" and the pervasive Catholicism of his early conditioning, that he was criticizing what he most loved, thus combining the roles of heretic and mystic, dissenter and knight-errant, critic and defender. As a patriotic Basque by lineage, birth, and education, unshakably faithful to his native region or *patria chica,* he could decry purely local allegiances, analyze the inadequacy of the Basque language, and suggest it be embalmed in research and given honorable burial. As a perfervid Spaniard and in his own eyes nothing less than a *pater patriae,* he could ridicule Spanish mediocrity, egotism, and false pride. As a professor he could vent his scorn for the professional intellectual and the unresponsive student. Lyrical in his love for Castile, he could call the Castilians "spiritual crustaceans";[21] as Salamanca's most eminent citizen he could describe the torpid university city as "a clutter of farmhouses giving the impression of pasture ground." [22]

The picture Unamuno presented to the world was that of the unquestionable patriot and *bon bourgeois* living at the highest coefficient through a spiritual discomfort that he would pass on to others for their own good. Lacking the finesse or urbanity to draw his audiences to him unobtrusively, he devised a technique of intellectual bullying and with the full weight of his authority made it clear that only those who were with him might climb to his heights, while those who were not might not even be vouchsafed admission to Hell: *non raggiamo di Loro—ma guarda e passa* was one of his favorite lines from Dante. Positive faults were to him more admirable than negative virtues, and in his exertions to magnify his personality to irresistible size and strength, he could not prevent his preoccupations from becoming manias. His obsession with the ultimate God-man relationship turned into tyrannical impatience with those whose purposes were more immediate. In his certainty that he was among the chosen valiant to wrestle with the Angel of God, he demanded from others complete deference to himself and submission to the tortuous meanderings of his thoughts, intuitions, and insights. He took fierce pride in tactlessness and compensated for the uncertainty of his belief with the certainty that those who did not writhe over the religious question in rhythm with him were of an unworthy species.

Irritated by the bland acquiescence which often parades as good manners, by the gregariousness that crowds out the need for self-knowledge, and the type of *politesse* that is a disguised form of cowardice, he cultivated his prejudices and indulged in that peremptoriness of the despot whose occasional concessions excite exaggerated gratitude. Nor did he make excuses for his indifference to the social graces, for his nonmusical ear, his aversion to the impersonality of large cities, his scorn for theater and cinema, his detestation of small talk or easy, categorical statements. "Against this and that" (*Contra esto y equello*),[23] he was anti-clerical vis-à-vis an unenlightened clergy and equally exasperated by hackneyed atheism; a Republican under the monarchy, a reactionary under the Republic, a rationalist dealing with irrationalities, he could truly echo Vigny's words, "I am not always of my own opinion." [24]

With a sort of inverted dandyism, Unamuno even strove for and achieved a unique, unmistakable physical appearance, and nearly always wore the same "civilian uniform" suggestive of the Protestant minister (to be the Spanish Luther had once been his ambition): a dark, double-breasted suit with vest buttoned to the neck and topped by the dramatic tie-less white of his shirt collar. With his small round hat, the gleam of his metal-framed spectacles, his thick-set body, his sharp aquiline nose and prominent cheekbones, he was caricatured as a cross between a man and an owl. Protestant in appearance in a country one hundred percent Catholic, a protester in a society which had known no serious religious cleavages in three centuries, goaded by an all-consuming desire for preeminence yet unable to find in life its own justification, existentially involved in every temporal question as it related to an absolute he struggled to define, Unamuno stands as a rugged monolith of our times, arrogant, contradictory, his enigmas and turnabouts inspiring love and contempt, respect and detestation, often in the same person.

## V  *1914-1936: A Short Summary*

On August 13, 1914, without previous warning or explanation, Unamuno was relieved of his rector's post. Towards the end of 1915 he refused appointment as dean, but in 1920 accepted the post of vice-rector which he held until his clash with Primo de Rivera's dictatorship and his deportation to the island of Fuerte-ventura, Canary Islands, in February of 1924. After several months Unamuno fled to Paris and in August of 1925 moved to Hendaye where he spent the rest of his exile until the fall of the dictatorship and his triumphal return to Spain in February of 1930.

On resuming his academic life he chose to teach only the second of the two courses he had taught until his exile, the History of the Spanish Language, and after the establishment of the Republic in 1931 he was reappointed rector and then elected deputy for the city of Salamanca to the *Cortes Constituyentes* or Constituent Assembly (Parliament). On turning seventy he retired from his teaching duties (September of 1934, just a few months after his wife's death) but continued as rector of the university until relieved of his post by the Republic in 1936 when he declared his sympathies for the Franco rebellion.

Soon, however, in a public ceremony of October 12, 1936, he raised his voice in protest over the philosophy of the Nationalist insurgents, was again relieved of the rectorship that had been restored to him by Franco, was confined to his home and died there on December 31, 1936. On January 1, 1937 he was buried in the cemetery of Salamanca next to his daughter Salomé and his wife. His headstone contains the verses:

> Receive me, eternal Father, on thy bosom,
>     mysterious home,
> I shall sleep there, for I come exhausted
>     from the difficult struggle.
> (*Méteme, Padre eterno, en tu pecho,
>     misterioso hogar,
> dormiré allí, pues vengo deshecho
>     del duro bregar.*)

"Of those who do not appreciate that the extinction of Unamuno's voice is in the nature of a national catastrophe," wrote the poet Antonio Machado, "one would have to say: 'Forgive them, oh Lord, for they know not what they have lost.' " [25]

CHAPTER 2

# *Religion and Immortality*

U NAMUNO does not provide very much information concerning the intellectual atmosphere prevalent in the city and university of Madrid during the four years (1880-1884) he spent there. Although we may certainly assume that the Catholic apologists Balmes and Donoso Cortés had ceased exercising much influence on his thinking, his country could offer no worthy substitute except for the popularity of a minor German idealist, Karl Christian Friedrich Krause (1781-1832). It was Julián Sanz del Río (1814-1869) who, after spending the years 1843 and 1844 in Brussels and Heidelberg studying with Krause's disciples and after ten years of quiet retirement, returned to the chair of Philosophy at the new Central University of Madrid and spent the rest of his life attracting many intellectuals to his version of Krausism.

Sanz del Río envisaged a new era of reform postulated on the ideal of humanity working out the harmony of God's creation through dedicated rational effort. "Humanity," he wrote, "is the harmonious synthesis of Nature and Spirit under the absolute unity of God." [1] Man is therefore obliged by a sense of individual responsibility to make every effort to achieve moral perfection and resolve differences and disparities. [2] Generally, the Krausists such as Don Francisco Giner de los Ríos, Joaquín Costa, and many other eminent educators and reformers, looked forward to a broad religious ideal informing all practical effort, but passing beyond dogma or revelation, indeed beyond Christianity.

In addition, and undoubtedly much more important in Unamuno's formation, the winds of positivism from abroad were blowing over Spain when the young Basque arrived in Madrid. Thought and effort were converging more on meliorism than on salvation; egregious minds all over Europe were concentrating more on physical and social engineering than on spiritual crises, for while the Church was embroiled in political strife and in defense of its enormous powers, worship was becoming more of a formality of the *bien pensants* than the renewal of the spirit through the scandal and paradox of Christ. Practical men relegated the mystery of religion to the background of the Unknowable, and hailed the accomplishments and potential to the quantitative sciences. The Romantic Revolution was a *cri de coeur* against the standardization encouraged by industrial output and middle-class norms, but spiritual despair was looked upon as an oddity, and acceptability was the general goal. The growing official outlook was an optimistic one, exemplified in the visions of ultimate resolution held out by Hegel, Comte, and Marx.

Herbert Spencer, especially, fascinated the young Unamuno and even when he eventually rejected the English thinker, the virulence of his reaction was indisputable proof of the lasting impression the entire scientific British school left upon him:[3] ". . . if positive knowledge constitutes the basis of what I have known as man or child, my knowledge is not me, nor am I a mere receptacle of that knowledge. Beneath such knowledge which, like all knowledge, always sticks to one, beneath such knowledge . . . there is me, me, me, my soul, my longings, my passions, my loves," he wrote his friend Pedro Jiménez Ilundain,[4] a few years after doing his translations of some of Spencer's essays.[5] His recoil from Spencer is symtomatic of his rejection of the entire scientific climate of Europe, and his liberation from the siren-song of facts. Scientists he would henceforth situate, like merchants, in the portico of the temple where they display their wares but beyond which they will not go.[6]

Already in 1886, Unamuno was working on a *Logical Philosophy* (*Filosofía lógica*) in which he broke down positivistic barriers by affirming the relativism of all subject-object relationships and stressing the importance of the concrete, total, irreplaceable individual in any epistemology. This unfinished little work proves how early in life Unamuno was already discontent with the purely rational outlook, and his need for a more encompassing, less restrictive reality.[7] The short story, "Seeing with One's Eyes" ("Ver con los ojos"), published the same year in *El Noticiero Bilbaíno* further reinforces that assumption. The protagonist, Juan, an antisocial, taciturn, introspective young man, asks himself twenty times a day whether life is worth living, makes much of his hostility towards popular beliefs, delivers himself of a homily on the vanity of human things and expresses his need for more consolation rather than more knowledge.[8]

I　*The Crisis of 1897: Conditions and Consequences*

In 1897, a spiritual crisis marked the definite turning point in Unamuno's life and determined the *sui generis* religious orientation of his subsequent work. A son, Raimundo Jenaro, born in January of 1896, contracted meningitis in early infancy and was left with a hydrocephalic condition which was bound to be fatal (he died in 1904). The father's grief over his child exacerbated his own pathological fear of death and culminated in fierce desolation: "What a terrible thing it is to cross the steppes of intellectualism," he wrote his friend Jiménez Ilundain on January 3, 1898, "and to find oneself one day . . . facing the image of death and total annihilation!"[9] Further on in the same letter he describes how the crisis came over him in sudden violent fashion, although it had been discernible in his own writings, and how, when he broke into tears, his wife cried out: "My child!" (*¡Hijo mío!*), a scene that inscribed itself on his sensibilities so ineradicably that it is incorporated in a good many of his writings and is recounted in several of his letters.

The anguish of a dying child, the heart palpitations he thought announced his own end, the attack of weeping, all attest to the completest experience of death, not in the abstract, but as personal annihilation. In this "limit situation" all reasonable thought seemed vain, unsubstantial, and insincere. He had lived like those who are called healthy in mind, strong, well balanced, those who consider death as a natural law and necessary condition of life. "And now I can no longer live like that and I view the years of courage, enterprise, struggles, plans, and happiness as years of spiritual death, of dreaming," he confided to the *Journal* (*Diario*) he kept in April and May of that fateful year.[10]

He took refuge in the religious practices of his childhood, but a reversion to retreat and prayer proved as unsatisfying as the positivism, scientism, and "atheistic" humanism he had rejected with his entire being. In short, the painful period that followed the apocalyptic experience of early Spring, 1897, made it abundantly clear to Unamuno that if, despite all longing, he could never again return to an undimmed belief in revealed religion, a total repudiation of the transcendental was inhuman and existentially untenable; if he could never again consider any alliance with tra-

ditional attitudes, he could never more live in the desert of total
rejection of Divinity. "I felt I was on the edge of the unending
Void and I finally felt that there are more ways of relating to
reality than reason, that there is grace and that there is faith, faith
which is finally achieved by really desiring to believe." [11] The command given to him in early adolescence to go and preach the
Gospel echoed again in his mind and he was convinced of the
apostolic mission put upon him to communicate to all his own
yearnings for faith.[12]

In 1898 Unamuno was preparing a series of *Meditations on the
Gospels* (*Meditaciones evangélicas*), but only one of these essays,
*Nicodemus the Pharisee* (*Nicodemo el fariseo*)[13] has come down
to us. A deeply subjective commentary on a few lines of the
Gospel according to St. John (3:1-24; 7:45-53; 19:38-48), it tells
how Nicodemus the Pharisee came to Jesus to express his faith
in Him, but only at night, for, unable to slough off the outer man,
the product of a society predicated on judicious, acceptable conduct, he dared to make his way to the Master only when secure
from prying eyes. It is, therefore, an admonition to the "enlightened" to connect again with the ground of all things despite the
pressure of timidity, custom, or propriety. Notwithstanding the
importance of those economic considerations which aim at and
even achieve material advancement, all of life converges on *one*
essential question: what is the purpose of all our strivings? And
if logical reason denies the existence of transcendental direction,
faith affirms it, because "faith consists not so much . . . in believing
what we have not seen as in creating what we do not see."

Faith, then, is not a matter of metaphysical or theological
principle; it is "an act of complete surrender, of total handing
over of the will . . ." in the certainty that ultimate truth is independent of the bounds of intellectualism. "I know what intellectualism is; I have suffered through it and even today, as I strike at
its crust of ice, I still suffer from it more than I should." It is a
sickness likened to the ulcerated stomach which, with the destruc-
tion of the epithelium, begins to feed on itself, and can only be
cured by a spiritual milk diet, the untroubled faith of childhood.
To Unamuno, caught in a deadlock between his role of man-in-the-
world and his supra-rational yearnings, the lesson was clear: a man
is enslaved only to his actions, not to his intentions; in the holy
freedom of spirit we find a bulwark against and refuge from

Pharisean morality, and even when we do ill, our salvation lies in the wish to do good.

*Nicodemus* is a tapestry of closely-knit reasoning that defines the liberation implicit in recognizing the availability of fertile unexplored spaces within us. Such vast inner realms are revealed to those who, having existentially experienced the vanity of life-for-life's sake, and having lost the savor of worldly gratifications, find themselves alone in a desert. For these there is egress: "religious faith has very deep roots in the innermost parts of the human spirit and can manage to provoke such a state of fantasy that it will penetrate the marrow of truths closed off to mere logical reason."

*Nicodemus* proves conclusively to the student of Unamuno's thought that his "conversion" of 1897 is in the nature of a religious purposefulness without strict content. The fundamental theme of all his subsequent work is stated in this essay-drama: the will to believe, along with the concomitant desire for God, may, and indeed must, replace theological faith, and as Father Moeller says, if Unamuno's faith rests on no philosophical foundation, it moves along the lines of hope.[14]

## II  *Liberal Protestantism*

At least as early as 1893 Unamuno declared that Protestantism appealed to him because it represented the death of the Church as a political institution and "the transference of religion to private conscience."[15] From Hegel, whose *Logic* he had read in his university days, he drew the theory of opposites, while the Kantian "postulate of practical reason which rises powerfully from the ruins piled up by pure reason,"[16] strengthened his arguments concerning the limitations of logical thinking when applied to areas beyond its powers.

And since voracious readers invariably find their way to books that will meet their needs, Unamuno read Schleiermacher and was moved by his notion of religion as a special experience of dependence, relegating dogma and ritual to secondary significance. He read further in F. C. Baur, Albrecht Ritschl, Renan, Wilhelm Herrmann, Julius Kaftan, Auguste Sabatier, Jean Réville, and even William Ellery Channing. These liberal theologians, in general, discounted the mystical experience, stressed the historical element in faith and the ethical content of the religious disposition, and de-emphasized the importance of dogmatics. In short, by showing that essential Christian truths cannot be vitiated by scientific change or biblical criticism, they defended both modernity and religious—not dogmatic—continuity.

Most representative perhaps of this school of thought was Adolf von Harnack (1851-1930), whose *Dogmengeschichte* in three volumes Unamuno read with particular care and admiration as early as February, 1897. Harnack's *History of Dogma* recounts with monumental erudition and detail the hardening process of Christian faith into dogma through its marriage with Greek philosophy and Roman law, how *pistis* and *gnosis* approached each other and fused into systematic dogmatics. If Gregory the Great incorporated the Roman pagan "inventory" into the Church in the form of statutes and carefully defined ceremonies, with the later popes ". . . juristic-scientific treatment of all functions of the Church became the highest aim." [17] Dialectic developed to reconcile contradictions, scholasticism took hold of the ecclesiastical reins, dogma solidified into law, causing "an inner dissolution, since it no longer satisfied the individual piety, or held its ground in the presence of new knowledge . . ." [18]

Although dogmatic-legalistic thought advanced mightily, there remained the stubborn desire for freedom of religion, kept in check by the power of curialism. It was Luther who reexamined God in the Gospel, and contested the doctrines that vitiated the *puritas evangelii*. He simplified religion, making it depend on faith, on the Christ available to every Christian longing for Him, and not on canon, hierarchy, or speculative definition. This Christ stands above prescription or miracle, above the web of decretals, bulls, and councils, in direct nexus with needful man.

But the Reformation inherited the struggle of dogma versus faith and Harnack deplored the "catholicizing of the Protestant Churches" and their involvement with "ordinance, doctrine, and ceremony," [19] a trend which made the masses indifferent and identified religion too closely with authority, hierarchy, and cult. The need is for a return to forces and principles of the Reformation: "Faith is to be the beginning, middle, and end of all religious fervor." [20]

Although Unamuno's important essay "Faith" ("La Fe"),[21] published in 1900 along with "Go Within!" ("¡Adentro!"), and "Ideocracy" ("La ideocracia") as *Three Essays* (*Tres Ensayos*), was already adumbrated three years earlier in some passages of "Pistis and not Gnosis!" ("¡Pistis y no gnosis!"),[22] he told the novelist and critic Clarín (Leopoldo Alas) that the nucleus of the new article was from the works of such Lutheran theologians as Herrmann, Harnack, and Ritschl,[23] and in a letter to Bernardo G. de Candamo, he said that he was certain that "Faith" would create a scandal since it decried dogma and affirmed living faith. "Faith," he says in the letter to Candamo, "is not the adherence of the mind to an abstract principle, but the surrender of confidence and heart to a person: for the Christian, to the historical person of Christ. Such is my thesis, at bottom a Lutheran thesis." [24]

Since faith is hope, Unamuno declares in his essay, it cannot be urged, but must be desired and awaited: it cannot be sought directly, but requires patient submergence in life. Unfortunately, for many Christians, *pistis* or the creation of what we do not see through our desire for it, has become *gnosis* or belief in what we have not seen. Knowledge or belief has provided a thick, choking overgrowth for faith, yet religion is pure faith in God and not in any special doctrine representing Him; it is not a concept but an imperative of the heart that hopes for immortality.

The belief of the ordinary man consists mainly of what he has been told to believe: having been given a closed book sealed with seven seals, he is commanded to accept what it contains. But such belief is a docile submission to earthly powers; it is the passive, unexamined belief of the charcoal-burner and a marriage of incompatibles: the Gospel and Roman law, feeling and codification. Because from Roman law came theology which consists not of spirit, but of shibboleths, and breeds categories, parties, sects, and factions. The flower has died but the petals which remain to be worshipped yield no fruit and retain no fragrance.

Finally, Unamuno demands that all living, spontaneous faith be respected regardless of the form it takes, since faith generates life, courage, hope, and consolation even when concepts are disproved and discarded. No corpus of doctrine has exclusive possession of truth; the human drive toward God transcends all organization and manifests itself in "sincerity, tolerance, and mercy," the sincerity of telling the truth under any circumstances, tolerance based on the understanding of the relativity of all *gnosis,* mercy that will convert the self-righteous to a knowledge of their criminal instincts.

The words of "Faith" are those of a latter-day, idol-breaking protest-ant, an impatient revivalist in the best sense of the term, one eager to restore God immediately to men of all persuasions. Toward that end, Unamuno breaks through the walls of discretion, expediency, spiritual monopoly, and coercion to restore the supremacy of one idea only: that intention, not dogma, marks the religious spirit. He foresees the resurgence of holy confidence in some universal supra-mundane ideal which indeed may never be realized but will maintain the incandescence of hope in the future, thus enhancing life in the present.

Without such a transcendental dream, life is the victim of practical ideals, all subject to obsolescence. Although eager to free men from the wall of dogma standing between them and their personal extension to God, Unamuno was equally anxious to free men from false faiths in worldly solutions, programmes, utopias, party lines, in short the ideocracy which makes for cold abstraction and with it, for heated fanaticism. "Truth is something more intimate than the logical concordance of two concepts, something more inward than the equation of the intellect with the thing . . . , it is the innermost union of my spirit with the universal Spirit," he says in "Ideocracy." [25]

An idea, he continues, whether practical or metaphysical, is true only when it is lived; when it becomes hieratic and congealed, it is of no further use and therefore false. The supreme obligation is to think, but "with the entire body and its senses, the entrails, blood, marrow, fiber, and all one's cells . . . and not only with the brain . . . to think vitally and not only logically." Man must be the master of thought, not its servant; intelligence is for life and not life for intelligence, just as the eye is made for sight and not sight for the eye. When we shake off the tyranny of ideas by thinking boldly, independently, and comprehensively, we become permeable to true living faith and charity. The greatest injustices are committed by those fully convinced they serve some immutable truth; it is, for example, only when the idea of "abstract" sin is forgotten that men become capable of pitying the sinner and dealing him compassion. Man must not be regarded too narrowly as the incarnation of given concepts—sin, virtue, reaction or revolution—but as the incarnation of something ineffable and divine, as an entity who not only cogitates, but also suffers and rejoices, loves and hates, lives and dies.

Thus, by 1900, Unamuno had clearly established himself as a party of one, a source of scandal both to the loyal members of the Church and to their equally convinced opponents. An enemy of all conventional, organized concepts, more because of the dangers they represented than of the good they did, he declared himself against every form of establishment, religious, rationalistic, atheistic: "I would not change this tormented position of my mind either for the absurdities of orthodox routine Catholicism or the absurdities of rationalistic free-thinking." [26]

## III  *Kierkegaard*

Since Unamuno soon felt that Liberal Protestant theologians tended to reduce the ineffability of the religious sentiment to ethical principles, it was with jubilation that, in the very year of "Faith" he discovered the Kierkegaard who was to provide a more intimate confirmation of his own ideological and sentimental contours. He first came across the Dane's name in the book by Georg Brandes on Ibsen which he read at the end of 1899 or beginning of 1900.[27] If he began to learn Dano-Norwegian by translating Ibsen's *Brand,* a play he never ceased to admire ardently, it was the work of Kierkegaard, his "spiritual father," which fully justified the effort.

It immediately became apparent to Unamuno that like himself, Kierkegaard had been witness to the dead letter of Christianity and therefore to the imperious need of reopening the issue of man's link to the infinitely unconditional. Kierkegaard's spirited attacks on the established Church of Denmark and on the certainties and comforts that are the denial of the essentially self-sacrificing Christian spirit, his scorn of bishops and parsons and professors who recount the effects of suffering without experiencing them, his contempt for the criteria of history, all proved for Unamuno the corroboration of his own special mixture of thinking and emotion.

Kierkegaard had foreshadowed Unamuno in preferring passionate heresy to luke-warm conformism and in denouncing the norms of judiciousness as opposite to the crusading rebelliousness of the New Testament with its call to lean living, self-searching, and above all, risk: "Without risk there is no faith. Faith is precisely the contradiction between the infinite passion of the individual's inwardness and the objective uncertainty. If I am capable of grasping God objectively, I do not believe, but precisely because I cannot do this I must believe." [28] His apostolic mission of being "something other than an author in the ordinary sense,"[29] his scorn for middle-class acquiescence in Philistinism, his suspicions of secular utopianism, his hostility to humanistic cultural activity as a substitute for faith, all these did Unamuno find amply expounded in Kierkegaard.

Further, the Spaniard agreed with the Dane that the supremacy of reason made for a "characterless" generation and that alienation from the kingdom of the pharisees could be a blessing and bear the seed of greater fertility, that one could reject the comforts of the middle-of-the-road for the greater glory of God. And in Kierkegaard he found such sentiments expressed with a strangeness and testiness congenial to his own temperament; here was a "chosen" polemicist for whom the sins of passion and of the heart were "much nearer to salvation than the sins of reason," [30] who had given up marriage and an ecclesiastical post, who had invited ridicule and had lived against the grain of his age since he could settle for nothing less than his own vision.

Since Unamuno was supported by Kierkegaard's distaste for the *Privatdocent's* Christianity,[31] by the Dane's disgust with attempts to explain the Christian paradox in any way other than through personal tension and suffering, by his opposition to systematic philosophy, by his stress on the inwardness of faith, by his distrust of the simple man who is too near religion and the educated man who is too far from it, it has been thought by some commentators that Unamuno's role as continuator of Kierkegaard's thought is of prime importance in the history of modern existentialism and that in our century Unamuno is the only existentialist "whose passion is worthy of Kierkegaard." [32] It would, however, be dishonest not to mention that while Unamuno's anguish stems from his inability to choose God, with Kierkegaard the choice was made and the central problem was to retrieve that belief from the hands of unworthy middlemen who exteriorized it. Yet, as Walter Lowrie said, "Soren Kierkegaard, who wanted no disciples, would surely have been pleased with such independent discipleship as this." [33]

## IV   *William James and Thomas Carlyle*

Between 1896 and 1908, Unamuno read William James and found further substantiation of the "will to believe" which creates its object, a defense of new criteria of truth over and above the empirical, and contempt for pretentious "scientism." James assigns to science its due, but keeps it within the bounds of the verifiable; he conceives of man as a complete existential being, made of reason and need; he understands the indispensable risk of choice and sympathizes as much with the personal as with the objective.

Thus, as James defends the autonomy of the religious choice which he calls the "leap in the dark," [34] he echoes almost exactly one of Kierkegaard's favorite images. And on the grounds that truth is possible but certitude impossible, James holds that "There are, then, cases, where a fact cannot come at all unless a preliminary faith exists in its coming. And where faith in a fact can help create the fact, that would be an insane logic which should say that faith running ahead of scientific evidence is the 'lowest kind of immorality' into which a thinking being can fall." [35] Here, in less passionate tones, is a conviction that runs like a major chord through all of Unamuno's production: we do not believe what we have not seen but rather create what we do not see, thus providing the basis for quixotic liberation from *adequatio intellectus nostri cum rê*.

Need creates desire, Unamuno understood even before his contact with James's pragmatism. Therefore, if the vital need for God reaches beyond the visible world, "why may not that be a sign that an invisible universe is there?" James asks.[36] If belief in the supernatural is such that life is enhanced, and if science cannot extend its dominion to that which will not be grasped scientifically, we have a right to believe in a nontemporal order and "faith based on desire is certainly a lawful and possibly an indispensable thing." [37]

The other fortifying influence which Unamuno discovered at the turn of the century was that of Carlyle. "Carlyle," he said in 1901, "is perhaps the one who contributed most to my finding my own style." [38] Carlos Clavería has pointed out that Unamuno knew Carlyle's work as far back as 1895 and that the Scotsman's preoccupation with Time and Eternity had made him congenial to the professor of Salmanca. In his essays on history and biography, Carlyle had stressed the importance of the "silent forgotten lives of thousands of obscure men who labor and create far from the battlefields, political meetings, and royal antechambers," [39] exactly as Unamuno maintained in *On Authentic Tradition* (*En torno al casticismo*), first published in 1895.

In Carlyle, Unamuno found other reflections of himself: the notion of the priesthood of the man of letters, impatience with *politesse,* with the mechanical view of society, with the vulgarization of religion. Like Unamuno, Carlyle was the antiaesthete: he exhorted his readers to turn away from fashion and orthodoxy to the deepest spiritual concerns, and especially denounced scientific materialism and its handmaiden, political science. Above all, Unamuno found in Carlyle confirmation of his conviction that men could be just and fair only if moved by higher insights and inspirations; as the enemy of logic-chopping, of dry-as-dust scholarship, of the "dismal science" of economics, Carlyle ratified Unamuno's position on the unifying power of the mysterious, the intractable, and the transcendental.


## V    *1900-1911*

From the beginning of the century on, Unamuno's work took on the unmistakable stamp of highly-charged personal confession orchestrated through copious quotations from his favorite authors. At the center of his writings stands the hunger for personal immortality which can find its "guarantee" only in the uncertain hope that Divinity exists. Although definitively estranged from the religious acceptances of his childhood, he was equally repelled by the purely cortical satisfactions of materialism and agnosticism which presented as institutionalized and smug a façade as organized religion.

Unamuno felt that the rigid structure of his country's religion engendered either complacency among the ignorant or resentment and incredulity among the enlightened. Such outmoded inflexibility as prevailed in the Spanish Church stood in the way of the sense of pervading mystery which, through its revelance on every level and speaking to the most skeptical souls, unites all men in brotherhood rather than dividing them on formalistic grounds. He drew the distinction between the free-thinker (*librepensador*) and the free-believer (*librecreyente*), the latter, like the author himself, agonizing with "Hamletian hesitancies and doubts . . . always on the basis of sentimental [rather than ideological] Catholicism." [40] Yet it was easy to pass from Catholicism to atheism in Spain since "false, absurd doctrines have a natural tendency to engender skepticism in those who receive them without reflection, since there is no one so prone to believing too little as those who began believing too much. It is usual to hear it said in Spain that if one is not Catholic, one must be an atheist and anarchist, since protestantism is a middle way accredited neither by reason nor faith. . . . Among us, the protestant seems to be, more than anti-Catholic, anti-Spanish. Atheism is more indigenous than protestantism." [41]

The protestantism which Unamuno most frequently refers to is in lower case; it is a disposition of the spirit, a religious intentionality beyond or above all official "shibboleth": "I do not take communion with official religion; but I . . . am a Christian and what grieves me most is the realization that here in Spain, for the most part, Catholicism is the element most active in the dechristianization of the people." [42] The spirit behind such a broad indictment of Catholicism is obviously that of Kierkegaard who indicted his own church in his desire to "reintroduce Christianity into Christendom." When the Absolutely Different is brought down to the cognitive level, it is denatured, objectified, or spatialized; therefore as another Kierkegaardian, Paul Tillich, was to say later: "The first word . . . to be spoken by religion to the people of our time must be a word spoken against religion. It is the word the Jewish prophets spoke against the priestly and royal and pseudo-prophetic guardians of their national religion . . ." [43]

The sacerdotal class, charged with watching over orthodoxy, defining it, and judging heresy, has been "without doubt, the principal cause of the blunting of the religious spirit . . ." [44] The Church, which began as a congregation of the faithful, both ecclesiastical and lay, has shrunk to the clergy; what started as a noble mission became a hierarchical, amoral gendarmerie serving the rich, the ministers more intent on preserving the status quo than the spirit of religion. Indeed, those most keenly actuated by the religious spirit—the saints—were not priests to any great extent. Like the military which confuses self-preservation with patriotism, organized religion is a sort of army that confuses hierarchy with Divinity.

The Inquisitorial spirit of organized religion has done away with that supreme freedom of choice which was primitive Christianity. To be a Catholic in a country that bans any other alternative is to forget that each individual must make his way to God in the despairing realization of his curtailed abilities and his participation in sin. Man's relation to God is not through gnosiological grasp but through his entire organic identification with Him. For man is not only a thinking animal, Unamuno repeats again and again, but a passionate being who desires, imagines, and wills, and since the finite mind cannot embrace the Infinite, he is left with the agony of personal decision. "We lean on authority outside ourselves in order to be free of the trouble of forming and affirming an authority of our own."[45] And since, in Spain, to be Catholic is to have been baptized a Catholic and to be averse to publicly abjuring that state, it simply means to be nothing else, to entertain an implicit belief, an external conformity to preestablished patterns—in short, it means to share in the ignorance of the charcoal-burner.

Truth, however, to Unamuno is what one believes with all one's heart and soul, and it must be made public, especially when it is most inopportune to do so. And Unamuno's truth was a strong leaning to Roman Catholic Christianity unbuttressed by allegiance to any doctrine. In his essay "My Religion" ("Mi Religión"),[46] the most succinct summary of his personal beliefs, Unamuno declares straightforwardly that a deep love and respect for Christ and His teachings is the sign of a Christian even if all proofs of God are found to be defective and all orthodoxies repellent. Unable to believe rationally in the existence of God and finding His nonexistence equally problematical, Unamuno rejects the eternal *ignorabimus* of the Spencerian school and posits the unattainable as his goal. In addition, he expects nothing from a culture that disregards the most fundamental question of life or turns it into a social issue, just as he expects nothing from a culture that blindly accepts dogma and precept. His hope lies in those who do not know but are not resigned to not knowing, who endlessly struggle in the knowledge that struggle is life itself.

The highest duty of every individual is, then, to plumb so deeply into self that he must desire to exist endlessly in space and time: that is the vitalistic *plenitudo plenitudinis et omnia plenitudo* that counteracts the *vanitas vanitatum et omnia vanitas.* "If religion is not based on the intimate feeling of one's own substantiality and the perpetuation of one's own substance, then it is not religion. It may be a philosophy of religion, but not religion." [47] As we enrich ourselves through self-knowledge, we become aware of an endless extension of self possible only through immortality, and God comes into existence through a sort of creative evolution; and by the same token, it is through the apprehension of His existence that our own existence becomes richer, more active, more meaningful.

## VI   *The Tragic Sense of Life, 1913*

On May 24, 1899, Unamuno wrote his friend Jiménez Ilundain that he had embarked on a work of great breadth which might take years, and into which he was pouring all his philosophy with the greatest sincerity possible. Mixing poetic fantasy and scientific induction, he would proceed from sociology and ethics to the problem of the "unknowable purpose of the universe, and from that to the concept of feeling of Divinity. It ends with the doctrine of the happy uncertainty which allows us to live." [48] It was only after fully assimilating and indeed *unamunizing* Harnack and other anti-mystagogues, along with James, Carlyle, and above all Kierkegaard, that Unamuno gave to the press the most fully elaborated expression of his religious thought in *On the Tragic Sense of Life in Men and Peoples* (*Del sentimiento trágico de la vida en los hombres y en los pueblos*).

Just as Kierkegaard had fulminated against Hegelian abstraction in favor of the individual apprehension of life's ultimate or religious meanings, Unamuno starts his book not with a statement of philosophy but with the concept of the total man, the man of flesh and blood, as the *fons et origo* of all speculation. If Kierkegaard's aim had been to salvage the authentic living being from the tidal wave of corporateness in social living and religious activity, Unamuno deplores the fracturing of man into the many interpretations and categories put upon him and seeks a basic definition of man *per se,* preceding any aspect of his performance in life or thought.

Some years after the publication of Unamuno's *Tragic Sense of*

*Life,* Heidegger would prove that man is revealed ontologically in *Sorge,* the disquietude or anxiety that is abated or trivialized by fleeing from oneself into generality or anonymity, or as Pascal put it, by placing *divertissements* between the self and the sense of the abyss. Unamuno, from the outset of his book, cuts through the outer or routine man to the integrated individual who must confront what ineluctably invades him when his defenses are down: in the words of the poet Antonio Machado, Unamuno's friend and sympathizer, "the impenetrable and opaque infinite."[49] Each individual starts with himself alone and ends with himself alone: thought only follows primordial life and life converges on death. When in the *Critique of Practical Reason* Kant reconstructed the God whose traditional proofs he had destroyed in the *Critique of Pure Reason,* he was motivated, Unamuno adduces, by the reasons of the heart; unable to resign himself to total extinction, he made the leap—the "immortal" leap—from one critique to the other. In the second of the two volumes, the existence of God is deduced from the immortality of the soul, rather than the reverse. "The categorical imperative leads us to a moral postulate which, in its turn, requires the immortality of the soul on the teleological or rather the eschatological level, and in order to uphold this immortality, God appears. All the rest is the professional sleight-of-hand of philosophy."

Unamuno then adds to his Greek chorus of "cardiac" *alter egos* Spinoza, the Portuguese Jew of Amsterdam, who in the sixth proposition of Part III of his *Ethics* maintains that everything exerts itself to persevere in its being or substance, and in the next proposition that the very effort with which a thing tries to persevere in its being is the essence of the thing itself. This is man, then, the creature who, whatever his disguise, wishes to continue on forever in his self. As he indulges in his various enterprises, as he constructs a society, expands his knowledge, and fills the world with numberless marvels, he must nevertheless return to himself and ask the capstone question: To what end? Those satisfied with merely worldly accomplishments are the professionals who think only with their brains *à la* Spencer, while the others think with all their organs and with their soul, "with their blood, the marrow of their bones, with their heart, their lungs, their bellies, their livers." To the first category belong the pedants and specialists, amputated beings, while the second consists of complete men who experience not only intellectual but affective or volitive needs.

Since the ground of all thought is life, *Sum, ergo cogito* is closer to the truth than the more restricted *Cogito, ergo sum,* and the philosopher might indeed say, "I feel, therefore I am" or "I wish, therefore I am," since to feel might be to feel oneself imperishable and to wish might be to wish oneself eternal, to wish not to die. It therefore follows that man seeks knowledge to subserve the instinct to live and the "variations of knowledge depend on the variations of human needs."

Yet man lives not only in isolation but in conjunction with other men and communicates with them through language; thus, reason comes into being as a social instrument. Philosophy therefore develops through the need of man to impart to other men what he thinks and feels, and ultimately what he thinks and feels about the final end of all things: death. No amount of frustration with regard to finding the answer to that question can cancel the question out, and our reaction to the enigma of death may be one of three: (1) if I die completely at death, I am in despair; (2) if I do not die completely, I am resigned; (3) if I cannot accept either of the two foregoing conclusions, then I must be resigned to despairing, or despair over my resignation. The third alternative leads to a conjugation of despair with resignation, a struggle that breeds hope and life.

Using Kierkegaardian categories again for his own purposes, Unamuno tells us that for the religiously concerned, escape from this unending struggle cannot come through the aesthetic mode of life, from immediate satisfactions, or from the ethical search for the mutable ideals of the true, the good, and the beautiful. Instead, the subjective man or "egotist" will exploit the "I" to that fullness where, as Sénancour said in Letter XC of his *Obermann,* death becomes an injustice. That is why the "I" must not be absorbed into the Whole, into God, but must envelop God into itself, and if this is pride, it is also the substance of the highest spiritual efforts, supported by non-reason or supra-reason. The proof that the hunger for immortality can in no way be disregarded but only disguised, lies in that herostratism which compels even the greatest non-believer to impress himself on posterity through some form of accomplishment, through "prolonging himself in time more than in space."

However, those who seek to quench their thirst for immortality in orthodox Christianity are confronted with the greatest of all dilemmas: faith must be rationalized and when rationalized, it is absorbed into theology. The earliest Christian theology was wrought by Paul of Tarsus who had not personally known Christ, and for whom the most important thing was that God had become man, had died and risen from the dead, thus promising the miracle to all men. Around this doctrine all Christology revolves: God became man so that man would become god-like, immortal. The purpose of redemption was to save us from death, rather than from sin, for Christ died and rose from the dead for each man, and as Malebranche said, Adam fell so that Christ might redeem us; He did not redeem us because Adam fell.

This shift of theological anthropology from the fallen state of man to Jesus Christ in whom God became Man in favor of man, indicates—as Karl Barth would show in *Christ and Adam*—that God's promise, and not man's sinfulness, is the ground of our hope. The Athanasian or Nicene Christ, says Unamuno, following in Harnack's wake, completed the view of the absolute "otherness" of Christ; Athanasius attacked the Arian view of Christ as the perfect man, since Christ conceived as anything else than God could not bestow godliness upon creatures of the world. Arianism or Unitarianism would have reduced Christianity to cosmology and ethics instead of the living communion with God.

Athanasius, Unamuno stresses, was a man of little education but of great faith and "had the supreme courage . . . to affirm contradictory things," so that after him, dogma takes leave of clear thought and follows the path of counterrationality. Nicaea represents the triumph of the *idiotas* or "simple men" who flouted reason because they did not wish to die and sought the guarantee of their longings in the sacrament of the Eucharist. Any other interpretation of Christianity inverts the equation of religion-immortality to the Kantian morality-religion. As Protestantism blurs the eschatological, it tends to become aesthetic, ethical, cultural, those stages on life's way which Kierkegaard called penultimate. Of course, Catholicism does not avoid the ethical and has indeed effected a compromise between the eschatological and the moral, but the former consideration predominates and genuine Catholic morality is embodied in monastic asceticism and the cult of virginity. In its struggle to defend the belief that man is an exception in the universe and destined for eternity, the Church denounced Galileo, opposed Darwin, and under Pius IX declared itself unalterably opposed to modernism.

Yet even when the Church upholds popular belief in the resurrection of the flesh and condemns all possible refutation, it must nevertheless lean on reason as the instrument for communication and diffusion of the faith. St. Augustine's *per fidem ad intellectum* was already a far cry from Tertullian's *et sepultus resurrexit, certum est quia impossibile est.* Faith had to seek concrete confirmation and the effort to find a rational basis for belief became scholastic theology and philosophy which reached its peak in Thomism. It was no longer enough to accept belief, one had also to accept its philosophical interpretation. Consequently, the priesthood became the repository of religious knowledge, and in answer to the difficult questions Father Astete's catechism affirms: "Do not ask that of me, for I am ignorant; the Holy Mother Church has doctors who can answer you."

Thus is the Christian caught on the horns of a tragic dilemma: he must believe in the existence of God, but also that such existence can be demonstrably proved. The substantive contradiction of Catholicism, involving the mystical experience of a living God on the one hand and on the other a "scientized" religion, makes of Catholic dogmatics a series of compromises between monotheism and polytheism, nature and grace, grace and free will, and the requirement is imposed on the believer that he believe everything or nothing. Consequently, it is understandable, as Channing said, that hordes of Frenchmen and Spaniards should reject Papism for atheism, since those who are not "simple" enough to accept "absurdities" cannot be made simple by fiat.

Yet atheists are spiritual eunuchs who pretend to be satisfied with this life only, just as the physical eunuch rejects the need to reproduce himself, and the man blind from birth disclaims any desire to enjoy the sights of the world. The tragic sense of life is embodied not in the spiritual eunuch but in the man whose powers of analysis fail when directed at mystery, the man whose needs break through the coherence of "truth" when the skepticism which feeds, not on uncertainty, but on itself, becomes intolerable. Yet when this man falls back on an inner belief independent of logic, he finds he must still use words to sustain his intuition. Thus, in his independence the religiously concerned man finds himself caught in a welter of antinomies: heart and mind, will and thought, mood and logic, and within this constant struggle or *agon,* he draws his comfort not from stupidly rejecting doubt, but from everlastingly defying it.

The battle of opposites is without resolution. To believe is in essence a matter of will, it is to wish to believe that God exists and in a manner of speaking, to create Him for oneself. The human being is so utterly removed from the absolutely "other," from the *Deus absconditus,* that rapprochement can be effected only through the creative act of wishing God into being for himself. So helpless is human reason in any form where apprehension of the Divine is concerned, that it must abandon itself to pure unsubstantiated will, which is the ultimate implication of the Christian freedom of choice. The living God comes into being, therefore, out of an unquenchable thirst for Him which breaks through the frontiers even of the imagination. Achieved through any other means, He becomes a theorem or hypothesis. And to wish God into existence may perhaps suggest that He created us to that end; to desire something into existence beyond contravention may mean that the "something" exists to exercise that loving pull.

It is in this sense that the knowledge of God is purely subjective and consequently anthropomorphic. As the individual strikes deeply into himself, he acquires the full consciousness of being or personality which embraces not only the many roles he is playing but also his inanity. He becomes increasingly aware that he is a fragile and truncated entity plunged into a precarious existence, in short a "nothing" (*nonada*), and along with the awareness of his nothingness comes awareness of and compassion for the wretchedness of his fellowmen.

So may egotism, or the plenitude of self-knowledge, lead away from egoism or vulgar selfishness and towards an intimate identification with all those condemned to the same pitiful state. Only through ourselves can we love others, for love personalizes all it loves. "And when love is so great and so deep, so strong and overflowing that it loves everything, then it personalizes everything and discovers that the complete All, the Universe, is also a Person with Consciousness, a Consciousness that also suffers, pities and loves. . . . And this Consciousness of the Universe, which love discovers by personalizing all that it loves, is what we call God."

The living God cannot therefore be an abstract principle independent of those human needs which, if they do not actually bring God into being, make Him so actual that "we can say that He is making Himself, in man and through man." Indeed, the popular Christian imagination is so far removed from abstraction that it conceives of God as man, and worships the child Jesus and His mother, the Virgin, "to complete the personalization of God by making of Him a family."

Yet the stumbling block remains: this is an intransitive God apprehended through the endlessly repeated "mortal leap" from denial, a *Dieu sensible au coeur* who can neither be enlarged by dogma nor reduced by scientific law. Just as we become aware of our physical organs—heart, stomach, lungs—only when they are a source of physical pain, so do we acquire knowledge of God only when we are in anguish over our perishable physical limitations, when we cannot resign ourselves to our short span on earth. And in what form can we perceive this immortality we hope for? Can we understand immortal life in terms other than those of this transitory, worldly one in which each personality strains to preserve itself? The beatific vision is Nirvana, a return to unconsciousness, and who would long for such a dissolution of self? "Is not eternal life perhaps eternal consciousness, not only seeing God but seeing that He is seen, seeing oneself at the same time and distinct from Him?" The desire to prolong one's life is the desire to prolong it in no other form but its own.

But in I. Cor. 15:26-28, St. Paul tells us that the last enemy to be destroyed is death and all things shall be subdued unto him and God will be all in all. This doctrine of apocatastasis is completed in the Epistle to the Ephesians: Christ is the head over all things and in Him we shall be raised up to live in the communion of the saints and to understand with the saints what is the breadth and length and depth and height of that love of God which passeth understanding. "And this gathering together of us in Christ, the head and, as it were, the summing-up of Humanity, is what the Apostle calls the gathering-in, the collecting, the recapitulation or gathering together of all things in Christ." Apocatastasis, or God's becoming all in all, resolves itself into anacephaleosis which means the gathering together of all things into Christ, making of Humanity the end of creation. If all matter, the principle of individuation, is done away with, everything becomes unthinkable purity which is even more than spirit, since spirit is supported by matter.

What happens, then, to each one of us in this supreme Christination? What happens to all the creatures who suffer and hope and believe in individual and separate eternization, as Unamuno interprets Spinoza's proposition? Must each of us be absorbed into Divine Consciousness? "But my soul, my soul, at least, longs for something else, not for absorption, quietus, peace, extinction, but an eternal approach that never reaches its goal, an endless longing, a hope which renews itself eternally without ever coming to an end. And with that, an eternal lack of something and eternal pain." The Unamuno who even as a child had considered the pains of Hell preferable to nothingness, opts for an eternal Purgatory, an eternal ascension, and not the obliteration of desire and suffering. One must believe, he declares, characteristically enlisting others arbitrarily to his own views, in an eternal life beyond the grave, "in which each of us is aware of his consciousness in the Supreme Consciousness, in God; one must believe in that other life in order to be able to live this one and endure it and give it meaning and purpose."

Paraphrasing again his favorite quotation from Sénancour, Unamuno adds, "And, above all, one must feel and act as if an endless continuation of our earthly life were reserved for us; and if nothingness is what is in store for us, we should not allow this to be justice . . ." Thus does Unamuno usher his reader into the field of ethics or comportment: can the uncertainty and doubt over our ultimate destiny provide a moral groundwork?

Morality rooted in certainty spawns intransigency, and when certainty weakens, it may plunge into immorality. If, however, each man feels that the afterlife may be an indefinite continuation of his particularity, he will strive to be worthy of that gift. It is the laborious, moral life which provides the symptom of hope, and therefore the basis for dogma, for it is the martyr who makes the faith, and not faith the martyr: did not Pascal advise taking holy water as a way to belief? The imperative, then, is for each one to make of himself something irreplaceable through vocation and duty and devotion, through the giving of himself in the highest degree. There are unmistakable Calvinistic overtones in such assertions: to act in such a way as to be worthy of eternity approximates the signs of election and provides the antidote to the sloth that was anathema to Unamuno, the reformer. Eternity is not contingent on conformity to any dogma; if any belief should earn eternal happiness, it is the belief in the possibility of that happiness through the highest individual exertion here on earth.

For most of us, then, the holy way is to partake in a sort of Eucharist through our calling, our profession, our work. But the meaningfulness of work cannot be made clear in salaries, in distribution of products, for then the soul is sacrificed to pure economics. The best way to handle the "social problem" would be to imbue the worker with a sense of the social or religious transcendency of what he is doing. How can the worker understand the importance of his work unless he is agonizingly aware of the eternal importance of the self? Caught up in the zeal of Carlyle and the German theologians Ritschl and Herrmann over *Beruf* or individual "calling," Unamuno concludes that "To work at our ordinary civil occupations, with our eyes fixed on God, for the love of God which is equivalent to saying for the love of our eternalization, is to make of this work a work of religion." Unless each man is impelled by what Tillich would later call belief-ful realism, a sense of the highest meaning of his calling, unless such passion informs the labors of man, reform is senseless.

## VII    *The Religion of Quixotism*

In a sense, *The Tragic Sense of Life* can be said to be a long commentary on innumerable quotations and resonances from a hundred authors. Such quotations are frequently used out of context, in scholarly gerrymandering; transitions are abrupt and arbitrary; deductions and conclusions are rash and bizarre; the theology is a slipshod juxtaposition of idea and fantasy, while Unamuno's diatribes against the inquisitions of Culture and Science are one-sided and cantankerous. It is therefore not surprising that the book should end with meditations on the supreme symbol of the rejection of unsatisfactory reality in favor of potentiating dreams: Don Quixote. If, for Unamuno, a clamoring need for eternity of a very personal sort provided the home-made weapons to storm all citadels of acceptable thought, it was the need to recall forgotten ideals that made Don Quixote oblivious to the "truth" of windmills, funeral processions, inns, and flocks of sheep. Man does not exist for appearances but appearances for man, according to Unamuno, and this introspective individualism, free from the restraints of proof, is the tragic sense of his nation, Spain, which produced not abstract systems of thought but mystics and conquistadors, the leaders of the Counter-Reformation and Don Quixote.

The latter represents the essence of Spanish-ness, since in his fidelity to himself, he could rise from defeat and face the ridicule of those "sensible" people who like the cultivated, skeptical, mocking Pontius Pilate brought shame on themselves rather than on their victims. In the name of life and its highest ideal, eternity, ridicule must be faced and incorporated into the *modus vivendi,* even the ridicule coming from those *Kulturmenschen* who denounce the philosophical validity of the will to "personal, individual, concrete immortality of the soul." The logical, aesthetic, and ethical norms which we adopt to distinguish between the true and the false, the beautiful and ugly, the good and bad, leave out the desirable and the undesirable.

The desirability of eternity is transcendental hedonism; in his religious mode, man seeks to eternalize his individuality, and to that end, avails himself of a new category of religious economics which deals with ways and means of satisfying the need for "enjoying forever the fullness of our own individual limits." This scandalous defiance of the sacrosanct rules constitutes Spanish philosophy, grounded in popular Spanish Catholicism which supersedes dogma, and is symbolized by Don Quixote who wished to bring into being a world of his own desires, a "medieval" world of simple faith struggling not only against the enlightenment of the Renaissance, Reformation, and Revolution, but against the "official" Catholics interested in nothing but their internecine quarrels. It is, in short, a denial of any sort of supine credulity, be it in Catholicism, rationalism, or agnosticism. "For my work—I was going to say my mission—is to shatter the faith of one party, the other party, and still the other, faith in negation and faith in abstention, for the sake of faith in faith itself; it is to wage war against all those who submit to Catholicism or rationalism or agnosticism; it is to make all men live in disquietude and yearning."

And if this has no immediate, tangible effect, neither did the efforts of Don Quixote; yet both Unamuno's efforts and those of his valiant knight stand as samples of the courage that flouts *Kultur* and "storms heaven, which suffereth violence." The survival of Don

Quixote among us guarantees the survival of Unamuno's book with its message concerning the value of despair as a "teacher of impossibilities," its reliance on the "absurd" hope that can come only on the other side of certainty.

\* \* \* \* \* \*

Standing alone with his questions and aided only by those kindred spirits in whose work he finds, often by a flagrant sleight of hand, confirmation and sustenance, the Unamuno of *The Tragic Sense of Life* carries on a highly-inflected monologue which ranges from whisper to rant, from tears to diatribe. Belief, doubt, and immortality treated as the personal torments of one man are not academic questions to be treated with delicacy, finesse, or *savoir-faire;* in Unamuno's hands they become cries of such agonizing sincerity that he awakens in even his most shocked readers feelings of sympathy that have been lost in the "civilizing" process.

Ortega y Gasset says that during the period when Europeans were most distracted from the essential human vocation which is "having to die," Unamuno made of death his beloved and deserves to be called a precursor of the inspiration which death provides for philosophy today.[50] If there is a lack of *pudeur* in Unamuno's style and a lack of care in his thought processes and associations, it can be said in his favor that extreme problems can be handled only in an extreme way, and that his thrust beyond good sense would only have been trammeled by decorum and discipline, "because the man who is really in pain, weeps and even cries out . . ." As anthologizer, demagogue, lyric poet, mystifier, and myth-maker, he persuades us that fallacy and disjunction may suggest a path to the ineffable when all other means have failed. Surrounding himself with a phalanx of "cardiac" writers ranging from Leopardi, Byron, Dante, and Comte to the pre-Socratics, the Greek classic tragedians, Swedenborg and Boehme, he leans most heavily on Harnack to trace the development of Christian thought and on the spirit of Kierkegaard in his insistence on the unknowability of God's attributes and the invincible need for His existence.

Above all, *The Tragic Sense of Life* presents the rare spectacle of an operation the author performs on himself; his work is "auto-surgery without any other anesthetic but the work itself. The pleasure of operating ennobled in me the pain of being operated on." Unamuno's direction, it must be underlined, is mainly inward: such words as "innards," "bones," "marrow," "abyss," "depth," "core of the soul," are repeated *ad infinitum,* for although his insistence on opposition, tension, and contradiction is suggestive of Hegelian dialectic, Unamuno recoils from impersonalizing the cosmos or finding a reconciliation of opposites in some absolute.[51] In Unamuno religious intentionality maintains itself flexed through constant inner struggle with doubt; it is his effort to overcome omnipresent perplexity through reasons of the heart, which he calls his faith. His concept of God is not one fixed for all times and situations, but a goal which retreats as implacably as he tries to reach it. His doubts are there always to be overcome, just as the saintly priests of Bernanos engage in combat with the evil ever abroad in the world. For Unamuno there is no way to battle with doubt except through personally rethinking the commonplaces of heritage and twisting them into shapes hitherto repudiated with disdain and horror. And if to Montaigne to philosophize is to learn to die, to Unamuno it is to struggle against death by thirsting after immortality in the most phantasmagoric and commandeering ways known to the imagination.

## VIII   *The Agony of Christianity*

It is the anomalous law of the spirit that it must continually disengage itself from the letter through which it has found its voice. While resting on structure and organization, religions of the spirit must also rebel against confinement and seek refreshment from the impurities of the institutional forms they are forced to adopt. Christianity developed in revolt against Scribes and Pharisees, against exclusivity and parochialism, and has followed the rhythm of acceptance and protest, continuity and upheaval, making of such contradictions the very nature of its vitality. Freedom of choice is the noblest and yet the most dangerous requirement it makes of its communicants, and since it is at one and the same time collectivist and personal, rational and mystic, authoritarian and forgiving, it sits on extreme absolute truths and accommodates itself to variants. The miracle of its inexhaustible strength is that it can and does engender apostles and reformers, exegetes and questioners, orthodoxy and dissension.

In this coil, Unamuno found the large pattern of his own discord. Never attracted to the substitute religions of art, science, or even politics that provide outlets for many religiously disenchanted souls, clinging to the conviction that religion is an "innermost disposition of the spirit" rather than a social shibboleth,[52] he was more of an unreconciled Christian than an unreconciled nonbeliever.

"The old mystic," says Paul Tillich, "went beyond cult and sacrament but he did not criticize them. The modern mystic, on the other hand, uses mysticism in order to set positive religion completely aside." [53] Standing before the mystery, but unaided by the "mysteries," Unamuno could neither go forward nor back. Fundamentally, he understood that the sense of Divinity, unsupported by authority and witnesses, may simply be the projection of wish or compulsion; he understood that the Church unifies belief which, if left unhandled, might encase each man in himself. On the other hand, if the Church makes faith intelligible to the gentile or uninitiate, in so doing it reduces absolutes to the sphere of relative knowledge and blurs the incommensurability of the eternal.

This is the impasse, consubstantial with Christianity itself, which Unamuno set out to explain in his *The Agony of Christianity* (*La Agonía del cristianismo*), written in Paris in 1924, during the early months of his exile there. The germ of the book lies in a short essay, "Pascalian Faith" ("La fe pascaliana"), which Unamuno contributed in 1923 to a special issue of *La Revue de Métaphysique et de Morale* in commemoration of the tercentenary of Pascal's birth. An expanded version of the essay became Chapter IX of *The Agony* which was translated into French by Jean Cassou as one of a series of monographs or *cahiers* on Christianity, and finally published again, in Spanish, in 1931.

It is a short, distraught book composed rapidly and disjointedly in the heat of a "spiritual fervor" brought on by the sufferings and loneliness of exile. The themes of *The Tragic Sense of Life,* "My Religion," and other essays achieve here a pitch almost of hysteria, as if the author had had no time to waste lest he lose the feeling of despair that was his hope, and sink back into a lethargy of hopelessness. The agony he refers to in the title and throughout the book is the tension between the feeling for a God who is incommunicable knowledge and the truth that is social and collective. Such a tension must not, and cannot, abate since agony means struggle, and so long as struggle prevails there is life, and death is fended off. It is not "struggle for life" but struggle as the definition of life itself, that provides the heat of existence, and peace comes only as it came to Don Quixote, in order to die.

Christ came to send not peace but a sword, for not only did he wish to separate son from father, daughter from mother, and daughter-in-law from mother-in-law, but to set man against himself in division and doubt. But Unamuno repeats that it is not the systematic, temporary doubt of a Descartes he refers to but the agonizing polemical faith of a Pascal. And in unending profusion Unamuno pours out the contradictions and paradoxes which are the very essence of a faith that reaches up to God yet must live in and of the world.

The Passion of Christ was the center of the new apocalyptic cult, and Jesus, believing in the imminent end of the world, had proclaimed "My kingdom is not of this world"; as a Jew, the author suggests, Jesus might have believed in the resurrection of the flesh rather than immortality in the Platonic sense. But when Jesus died and Christ was reborn in the soul of the faithful, there was born the agony or the conflict of the two dogmas, one Jewish, the other Hellenic and illustrated by St. Paul, the Hellenized Jew. And when the world did not come to an end for the witnesses of Jesus, each man started to anticipate his own end, that death which each man, living in society, can face only alone. To support this unbearable loneliness, each one had to make for himself an individual religion, a *religio quae non religat*.

Eventually the new religion took on the agony which is its strength and its torment: the conflict between the spirit or word which is a vivifying oral tradition on the one hand, and the letter which is the book that kills the spirit, on the other. In St. Paul the word became letter, in the Gospel it became the Book. And as the letter became dogma, the latter found its definition through differences, through heresies, and through negotiations. Even the Protestants, in their movement back to the word or spirit, enslaved the spirit in the letter, but as the Reformation began to Romanize itself, the Roman Church began to Protestantize itself. Gradually the ecumenical idea was transferred to nationalism, and Spanish traditionalism hoisted the motto of "God, Country, and King," while Mazzini would exclaim "God and Country," neither one in the spirit of Christ who fled to the solitude of the mountain when the crowd wished to proclaim him King.

As the spirit struggles to survive debasement amid the tumult of politics, both temporal and ecclesiastical, so did Abishag the Shunammite try to warm the body of the ancient King David. And she slept with him and served him but he did not know her. And when Adonijah rebelled against his father, Nathan told Bathsheba to extract from David the promise that her son Solomon would reign after him, and the priest Zadok was sent by David to anoint Solomon. Yet, oblivious to all worldly tumult, Abishag ministered to the King, but in vain. And when David died, Adonijah asked for Abishag's hand and Solomon was greatly vexed, and from there on nothing more is heard of the virgin Abishag and her unconsummated desire, although Solomon lived on with a harem.

So are we all Abishags, embracing our hope in an attempt to warm it into true faith, a faith belonging to each one of us, while the transactions of Church and State tend to temporalize pure essence. Minerva, the goddess of wisdom or practical intelligence, was born full-blown from Jupiter's head, but Christ who must constantly be won again in an agony of frustration, was born in suffering from woman's womb. Civilization, the temple, history, and politics seek to guide men's ineffable yearnings for immortality into channels of lucidity, cooperation, expedient action, but Abishag knew David only in unfulfilled desire, not in consummation, and if her love met with despair only, she did not trade her despair for family, power, or friends.

In a word, the Christian life is a purely personal problem, epitomized in the isolation of the monk. For just as Christ was anti-patriot to the Scribes and Pharisees, the pure Christian spirit turns away from the vanity of worldly things. With Romanization, however, came the paganization of Christianity, and the letter—not the word—was converted into canon law, and Christianity became juridical and mundane. And perhaps inevitably so, since no religion can survive in the monastic ideal alone; the race must be propagated and with society comes the assessment of right and wrong in law. Did not Dante pour out his contempt on that Celestine V who made the great refusal? How then can Christianity turn its back on matters of the world? And there again is the agony of Christianity, its innate contradiction, its tension, its discordance, and its vitality.

We are left, then, with this anomaly: that in the midst of the transactions of the world, to desire God is to try to create Him into existence, as Abishag tried to warm David. The Spanish word for "to wish," *querer,* derives from the Latin *quaerere,* to seek. Faith emerges from the search, from the desire for faith, from the simple fact that "I believe because I feel like believing." This is the personal agony—the Abishag agony—that must be sustained at the core of society and politics, at the core and within the framework of Solomon's realm.

And this contradiction is best exemplified in the Jesuits who, in order to combat the Reformation, dedicated themselves to the education, not of monks or solitary men, but of citizens and heads of families. And the cure of souls became in their hands secular education, the "pedagogical industry." The Jesuit is antimystical and his doctrine of passive obedience "is an anti-Christian doctrine . . ." The great adversary of the Jesuits, Pascal, drew the contrast between pure religiosity and the Jesuitical "accommodating policies . . . their casuistical morality." Pascal, the man of agony, understood that the Jesuits, with their rule of unquestioning obedience, killed agony, the very life of the Christian spirit, yet he also knew that without the accommodations of Jesuitical casuistry, a moral secular life would be impossible.

Since the will to believe is the only possible faith in a man with a lucid mathematical intelligence, for Pascal, the mathematician, as for so many others, God could not "ex-ist" but rather "in-sist" in the heart. Thus Pascal flew in the face of the anathema made official centuries later by the Vatican Council of 1869-1870, an anathema directed at anyone who denied that the existence of God can be demonstrated rationally and scientifically. Pascal might have chosen the middle way of the Pyrrhonians, but he could not resign himself to doubt, negation, and *scepsis,* and sought a solution not in synthesis but in the contradiction between faith and reason. "The cruelest war that God can wage against men in this life is to leave them without that war which He came to bring."

In this connection, Unamuno points out, it is significant to remember that we call Pascal's most important work *Thoughts,* which are fluid and free, and not *Ideas,* which are as solid and fixed as dogmas. And in one of those thoughts Pascal, who fought the passive mental obedience required by the Jesuits, advises abdication of reason, an *abêtissement.* This is again a personal task, for one can commit the suicide of reason only for oneself, never for others, although this latter is what the Jesuits try to do. However, in their endeavors to infantilize others, they themselves have become like children: "And today there is hardly anything more stupid than a Jesuit, at least a Spanish Jesuit. All the business about their cunning is sheer legend."

Therefore, with the Jesuits, Christianity no longer struggles and agonizes but is dead and buried with an epitaph consisting of the words of the most widely used catechism in Spain, the catechism of the Jesuit Father Astete: "Do not ask such questions of me, for I am ignorant; the Holy Mother Church has doctors who can answer you." But Pascal faced all the questions and made them his own; of ideas and dogmas he made thoughts, living truths for himself and others who conceive of Christianity in terms of irreconcilables, and who do not seek peace in codified doctrines.

Attached by tradition and nostalgia to the faith of his fathers, but cut off from innocent belief by his gnawing doubts, Unamuno sought consolation in the study of those who, like Kierkegaard, or the apostate priests Tyrrell and Loisy, had been denounced by the church authorities, had been declared outcasts, and had yet clung with greater passion to a personalized belief. He had long found comfort in the example of a Lamennais, who, at odds with orthodoxy, but holding fast to his need for God, had claimed in his *Essai sur l'indifférence en matière de religion* that absolute certainty and absolute doubt were equally untenable.[54]

He was, above all, fascinated by Father Hyacinthe Loyson whose life he read while writing *The Agony of Christianity,* and who had left the Church in order to marry and beget children so that he might perpetuate himself in the flesh. The Loyson who confessed that "I bear doubt at the bottom of my mind; I have always had it . . ." won a secure place among Unamuno's "cardiac" writers. For Loyson had lived, like Unamuno, with God in the mind and soul not as irrefragable truth, but as a working hypothesis; God, for the Frenchman as for the Spaniard, was the premise from which he proceeded but which he doubted. Like Unamuno, furthermore, Loyson abhorred politics, yet had to concern himself with the matters of the world. Torn between solitude and the exigencies of social living, between religion and its abuses, Loyson was, like the Unamuno who interpreted him in his own image, a

church of one, the church of contradiction and paradox, of flesh
and spirit, of allegiance and reservation, of loyalties joined to dissent.

* * * * * * *

The *Agony of Christianity* might be considered a pendant or
codicil to *The Tragic Sense of Life,* for the poetry engendered by
the emotion is equally irregular and fitful, lending itself only with
difficulty to critical parsing. The recently exiled Unamuno, shaken
by doubts over his role as political martyr when his true concerns
were supramundane, is in this book erratic and gratuitous, tortuous
in thought, wayward in perception, addicted to purple patches,
biblical not only in allusion but in color and tone.

Yet the boldness and relevance of the themes cannot be gain-
said: the deemphasis of properly established ecclesiastical media-
tion, the greatest affirmation of active faith in the face of denial
or indifference, the stress on the pain and grandeur of personal
awareness. Still bearing the earmarks of the latter-day Lutheran,
Unamuno strained to inspire a "Spanish Catholicism" resting on
the twin pillars of despair and hope: "We may cease being Catholics, we shall cease being [Catholics] in the orthodox sense of the
Roman Church—such is my faith and most ardent wish and
desire—but with any other belief we shall show the same spirit
which as champions of the Counter-Reformation our ancestors
showed."

Whatever shape Unamuno had in mind for this indigenous
reform, we may be sure that he meant its core to be what St. Teresa
called the "exquisite pain" (*dolor sabroso*), so differentiated in
Unamuno's mind from the religion of jurists and counselors and
cataloguers, or that of the *honnête homme* who combines the good
life with good sense, and personifies the compromise of logic
rather than the truth of paradox. Like the mystic Franciscan monk,
Juan de los Angeles, who exclaimed "Me for God and God for
me . . . ," to Unamuno theology was "egology":[55] to believe in
God was to monopolize Him and so return to that pristine Christianity which stressed God's nexus to each separate man. To come
to God with the intense love of the protomystic is to be unable to
share the knowledge formally with anyone else; it is to devour
Him intimately as lover devours lover in the ecstasy of junction.
And like all lovers, Unamuno would not consent to having his

beloved chosen for him by agreement, common sense, council, or even Revelation.

Kierkegaard had emphatically stated that "the more spiritual the aim is, the more one can exalt doubt," [56] and Unamuno sums up his own thought in the words of the tormented father in Mark 9:24, "Lord, I believe; help Thou my unbelief." By thus propounding his personal ethic of strife (*moral de batalla*) he widens the definition of religion to embrace those who, disenfranchised from sectarianism, are left only with what Tillich has called "an ultimate concern." The dynamic revisionist attitudes of our day may very well weaken the mysteries of religion without weakening the concomitant religious need which, Unamuno repeated, starts with man and not with what he knows. "Religion," writes A. N. Whitehead, "is the vision of something which stands beyond, behind, and within the passing flux of immediate things; . . . something which is the ultimate ideal, and the hopeless quest." [57]

Writing in a country long refractory to developments elsewhere, Unamuno nevertheless understood and dramatized the nostalgia of the intellectual anywhere who is compelled to uphold what he most needs in the face of wave upon wave of denial. The balm he pours upon this dilemma is the reassurance that as faith seems to lose ground, it loses only that which is most unnecessary to its strength. We are left with the passion, but since we are always wrong "as against God," [58] we must accept the offense to our understanding and embrace both offense and paradox in infinite longing.

As Unamuno transmuted the ontology of disproof and despair through affirmation of the "impossible," he did not banish conceptual knowledge out of hand, but reduced its status from definitive to *ad hoc*. The crucifix he wore under his shirt and close to his heart was not so much a symbol of Christian certainty as a statement to the effect that "so much have I honored Christianity that I have employed every hour of my life in pondering it." [59] Since this Christian concern is an existential contradiction, it brings no surcease ever: "I prefer to be an unhappy angel rather than a satisfied pig." [60] For the "aesthetic" or even the "ethical" individual, suffering is a transitory state from which he aims to set himself free; even if the suffering persists, it "stands in an accidental relation to existence." [61] Religious suffering, on the other hand, is

to remain in agony, to derive strength from a deepening sense of
approximation to truth. The difference between the comic and
tragic apprehension is that the comic has in mind a way out,
making the contradiction painless, while the tragic "sees the contradiction and despairs of a way out." [62]

## IX   Some Comparisons

Unamuno's views coincide with a substantial segment of modern
thought that again recognizes a primordial mystery which, as it
gains freedom from the superstitions of worship, nevertheless
remains invulnerable, omnipresent, but happily shrouded in mist.
Not only Unamuno, but other thinkers stress the unknowable, not
as a margin of the knowable nor a subsidiary element of life, but
as that vast area in which "the real man and all being which he
touches [is free] from a supposed identity with its knowability, or
fixed knownness." [63]

Central to Gabriel Marcel's philosophy is the distinction he
draws between "mystery," which is impenetrable, and "problem,"
which, like Kierkegaard's and Unamuno's "comic" sense of life,
is the unknown only so long as it is not penetrated. Being, immediately apprehended, always precedes "problem" and always
surrounds it; no knowledge can therefore substantiate being "for
which no epistemology can account because it continually pre-
supposes it." [64] Thus only by detachment from experience into
recollection do we rise to the level of mystery where we apprehend
a reality that cannot be "summed up." Furthermore, Marcel insists, as the disproportion grows between proud technical intelligence and the continuing fragility of life, our pessimism grows and
can be counteracted by a creative hope that recognizes man's
liberty from perishable things through his permeability to a higher
unparticularized presence. Such an openness may be fertilized by
Christian data but does not "presuppose it";[65] indeed, the facts of
revelation may become meaningful only to those who have first
ventured beyond the frontiers of the problematical to the point of
recognizing mystery.

Unconcerned with the problem of religion, Martin Heidegger has
as his goal the return to the vital center or ground and the rescue
of the spirit used as "tool." In pre-Socratic thinking, *physis* and
*logos,* unfolding being and the word (or thought), were one and

the same, but *logos* seceded from being and the idea became the "whatness" of the thing. In other words, appearance or phenomenon was no longer *physis,* but a deficient copy. When being becomes *logos* and *logos* is incorporated into language, language becomes the custodian of being and truth becomes an "attribute of statement," a shifting thing determined by "properties, magnitude, relations," [66] in short, categories. Statement assumes such supremacy that *phasis* or speech will not tolerate *antiphasis* or contradiction, and spreads "by way of discussion, teaching, and rules, becoming steadily broader and flatter." [67] *Logos* has become logic, a tool to constrain being within its rules and so degrade it. To counteract such degradation, one must set something *"above* being, something that being never is yet but always *ought* to be." [68]

It becomes evident that at this point Heidegger hovers on the edge of some religious incursion, but as Professor Collins explains, refrains from saying anything about God "not out of indifference but because of a respect for the limits of philosophical inquiry." [69] Unamuno would agree, of course, only insofar as he would recognize that philosophers and theologians are not necessarily equipped to trace the delineaments of God, but not to exempt them from a preoccupation with the problem. More central to Unamuno's thought is the consideration that reason is an usurpation of the whole by the part, an arbitrary breaking-up of an indivisible unity into discrete parts. Reason is skeptical for it cannot accept any truth that is not coherent; outside the formal arrangements of sense perceptions, the spirit of geometry is not only impotent, but annihilating.

It is Unamuno's emphasis on the insufficiencies of life's tangible offerings that establishes his affinity with Karl Jaspers. The latter argues that despite man's immersion in the penultimates of business, family, society, love, entertainment, he cannot escape those "limit [ultimate] situations" where he faces his own destiny unaided. Whatever his background, whatever the expectations that progress and change hold out to him, he cannot escape the omnipresence of contingency, guilt, and the cancellation of the best intentions by death.[70] Thus compelled to think of mystery in terms not contained in facts and figures, man is yet earthbound and can only handle the mysterious in inadequate non-mysterious terms. Since modern theological philosophy combines the Greek concept of God with the Ineffable God of the Jews, man can soar up to pure being only as he frees himself of existents or pure objects. When Unamuno places God qualitatively beyond the limitations and errors of the human purview, he not only confirms Jaspers' suggestion that what matters is "not our knowledge of God but our attitude towards God," [71] but agrees with Chestov that "one cannot say of God that He exists, for in saying 'God exists' one loses Him immediately," and with Karl Barth that "God is a subject and not an object." [72]

When Unamuno declares, then, that theology is a basic contradiction since there can be no compatibility between *theos* and *logia*,[73] he is nearer to many of his contemporaries than has hitherto been acknowledged. The magnitude of God lies in His superhuman demand; His might lies in His freedom from all exegesis. His majesty is greater than the Summas compounded in His name and greater than the errors discerned in "divine" books. He cannot be possessed or dispossessed, He is infinitely beyond. As our unlimited devotion to God lifts us above interpretation, we escape both the trap of fanaticism and the trap of despair over ephemeral truth infinitely open to correction and supplementation.

\*   \*   \*   \*   \*   \*   \*

Even in scientific thought contradiction is no longer considered an error in calculation, and tentativeness is the very nature of advancement. If Unamuno said that there are as many philosophies as languages and dialects, including the dialect of each individual,[74] Werner Heisenberg would say "we can no longer talk of the image of nature but the image of our relations with nature," [75] and Niels Bohr has provided an aphorism that might have been formulated by Unamuno the poet: "There are the trivial truths and the great truths. The opposite of a trivial truth is plainly false. The opposite of a great truth is also true." [76]

Unpredictability has crowded out determinism, irregularity has in many instances refuted causality, and the idea of the working hypothesis is replacing the finality of the "rules" of nature. Eddington called exact science "pointer-reading," and Jeans thought that "all the pictures which science now draws of Nature, and which alone seem capable of according with observational fact, are mathematical pictures." [77] The subjective factors play as paramount a role in scientific elaboration as in philosophic, and it is recorded that Einstein disliked Eddington's theory but could not disprove it, while Eddington said of Einstein's theory that it was a matter of taste.[78] With typical appropriateness, Ortega once said that as poetry is a form of knowledge, so physics is a form of poetry or fantasy, ". . . a mutable fantasy which imagines today a physical world different from yesterday's and will imagine tomorrow [a physical world] different from today's." [79]

While such views have contributed to breaking down the concept of a clear, organized universe, the increase of physical comforts has yielded only partial dividends; exploration carries with it malaise, extension of height and depth has emphasized endlessness, and the increase of amusements has heightened the awareness of triviality. The purely material and calculable may indeed, as Unamuno pointed out, feed on itself like the ulcer and produce a sense of despair over the possibility of egress. Life's expanding facilities generate a need for something they cannot supply, for an inspiration and meaning not contained in tangible achievements or potentialities. Addressing himself to this existential agony, Unamuno proposes a broadening of all views to the point where the despair over the indispensable and unratifiable may be absorbed into life through recognition of its permanence.

To this end, Unamuno uses every means at his disposal—authority, myth, metaphor, fantasy, dream, command—and carries the philosophical essay to its highest poetic power as he evolves thought from emotion and possibility from desire. As a supreme personalistic thinker, putting life before abstraction and finding the ultimate significance of life not in life itself but in its unconfirmed extension into the endless, his voice becomes more compelling all the time as men question the postulates of tradition and revolution, of faith and reason, of conformity and libertarianism.

## CHAPTER 3

# History and Eternity—I

UNAMUNO was always fond of pointing out that Dante, the supreme other-worldly poet, was nevertheless a great Florentine patriot. The sage of Salamanca who purported to be a teacher to all men was likewise a passionate lover of his country, and like the egotist who enriches himself to the point of being able to give of his abundance to others, Unamuno felt that only by saturating himself in knowledge of every facet of national culture could he separate the gold from the dross and suggest what Spain had to offer to the rest of the world. First, however, he had to delve into Spanish history in order to distinguish sanctioned distortions from solid truth.

The advent of the Bourbon dynasty at the very beginning of the eighteenth century accentuated the split between what has been referred to, at least since Larra, as the "Two Spains." On the one side stood the traditionalists or *casticistas* whose mission was to combat denaturalization of the Spanish spirit and modalities, and on the other the progressives who looked to the rest of Europe—and especially to France—for guidance in renewal or revitalization. The debate centered essentially about the question whether Spain could best serve herself by marching abreast of the rest of the continent, or by vigilant fidelity to the tradition of the sixteenth and seventeenth centuries.

Despite very worthy resistance, the strong feeling created by the Counter-Reformation that the Spaniards were a chosen people invested with the holy task of restoring the universality of Catholicism, or at least of keeping religion within Spain's own boundaries untainted by heresy or qualification from abroad, was not allowed to die. Church and State continued more closely allied in Spain that anywhere else in Western Europe, and any challenge to the political status quo was interpreted as a blow aimed at religion. If, on his visit to Spain in 1840, Gautier concluded that the

country was no longer Catholic, the Spanish moralist Jaime Balmes
asserted that Catholicism was the greatest hope of Spain and his
fellow countryman Juan Donoso Cortés denied any value to liberalism. Marcelino Menéndez y Pelayo believed the national decline
had begun with the expulsion of the Jesuits in the eighteenth
century, and Ramiro de Maeztu (1875-1936), who had swerved
from extreme radicalism to extreme reaction, dated the decline
from the middle of the eighteenth century when the country turned
away from the *philosophia perennis* to imitate France. When Alfonso XIII visited Rome in November of 1923, he advised
Pope Pius XI that in any fresh crusade against the enemies of
Catholicism he could count on Spain, yet after the Republic was
declared, Manuel Azaña proclaimed that Catholic Spain had
ceased to exist. "This," Menéndez Pidal says, "was the fatal destiny
of the two sons of Oedipus, who would not consent to reign together and mortally wounded each other." [1]

The members of the so-called Generation of 1898, born around
the third quarter of the nineteenth century, were beset by the
quandary of love for a country that did not inspire pride. As they
set about rediscovering the history-drenched towns, cities, and
countryside, they found not only poetry but sadness and decay,
ignorance, baseless vanity, and paralyzing envy. Azorín, who in his
youth had clamored for reform, sank back into conservatism and,
sitting at the windows of inns, cheek in hand, he looked out at a
melancholy landscape soaked in the past but closed to the future.
Baroja, among the fiercest of his contemporaries in his condemnation of the country he loved, asserted that no worthy Spaniard
could be anything but a solitary, for if the traditionalists were im-
mobilized in the posture of Lot's wife, the intelligentsia were
grotesquely inept. One of Valle-Inclán's fictional characters calls
Spain a grotesque deformation of European civilization, while the
greatest poet of his generation and a liberal thinker, Antonio
Machado, gave vent to his sorrow: "Wretched Castile, yesterday
triumphant, / is wrapped in rags, despising what it does not know."
(*"Castilla miserable, ayer dominadora, / envuelta en sus andrajos
desprecia cuanto ignora."*)

For over two centuries Europe had been witnessing the distress
of the Iberian peninsula stripped of territory and power; and
especially mortifying for the Spanish intellectual was general European indifference to the culture of Spain except for an occasional

glance southward for the picturesque detail, the exotic pose, or the archeological find. It was therefore the mission of the gifted Spaniard, Unamuno held, to utter with every power at his disposal a resounding Yea. More than any of his contemporaries, Unamuno took up the gauntlet and in thundering tones announced *urbi et orbi* that his beloved Spain was neither an anachronism nor a function-less organ in the body politic of the world. In speech, essay, verse, and book he designed major metaphors to help his fellow country-men overcome a deep-rooted sense of inadequacy and to define a Spanish mission strong enough to shake Europe into admitting the possibilities of values not dependent on industrial output, territorial expansion, political power, or fashion in arts and letters.

As grandiose as Unamuno's metaphors may be, their applica-bility to any given situation is limited. Almost from the very first, he strove to make of himself the acknowledged spiritual legislator of his country, yet remained fiercely in opposition to all entrenched power of whatever persuasion, and restricted his counsel mainly to the poetic mode. Since, in the long run, any concrete programme struck him as false, and since his viewpoint was life-in-struggle rather than struggle-for-life, his message is animating rather than regulative, virtual rather than specific.

Nothing bears this out so much as Unamuno's connections with the Socialist movement in Spain. Even before joining the Socialist Party (*Agrupación Socialista*) of Bilbao in 1894, he had enter-tained sympathies for radical thought, and although he contributed a good many articles to the party organ *The Class Struggle* (*La Lucha de Clases*), especially between 1895-1897, he could not subscribe to their anticlerical or antireligious leanings. In a letter to Clarín dated May 31, 1895, he wrote that his mystical ten-dencies were taking the shape of a Socialist ideal "such as I see it. I dream that socialism may become a true religious reform when Marxist dogmatism fades away, that it may become something more than purely economic." [2] Several months before his crisis of the Spring of 1897 he had already left the Socialist Party, for as he wrote in October 30 of that year, pure socialism "sets itself up as the one single doctrine and forgets that after the problem of life comes the problem of death." The task of making life easier and more pleasurable increases the pain of death and results in *noia* and spleen, in *taedium vitae*. "From the very bosom of the resolved social question (will it ever be resolved?) will surge the religious question: is life worth living?"[3] If the one keystone to the spirit of a nation was its property system, the other was the attitude towards the ultimate goal in life, that is, how the peasant receives his last rites.[4]

After his withdrawal from the Socialist Party, however, Unamuno did not totally cease his criticism of economic injustice and exploitation. He took capitalism to task for quoting human effort in terms of production value, he condemned bourgeois greed as being responsible for war, and approved of pressures exerted by English trade unionism on capitalism as one of the great forces of progress. He fulminated against the use of excess capital for interest instead of for the improvement of agriculture (here the influence of the economist and agrarian, Joaquín Costa, is unmistakable), and pinpointed the maldistribution of property as the weakness of Spanish economy. He called upon the State to pass labor legislation and even exhorted workers to win over public power, but peaceably within the framework of law and order. In *The Life of Don Quixote and Sancho* (1905) he points to the Sancho who accepted money to whip himself in order to "disenchant" Dulcinea, but in reality whipped a tree, as the perfect symbol of the laborer on whose work society lives. When the Sanchos rebel, their masters offer them higher fees for their troubles, but the Sanchos deceive their masters by giving themselves seven or eight blows and then applying the rest to a tree trunk. Behind the play of exploitation on the part of the monied classes and the retaliatory tricks of the working classes, lies the system of property rights, and Sancho would do well to turn on his masters and whip them instead of the trees.[5]

But such pronouncements became rarer with time for, to his mind, the regeneration of Spain could not come from any specific prescriptions. Such solutions were for sectarians, and although habits of hard work and educational reform were well and good, ". . . it is not enough for us, nor can it be the basis for our renovation. . . . I think that any future aggrandizement of Spain . . . not based on a [special] way of conceiving and feeling religious life and liberty of Christian conscience will be misleading and only superficial . . ."[6] Unamuno the extremist could condemn the aesthetic man for living in too close a relationship with himself, and he could exalt the religious man for living in the closest God-self equation, but the ethical stand was always to be for him a half-way house. The intermediate position adopted even by the Church in its concern with temporal questions through "social Christianity" was, in his eyes, an attrition of its primary purpose, while his emphasis on "dedicated labor" in *The Tragic Sense of Life* is more closely related to his preoccupation with the deepening of subjectivity than with anxiety over material benefits. Basically his economic views were the same as his religious views, those of a "heretic even within heresy. Anything but dogma." [7] And Father Benítez is justified in saying that "Unamuno's Socialism has . . . as much to do with [orthodox] Socialism . . . as the love of St. John of the Cross with the love of Don Juan Tenorio." [8]

## I   En torno al casticismo (On Authentic Tradition)

If Unamuno held to any established view concerning healthful change for his country, it was that such change had to develop organically from the bedrock of the nation, and it was therefore necessary to disentangle what was genuinely and authentically Spanish from what was ancillary or even spurious. If change was antithesis, it was indispensable to find the basic thesis in order to arrive at some middle way. "There will not be any healthy public life," he wrote, "so long as the essence of our nation does not find agreement with its exteriorization, so long as adaptation does not fit in with heritage." [9] It was vital to define the genius of Spain if, in consonance with that genius, she were to conjugate with the nations north of the Pyrenees and recover her station in the world. The practical regenerationist, Joaquín Costa himself, had advised Europeanization, but not at the cost of de-Hispanization.

Only two men at the end of the nineteenth century were to make permanent literary contributions in their attempts to define the character of Spain in terms of comprehensive strengths and weaknesses for the express purpose of therapy and renewal. These were Angel Ganivet (1865-1898) whose *Ideas on Spain* (*Idearium español*) appeared in 1897, and Miguel de Unamuno who two year earlier, in 1895, wrote five articles for the review *La España Moderna,* published in book form as *On Authentic Tradition* (*En torno al casticismo*) in 1902. The attitude behind such enterprises was to ferret out what was irrefutable and eternal in Spanish tradition, and by so doing, to "vitamize" it. For Ganivet, the origin of Spanish decadence and prostration lay in excessive ambitions, in having attempted actions incommensurate with the real strength of the nation. "Since we have exhausted our possibilities of material expansion," he concluded, "we must change our tactics and tap the intellectual strength that never gives out . . ." [10]

Similarly, Unamuno in his book turns away from what he called *condenada historia* or "accursed history" which, by emphasizing past glories, draws attention to subsequent ineptitude, blunders, and defeats. For the recorded events in history, both flattering and ignoble, are to the continuity of history what disparate moments in time are—we may say—to Bergson's fluid, indivisible time: a distortion or falsification. Unamuno attacks false national pride which, contemplating its own navel, will assimilate little or nothing from abroad, contrasts the petrified aristocracy with the vital energies of the masses (*pueblo*), the true repository of national strength, calls upon Spanish youth to study the people as much as it does national history, and invites compatible foreign influences to tear up the ground in which the new seeds are to be planted.

Even to the most perspicacious, history dissembles the fact that humanity goes on living and working like the silent sea over which the waves of cataclysm break. Tradition lives in this humble unspectacular world and is therefore always present; to seek it in the past is to seek eternity in the past only, which is a form of death. Genuine, unshakable tradition resides in the persistent, inexhaustible rhythm of humanity which is ever fertile and provides the strength for victory and for survival in defeat. Drawing upon German Romantic concepts, and particularly the Herderian *Volksgeist,* filtered through Joaquín Costa, Unamuno calls this intrahistory (*intrahistoria*).

The work of intrahistory—which he compares with suboceanic coral—is to provide the bases for the islands of history. The eternal Spanish tradition, consequently, is fundamentally the tradition of all people; it is a common and endless reservoir of vitality and any quality that so deeply affects a race as to alienate it from the rest of the world is by definition a defect. To know one's roots is to discern where those roots join others; to receive fresh currents of air is not to renounce one's heritage but to revitalize it. The affection the Spaniard devoutly professes for his *lares* would not be diluted by foreign influences but rather strengthened, exactly as the parts of the human organism are invigorated, not debilitated, when the lungs breathe deeply. The study of national history, therefore, like the study of national religion, should not turn into a solid wall against "regenerating penitence" or into an apology for racial defects like the sentimental old lady of Larra's anecdote who harbored a passion for hunchbacks because her beloved had been one.

In his analysis of such national defects, Unamuno often coincides with Ganivet. Like his friend, he centers Spanish history in Castile and deplores the depletion of national strength in military conquest. As Castile pursued its goals of conquest and expansion, it slowly destroyed its political power, but in the realm of spirit and art Castile left lofty, enduring monuments. Yet Castilian literature is very much like the soil and climate from which it sprang, poor in nuance, made up of sharp contrasts of light and shadow, austere, polarizing flesh and spirit.

The Castilian temper is foreign to soft gradations and slow unfoldings; consequently, its theater, the quintessential manifestation of its spirit, is rich in abstractions and mighty concepts presented hieratically. Calderón's theater, which best represents the Spanish Golden Age, is a storehouse of abstruse, categorical ideas with no room for the unique, individualized character. Calderón's talent is signalized both by a lightning intuition and the absence of that balance and calm which Ganivet also deplored as a weakness of the Spanish temper. Instead of delineating men of flesh and blood, Calderón divorces the ideal from the real and resolves the enigmas of life unhesitatingly, without doubt and without antinomies. This inability to suggest nimbus, shadings, muted colors, leads to the extravagance of "apoplectic" rhetoric, epilepsy of the imagination, gongorism. The characters of such a theater are constructed from the outside in; they crystallize into complete form *ex abrupto* and lack the rich texture of a Lear, Hamlet, or Othello. Where those Shakespearean creations embody psychological truths germane to all times, Calderón's heroes express the ideals of his own time: they are hard, of one piece, the projections of established dogma and the counterparts of the proud, unbending fierce hidalgos and conquerors of the seventeenth century. "This is the traditional [Spanish] soul, warlike and indolent, passing from impulse to impassibility, without gradation which makes for the sustained, unspectacular, diffuse, slow heroism of true labor."

Similarly, love is treated in Castilian literature as either gross or austere, and since the Spanish troubadours were Galician, Catalan, Valencian, rarely Castilian, the "erotic casuistry" of the Middle Ages finds no place in Castilian letters. Remote from the European tradition running from Abelard to Werther, passion in Castilian writing is represented either by the profligate Don Juan or the vengeance-seeking husband.

In religion, too, the strain is towards unity: one persuasion into which all contraries must be forced and from which all dissidents must be ejected. Such intensity does not indicate so much a strength of mind as an inability to cope with complexities and an intransigency that condemns all differences. Monistically, it must conciliate this world with the next in one supreme ideal, the mystical, which embodies true Castilian philosophy, the "perfect adequation of the inner with the outer, the perfect fusion of knowledge, feeling, and desire. . ." Castilian mystics shut their eyes to intrusions from the world of facts, induction, experimentation, to find an absolute in the heart, in the "inner castle," and when as late as the nineteenth century, the winds of philosophy began to blow, a mystical, nebulous Krausism found propitious soil in Spain.

Implicit in the mystic's withdrawal from the world is a strong dose of egoism, for if the solitary seeks personal salvation through renunciation, the *fraile* or *frater* seeks to save himself by redeeming others. If the symbol of the Spanish St. Teresa is the arrow of God in which she alone rejoices, the religious symbol of the Italian St. Francis of Assisi is the stigmata, the signs of the crucifixion, or the sacrifice of self for others. The Italian mystics bequeathed to the world the popular art of the "little flowers" while the Spaniards found expression in the highly involved allegorical *autos sacramentales* or in the arcane poems of St. John of the Cross; if Giotto, Fra Angelico, Ghirlandaio and Cimabue painted in the rosy hues of dawn, Zurbarán and Ribera concentrated on tormented anchorites.

Thus does the dissociative, antisocial spirit work to the detriment of Spain. The peasant, sunk in his torpor and ignorance, clings to his old ways; the middle classes pursue the ways of security and ape the French; the aristocracy dreams of some miraculous return to the Golden Age; the military strives for might in Africa; and the ascetic concentrates on his own salvation. Spaniards are still governed, Unamuno explains, by spurts and spasms of discontinuous energy or fatalistic resignation, attitudes which are two sides of the same coin: abulia. Spanish society is too slow in reacting to impressions, but once the Spaniard has accepted an idea it becomes what Ganivet would call a fixed idea: the vital inner currents become marshes of stagnant waters sucking down even the young who should provide the impetus of renovation. Instead of evincing daring vitality, Spanish youth expends itself in seeking security within stagnation, in seeking adjustment and reassurance rather than risk.

Such are the dikes set up by a rancid historical spirit against renewal, for even though the Inquisition as an institution is dead, it has deep roots in Spanish conservatism. If, in the past, it suppressed the rich flowering that had taken place in the Reformation countries, today its spirit isolates Spain from the rest of the world in order to protect an ill-defined "purity." Help will come only with the opening of windows to the rest of Europe: "Spain is still to be discovered, and only Europeanized Spaniards will discover it." Hence, efforts must be exerted simultaneously in two directions: to break down Tibetan isolation in order to assimilate the best from abroad, and to encourage a dedication to plumbing the potential incarnate in the Spanish people. Since the principle of international continuity is coexistential with the masses in intrahistory, a broadening of vistas can never run contrary to the Spanish personality if rightly understood. "I regenerate my blood with air from without, not by breathing in the air I exhale."

Unamuno confesses that his five essays are "disjointed ramblings"; had he already discovered Kierkegaard, he might have called them "scraps" or "fragments." Despite inconsistencies and egregious errors, the lesson he seeks to teach in *On Authentic Tradition* is clear. Spain must shake off its inertia, the aftermath of an historical trance; it must shift from narcissistic pride to pride in aims common to all men. History is a limber force which derives from the past but is not shackled to it, and if not held back by selfish thinking, it points to the future. Hope lies only in those Spaniards who will galvanize the untapped energies of the collective spirit which, freed from bondage, can join forces with the "common soul" of all nations. Beneath national forms lies the pristine vigor of universal forms; beneath the crust of caste lies an elastic material ready to take on infinite numbers of shapes.

Since Unamuno's time a great deal of scholarship has gone into teaching how warily one must tread in drawing the spiritual, intellectual, and historical profiles of nations and races, and how writers in these fields are impelled by motives other than objective research. We have learned how hypertrophied nationalism grows pathologically from contempt or mistrust of heterogeneity, how the passion for racial or ideological purity becomes the rationale for brutality and carnage, while the needs of the laborious, inarticulate masses are either disregarded or exploited and misled.

Therefore, despite turbidities of style and misuse of fact, Unamuno stands with those philosophers of history who, like Nietzsche, directed their animadversions against the idolatry of an antiquarian or aggrandized past that breeds a helpless feeling of decline or encourages futile attempts at emulating bygone glories. A pious attachment to history, we have seen most recently, can lead to a worship of sham "innate" values in a race or nation, and imbue it with a sense of specialty that derives more from pride than truth. Against the "malady of history," Nietzsche proposed the "unhistorical" and the "superhistorical," the first being the art of forgetting history, the other being attention "to that which gives existence an eternal and stable character, to art and religion."[11] Unamuno's antidote is intrahistory, that immutable substratum which supports all vicissitude and is always ready for further development, and he therefore inveighs against "presbytocracy," against the confinements and smugness of the family unit, against passive obedience to authority, against routine and superstition. He arouses the anxiety that must precede reexamination, and exhorts the Spaniard to raise his own status by partaking of the general European patrimony. In short, his book is an attack on blind loyalty to obsolete norms which parades as constancy, and on that impracticality which calls itself idealistic.

## II   *Intrahistory and Landscape*

If the admonitions and analyses of *On Authentic Tradition* make it one of the pivotal works of the Unamuno canon, it is also significant for containing the seeds of dilemmas which would plague the author for the rest of his life and provide the dramatic malaise of his subsequent work. In his discussion of Castilian mysticism, for example, he is confronted by the problems of integrity: is personal salvation a self-sufficient task or disguised selfishness? On the other hand, to what extent does engagement in the world constitute a peril to one's own personality? How far can convictions be exposed before they become diluted in words, and how far can one temporize with circumstance before the latter assumes the lead?

Similarly, in his exhortations to his countrymen to receive and absorb fertilizing elements from abroad, he stops short to warn against subservience: foreign influences, he holds, must serve not as invaders but as catalytic agents for native resources. Furthermore, as he welcomed fresh suggestions, he understood from his own experience the high price paid for such change in the form of restlessness, agitation, upheaval. The antidote to such possible ideological homelessness, he came to understand, is to anchor oneself firmly in one's country, in one's region, in one's home, and thus to establish a confidence and balance on which to build. A broadening of horizons could only be healthfully achieved on a firm basis of deep, personal love of one's country, an understanding of its people, its geography, its languages and dialects, its legends and folklore. An intimate contact with intrahistory was necessary not only to prove that "Spain is amiable while its history is not, for Spain is not its history,"[12] but for a love of the universal human fatherland.

Intrahistory could only be apprehended by steeping oneself in it, and Unamuno took every opportunity to travel widely in the peninsula, especially to out-of-the-way places, as if in answer to Ganivet's injunction, adapted from Augustine: *Noli foras ire, in interiore Hispaniae habitat veritas.* So closely did he identify with the landscape and the people inhabiting it that they became vital parts of his own being, and when on more than one occasion he exclaimed, *Me duele España* ("Spain hurts me"), it was as if the sorrow of Spain were as much a source of personal suffering as any organ of his body. Alleviation of that pain came to him through compenetration with the entire peninsula where he sought out those beauties and meanings that could never be marred or discounted by history.

It was true that the country was limp with apathy, scarred by poor taste, hypocrisy, superficiality, imitativeness, but it was nonetheless alive, not in its monumentalized past, but in the untapped strength of its population, in the variety of its provinces, in its physical and spiritual configurations. In innumerable essays devoted to his excursions to the various regions of *his* peninsula, Unamuno recounts how he assimilated them into himself—into "landscapes of the soul"—and pours forth the tenderness and understanding of the true patriot, not of the professional "patrioteer." By submerging himself in a spiritualized geography of Spain and Portugal, he is again sure of the undiminished strength of a continuum upon which history descends only at disparate moments, just as paleontology records the steps of dinosaurs but not the flight of birds.[13]

The many trips he made to the various points of the peninsula were undertaken, of course, to refresh his overburdened spirit and mind, to relieve the satiety so familiar to bookish men, and, like the Fray Luis de León, whose statue benignly faces the plateresque façade of the old University of Salamanca, to leave behind the friction of academic life, the noise of students, and follow the path "that lies/apart, where wise men go–/ The hidden path the earth's few sages choose!" (*Noche Serena*). There he sought out the "eternal Spain" so utterly different from the operatic Spain of gypsies, bullfights, and castanets created by native and foreign artists for general delectation.

And there he found the materials for admonitory sermons directed at those who sought the false cosmopolitanism not only of Madrid and Barcelona, but of Rome, Berlin, and above all, of Paris. For the overly urbanized he advised dropping the decorum of society, leaving behind the civilization of railroad, telegraph, telephone, and WC, and permitting the body the relaxation of physical exertion. Undeterred by the hardship of rural travel, he penetrated hidden places "full of history, legend, poetry, and peace in Castile, Aragon, Extremadura, or Andalusia"[14] to immerse himself in the soul of a nation compounded of trees, mountains, and rivers, and the people living among them. And he found that silent expanses did not necessarily bespeak atrophy, the monuments were not museums, the grave peasants were not boors, and the Castilian steppes were as rich in spirit as they were denuded of vegetation. This was the same Unamuno who contradictorily on many occasions deplored the ignorance, the avarice, and brutality of rural life and exclaimed "Ruralism is ruining us,"[15] but in the main preferred the countryside to large cities where he was assailed by an invincible "Platonic" fear of democracies based on numbers, and recoiled from the seas of unknown faces involved in collective activities which raised the lowly and degraded the lofty, where mediocrities were acclaimed and summits flattened out. To the noisy Madrid or the pretentious Barcelona, he preferred Guadalupe, Avila, Yuste, Zamora, Palencia, the Canary Islands, Mallorca, and to Lisbon he preferred Braga, Guarda, Alcobaça.

Only four times did Unamuno go abroad: once as a young man in 1889 to visit Italy and France; the second time in September of 1917 as a member of a Spanish group visiting the Italian front; the third time, from 1924-1930 as a political exile in France; and the fourth time to England in 1936 to receive the degree of doctor *honoris causa* from Oxford. If he welcomed foreign culture in the form of books and magazines, and maintained epistolary friendships with important foreign figures, he was reluctant to travel beyond the boundaries of the peninsula and instead made of his excursions through Spain and Portugal a regular invigorating phenomenon of his life and of his travel impressions a remarkable part of his output. The articles collected in such books as *Landscapes (Paisajes), 1902, From My Native Region (De mi país),* 1903, *Through Regions of Portugal and Spain (Por Tierras de Portugal y de España),* 1911, *Spanish Travels and Vistas (Andanzas y visiones españolas),* 1922, or the posthumous *Landscapes of the Soul, 1892-1936 (Paisajes del alma),* 1944, are effusions of love, sympathy, and occasional stricture, interlarded with snatches of history, legend, anecdotes, and even tales of varying length.

As his lyrical descriptions flow naturally into literary reminiscences, autobiography, and meditation, the author not only extracts the temperament of place, person, and thing, but makes them into something peculiarly his own. Sometimes the sketches of tranquillity, of the hospitality of fields, valleys, churches, and of chance encounters with the wisdom of the ages incarnate in people and places, are too patriarchal and smack of the romantic dichotomy of rustic virtue versus urbane artificiality, but in general Unamuno imbues these vignettes with substantial meanings by humanizing the purely pictorial with regional customs and patois, along with philosophical, linguistic, and historical digressions.

Frequently he will linger over ethnic considerations: among the best of these are his analyses of Portuguese melancholy dramatized in the *fados* and the suicidal propensities of Portuguese writers, or of Castilian austerity growing from its bleak country-side and distilled in the writings of its ascetics and mystics. Through Bilbao and the Basque country, Catalonia, Galicia, even the Canary Islands and the Balearics, he enfolds the peninsula in an enormously tender embrace, fusing personality and landscape symbiotically: the earth, sky, and vegetation enrich the writer, while he, in turn, conjures out of them poetic meanings in auto-dialogues that are more like blessings.

### III   *The Myth of Don Quixote*

By the time he wrote his prologue to the first edition of *On Authentic Tradition* in 1902, Unamuno's views on the need for change in his country had evolved radically. Sated on the breast-beating of the Europeanizers, urged on by the desire to restore a national self-confidence that had dissolved into acute hypochondria during the aftermath of the Spanish-American War, he was more ready to exalt the uniqueness of the Spanish soul than to recommend it for change. Although holding firm to his duty of shocking his fellow countrymen out of their lethargy, he was convinced that the aim of such awakening was not so much to transfigure Spain on European models as to sharpen her self-awareness and self-respect.

If the Treaty of Paris deprived Spain of Cuba, Puerto Rico, the Philippines, Guam, and the Marianas, it might also have been the hand of Providence emphasizing Ganivet's conclusion that Spanish supremacy lay not in physical domination or territorial holdings, but in those ideals which had once given it spiritual and intellectual preeminence. Spain, Unamuno saw, need not bow before historical determinism, and could counteract the shock of colonial retraction and loss of prestige only if it exploited its inner strengths. Wounded in his capacity as archetypal Spaniard by the recorded historical fact, his sympathies turned more emphatically to the poetry that aims not at accuracy but at the expression of possibility.

The country, he argued, could absorb from the Anglo-French-German axis the technology that provides for a dignified level of physical existence, but she in turn had a great gift to bestow: the corrective view of the autonomy of man and of his transcendental status. Spain, in short, could assume the mission of calling man back from his labors to himself. Indeed, the so-called backwardness of his country was perhaps the very factor that kept it aware of the danger of excessive progress leading away from the primacy of man to the primacy of artifact. The collective way of life, the annihilation of the individual in the system, the assessment of each man only in terms of tangible contribution, the imperative of conformity, were pitfalls far more serious than indifference to industrial advancement. "The very qualities which have made Spain refractory to the type of civilization prevalent today," Unamuno claimed, "may qualify her for propagating the civilization to come; perhaps we should, like Don Quixote, dream of a purified Spain, separating, exalting, and sublimating that part of humanity reserved for her, in order to undertake the spiritual conquest of Europe and the world."[16]

In one of his most famous essays, "Life is a Dream" ("La vida es sueño"),[17] written one month before the signing of the Treaty of Paris, Unamuno declares his opposition to those "regenerationists" who, not unlike the traditionalists, were dinning such intoxicating slogans as "the glory of Spain" and "national progress" into the ears of the people, and shutting out the sound of the "deep waters of the unfathomable depths of spirit, the voice of Eternity." These progressivists were the slaves of time because, having lost their Christian faith, they sought a specious immortality in History; and if we die only to return to the unconsciousness from which we came, we are "simply an unhappy procession of ghosts going from nothingness to nothingness, and humanitarianism is as inhuman as it can be."

"Life is a Dream" may be taken as a classic example of the technique Unamuno would use repeatedly: that of conjuring away facts by execrating them. Motivated undoubtedly by the charitable desire to pour balm on national wounds, he could turn his back at will on native poverty and sluggishness, on economic injustices, on the lack of an enlightened public opinion and a responsible press, in order to compare a godless Europe bent on inventing monstrosities with an idealized Spanish peasantry dreaming life away in expectation of glorious eternity. Yet only two years earlier he had argued that dignity is stifled by the squalor produced by capitalism and that the "spiritualistic" reaction of the *fin-de-siècle* was the work of a desperate bourgeoisie "looking for a God to chain the working class to machines. . ."[18] Life he had then regarded as autoteleological, aiming at the greatest expansion of itself, and he had urged that the masses be afforded the means to buy more and more and thus stimulate production for the greatest satisfaction of the greatest numbers.

When the great dénouement came in 1898, Unamuno interpreted his work to be that of salving the wounds of his mortified countrymen by offering them a philosophy of compensation, and adopted the role of the father who comforts his cudgeled son more often that he berates him for having been so easily defeated. In essay after essay he was to reiterate his conviction that his country must rebuild from within that special national genius which it was his task to encourage. His essay "Go Within!" ("¡Adentro!")[19] is a clarion call for inwardness, the surest way of developing the originality or uniqueness which subsequently serves others. The stress is now more often on the need for digging deeply into the precious vein of Spanish-ness, that awareness of self which has been called the search for the intra-man or *intrahombre*.[20]

In "Solitude" ("Soledad"),[21] Unamuno reminds his readers that apartness is often the surest way of bringing people together: the groan from the next room heard through the wall penetrates the heart more acutely than the actual presence of the sufferer. Interest in the larger social, moral, and political questions may desensitize one's reactions to individual men, exactly as the din of conviviality deadens the meanings of words. Solitude is therefore a precious retreat wherein we store up the strength to break through our shells and even collide with our fellowmen rather than brush against them indifferently. In the long run, subjectivity does not make for detachment but rather for a deepening self-knowledge which can face up to the greater issues without loss of personal moorings. If, in Hegelian terminology, there was to be an ideal state based on the communion of men, it would have to proceed from a deepening individuation and not simply from legislative fiat.

In his obsessive fear over the recession of the individual in favor of the social cog, Unamuno is one of a long line of nineteenth-century European and American moralists, while in his own country he anticipated the Ortega y Gasset who, in his *Revolt of the Masses* (1926) and other works, makes a most convincing analysis of the tidal wave of totalitarian democracy which will overwhelm the select man. But while Ortega stresses the noble life as one lived in perpetual tension, and distinguishes between the élite as intellectually active and the masses as simply reactive, Unamuno warns that the ideal of intellectualism which is a perpetual strain to investigation and knowledge, will exteriorize the individual into pure energy. Both thinkers are disturbed over the vulgarization of modern life, but while Ortega is concerned with the atrophy of the sense of function, Unamuno is concerned with the atrophy of the soul. Within man, says Unamuno, lies the deepest truth, and he exhorts his readers to take precautions against ready-made formulas, dogmas, and parties. It is not by going out into the forum that one sprouts wings, but by straining upward.

Spain, Unamuno makes clear, was ready to uphold such all-encompassing truths now that historical events had forced her back on her innate disposition. The Spaniard has been accused of being too preoccupied with death, but Unamuno holds the contrary view: his countrymen have gone too far in renouncing such concern in favor of European coloring and have become spiritually half-breed. It is true that Spain is more or less impervious to what goes on under the name of European culture, yet the choice is not between Europeanization or barbarism, technology or ignorance. If knowledge has as its object ease and the prolongation of life, wisdom has as its object the final meaning of life. The modern Spaniard can outstrip his European counterpart by learning to incorporate the mystery or supreme anguish into life rather than turning his eyes away from the Sphinx.

In 1895 he said: "The national characteristics of which each European nation boasts are often its defects. We Spaniards are guilty of the same sin." [22] Eleven years later he would say, "Our defects, or what others call our defects, are in the main at the root of our outstanding qualities: what they derisively call our vices, are the basis of our virtues."[23] Taking exception to Pío Baroja's complaint that Spaniards are incapable of joviality or frivolity, Unamuno retorts that such an inability is the consolation and glory of his country; if Spain were like its neighbor to the north, it might have subtler wines, more delicate oil, and better oysters, but it would have to give up the possibility of another *Don Quixote,* another Velázquez, or St. John of the Cross.[24] Passion, extravagance, preoccupation with death and its meaning for life, these are what the world called Spanish weaknesses but these very qualities form the foundations of Spanish uniqueness and to twist them to fit foreign molds would be to falsify the native temperament and give it a hybrid identity.

One of Unamuno's principal aims, therefore, at about the turn of the century, will be to distinguish between the Spanish genius and that of the rest of Europe by arguing forcefully that the kinetic principle as embodied in technological progress is not the only valid one, and that the superimposition of such ideals on the Spanish temper would denature it and remove it from its center of meaning. "I know and recognize our ills but I am ever more enamored of the vigor of our soul, of our contempt for fate. There is something great in our very poverty. It would be better to diminish it but please don't think that I wish upon my country the satiety of other nations nor am I enthusiastic over those nations who, surfeited on material goods and comforts, end up with collective diabetes."[25] Instead of urging his countrymen to lean towards that disciplined logic and symmetry so precious to the French, or the industriousness and systematic thinking associated with the Germans, he tends to defend Spanish intensity and emphasis—even in the form of conceptism and culteranism—as equally significant. The Spaniard is given to outbursts, to antitheses, to paradox, because when his passions are obstructed by logic, he must override that logic. And so, as Unamuno identified his hunger for immortality and the meanderings of his own tormented "logic" with that of all Spaniards, he elevated his own propensities to the status of a racial incumbency and stressed that to be first-rate Spanish was infinitely superior to being third-rate European.

There is no better way of dramatizing the evolution of Unamuno's thought with regard to his country's status in the world than to trace his attitude towards the symbolic meanings of the "Spanish Christ," Don Quixote. Rankled in his earlier period by the cultural lag under which his country was laboring—a period that coincided with his own uncertainty about the preponderant role he so longed to play in his society and time—he had urged quiet, unspectacular diligence, application to the workaday task, to replace that indolence which followed the disappearance of heroic opportunity. In the essays of 1895 known as *On Authentic Tradition*, he professed his preference for the "sublime ending" of *Don Quixote* in which the mad knight, confessing his mistakes, again becomes the unassuming Alonso Quijano the Good. For Don Quixote's error had been to render his endeavor futile and even harmful: he had tried to revive a chivalry that was dead, exactly as Spain clung to obsolete ways on the grounds that they were "authentic."

Even in 1898, when his sensibilities were further exacerbated by the sorry defeats of Spanish forces at the hands of the foreign Colossus, he thundered: "Don Quixote Must Die!" (*¡Muera Don Quijote!*).[26] The spirit of madness must be extinguished to leave room for a clear-sighted realism; the Spanish people must be cured of a desire to duplicate a glorious past under circumstances totally different; they must sweep out the tinsel of tales endlessly retold just as Don Quixote finally repudiated the romances of chivalry that had lured him to his fruitless adventures.

By the next year, Unamuno had already drastically altered his view of Cervantes' creation: let Don Quixote die, he states, but only the Don Quixote dissected by professional Cervantists, for then the quixotic spirit will be free to speak to every Spanish soul and will provide the ideal for spiritual rejuvenation.[27] And by 1905 Unamuno was ready to refute his earlier harsh statements completely by recognizing as the symbol *par excellence* of Spain, not the remorseful Alonso Quijano the Good, but the noble, reckless, ludicrous, and lovable benefactor of the needy: Don Quixote de la Mancha. In *On Authentic Tradition* he had tried to make it plain that true tradition consisted of those features of national character that coincided with the features of universal human character; now it was time to demonstrate that Spain had evolved a myth so broad in connotation that it could spread much needed light to a world in bondage to technocracy and a simulacrum of religion. This Spanish national idea had a radiance so boundless that not only could it restore to Spain a special sense of mission, independent of material triumph, but could compel recognition from all other peoples.

The year of the publication of Unamuno's *Life of Don Quixote and Sancho* (*Vida de Don Quijote y Sancho*), 1905, was the three-hundredth anniversary of the publication of the First Part of the "Bible of Spain" and was celebrated with the rash of academic homages that always accompanies such events. In his own book, Unamuno, always the critic of officialdom, set out to save the noble hidalgo from the dead hand of "carpenters of definitive editions," or errata-sniffers and monograph compilers; in short, his aim was to raise Don Quixote from the dead into an ever-living presence. Coincidentally, what Ortega y Gasset said with regard to Goethe over a quarter of a century later, summarizes the purpose of Unamuno in his book: "There is but one way to save a classic: to give up revering it and use it for our salvation—that is, to lay aside its classicism, to bring it close to us, to make it contemporary, to set its pulse going again with an infusion of blood from our own veins whose ingredients are *our* passions . . . and *our* problems. Instead of becoming centenarians in a centenary, we must attempt to resurrect the classic by resubmerging it in existence."[28]

In this spirit, we can consider Unamuno's *Life of Don Quixote and Sancho* one of the most audacious attempts at poetic reconstruction of a hallowed classic. For the student who has made his way through oceans of footnotes and references, formal exegeses, endless background material, stylistic analyses and other academic approaches to *Don Quixote*, Unamuno's work comes as a refreshing experience. No longer does the reader have to identify himself with the knight over a chasm of three centuries; Don Quixote is made immediate and contemporary, freed from the formidable sanctity of the museum. Just as Unamuno made his religion Christ-centered so that it might speak to human needs directly, without the intervention of convoluted theology, he frees his Don Quixote from the texts that are the special competence of the scribes and commentators, in order to make him available to the heart—Don Quixote *sensible au coeur.*

It follows, therefore, that those portions of the original text which do not elicit a subjective reaction are peremptorily disregarded: in addition to passing over the interpolated novels (*The Story of the Ill-Advised Curiosity* is airily dubbed ill-advised), Unamuno is unconcerned with the farcical elements of the book, the slapstick humor, the pummelings and falls, all the episodes designed to excite laughter. To Unamuno the novel is too serious, indeed too tragic, to justify attention to any aspect that cannot, for the author, be pressed for deeper meanings. As in the case of most individualists, Unamuno concentrated so passionately on what appealed to him that he was convinced of the insignificance or wrong-headedness of the rest.

Unamuno's text is a tapestry of ingenious paradoxes, diatribes, poetic prose, and arbitrary conclusions drawn from the best-known episodes of the original. But the identification of the author with his subject is so intense, the need to find magnificent meaning in the mad knight's adventures so poignantly stated, that we are swept along into accepting these variations for what we know they are not: logical inferences. Instead of objecting to the gratuitous liberties he takes, we forgive Unamuno his poetic licenses and are persuaded to say: *se non è vero, è ben trovato.*

For Unamuno, the Nietzschean despite himself, Don Quixote's grandeur resides in the scale of values he devised for himself and upheld, notwithstanding the sly bachelors from Salamanca, the priests and canons, the *hommes moyens sensuels.* Don Quixote lived, like Christ, against the grain of his time, in the "madness" that will not sit down to table with expediency or good advice. Like Christ also, his sympathies lay with the outcasts, the publicans, sinners, prostitutes, and thieves; like Christ, he died but is contemporary with all those willing to accept his spirit and heed his word.

Born a poor hidalgo in a country where poverty precludes satiety and ferments hope, he overcame the dinginess of his life by steeping himself in the romances of chivalry and conceiving the design of winning eternal glory. Thus, by losing his mind he found the heroic reason of non-reason; by fervently believing in his mission to right wrongs, he made the mission come alive. For the will to achieve may triumph over handicap as the will to believe may triumph over the disapproval of good sense. But first one must descend so deeply into self as to be willing to surrender even one's social identity, and Alonso Quijano the Good was reborn as Don Quixote de la Mancha. And when his neighbor asked him who he was, he retorted, "I know who I am!" He alone knew what he was bound to do, as Abraham, Kierkegaard's hero of faith, alone heard God's command to sacrifice his son Isaac, and was resolved to obey even though he understood that in the eyes of others his action would be either mad or criminal. It is only with total faith in inspiration that one can make merchants appreciate what they cannot see or measure, and if, in such an attempt, Don Quixote falls to the ground and is beaten, it is not defeat but the daring and the ability to rise above the unhappy consequences that matters.

Never loathe to enlarge the national and religious meanings of his book, Unamuno not only compares his hero with Christ Himself but draws analogies between Sancho and St. Peter, Maritornes and Mary Magdalene, and especially between Don Quixote and St. Ignatius Loyola. As Don Quixote lost his mind by reading too many books, and as indeed St. Paul was accused by Festus of having been made mad by too much learning (Acts 26:24), so did the founder of the Company of Jesus awaken to the "mad" imperative to renounce the life determined for him by his birth and training, in order to follow an unknown but irresistible path. It was only after being wounded at Pamplona that he spent his convalescence reading the lives of Christ and the saints and became the Knight-Errant of Christ. In his youth he, like Don Quixote, had been addicted to novels of chivalry and later, like the Don Quixote who struggled with fear, he struggled with demons, and with as much dignity as the mad knight suffered the reprimands of churchmen.

Sancho was the beloved of Don Quixote as Simon Peter was of Christ. Sancho was low-born, unprepared for the mystifying impulses of his master, but he clove to him out of simple faith. Living close to his knight, Sancho the empiricist, Sancho the naturalist, was quixotized, just as we, by dint of believing in God, become godlike and find solace in the loneliness of our extreme situations. When, at the beginning of the Second Part of the book, Don Quixote's housekeeper and niece upbraid Sancho for misleading his master, they are not completely unreasonable, for the hero is always sustained by his followers and feeds on the faith of those to whom he has given faith. Perhaps even God feeds on the faith men have in Him; indeed, God may simply be the equivalent of the collective, vibrant, vital faith of men. Did not Jesus exist first in the eyes of the Simon Peters, the Sanchos of Galilee? And if Don Quixote separated Sancho from his wife and children, offering him a life of difficulty in exchange for one of animal comfort, so did Jesus summon His disciples to leave family and possessions behind. For what is the comfort of blissful ignorance but the comfort of cowardice, the puny faith of the charcoal-burner? Sancho's faith in his master was not supine, but the real faith that feeds on doubt and even on occasional disaffection, that affirms itself at every instant like life fighting death, in continuous self-creation.

Of the women in Cervantes' novel, Unamuno tells us that Maritornes, the serving-wench who gave freely of her body, is redeemed for having succored the blanketed Sancho. Like Mary of Magdala, she loved not wisely but too much, for it was, according to one of Unamuno's transpositions, in a spirit of mercy and not lust that she gave herself to the carters. She was no inciter to vice, no coquette or tease; she came naturally to the men who stopped at the inn and freed them of the sluggish humors of their desire. Never greedy, her purpose was not easy living in preference to hard work, and it was out of her own pocket that she paid for the wine which the victimized Sancho drank. Even the whores who laughed at Don Quixote and helped him off with his armor remind Unamuno of Mary Magdalene washing and anointing Christ's feet and wiping them with her hair.

That Dulcinea was, in fact, Aldonza Lorenzo, a strapping evil-smelling wench who could do more than a man's work, was of little importance to the Knight of the Woeful Countenance. Transformed by his need for inspiration, she became the noble princess of delicate fiber who provided the incentive for his great deeds. "Any belief that inspires life-giving deeds is a true belief, and false belief is that which leads to deeds of death." When the barber wishes to reclaim his basin, Don Quixote insists that it is a helmet, for "The more one believes in a thing the truer it is; it is not the intellect but the will that makes it be." And because Sancho effects a compromise, calling the object *baciyelmo* (basin-helmet), Unamuno takes him to task for doing what most men do when they identify virtue with the Golden Mean, and he advises him that a thing is a basin or helmet, depending on who makes use of it. And with regard to the dispute that ensues, Unamuno adds wryly that similar questions of identity have provoked bloody antagonisms: e.g., whether bread is bread or wine wine. Ironically enough, those who will argue to prove that an object is a helmet, are secretly convinced that it is a basin. So it is that men fight for a faith they do not share, and it follows that martyrs make faith rather than faith martyrs.

It is because such blind faith is lacking in Spain that the country is paralyzed. It is the fear of failure, a moral cowardice, that accounts for the lack of irrigation canals and poor crops. There will be no commerce, no industry, no agriculture so long as there are those so poor in spirit that they will not recognize the possibility of rejuvenation in the most extravagant, self-assertive, quixotic forms. Spaniards are willing to accept the unfavorable verdict of history in order to keep a peace for which they pay the price of soddenness, just as Don Quixote was shut up in a cage by those who envied him his inner freedom and wished to bring him down to their level.

And for those who would accuse him of tergiversation in transmuting fiction into reality, Unamuno's answer is that documents and archives enclose dead weight, while myths contain the power to set men's hearts on fire and console them for the meagerness of their existence. Furthermore, the strain after illusion may be so great as to give that illusion a dimension of truth: Dulcinea was fiction, but a fiction that inspired Don Quixote to the loftiest of conceptions, and earned for him a fame that made of death an injustice or at the very least mitigated its total destructive effect.

The Scriptures themselves may be books of divine chivalry and the madness of the Cross may be the madness of knight-errantry. Indeed, it is quite possible that the Gospels and the entire structure of Christianity constitute a mighty fable unproved in fact but validated by an inner fire, by a truth that lives only because its inspiration of goodness and charity, humility and hope, is never spent. It is therefore not implausible to consider Don Quixote as a poetic reincarnation of the Christ who, although He suffered a moment of what the rationalists call pure lucidity when He cried out, "My God, my God, why hast Thou forsaken me?" yet, throughout his life, rejected arid reason for the love and consolation His teachings would spread. And those "reasonable" canons who teach the letter of the law, who reduce the "madness" or scandal of faith to catechisms, rituals, and ceremonies are as inimical to spirit as Cervantes' canon was to the hero of the book. Even as Don Quixote believed fervently in the perfection of Dulcinea's face and breeding so that he might conquer in the name of a superlatively worthy being, it is possible that Jesus Christ created the God in whose name He could establish the Kingdom of Heaven for those whose kingdom on earth is too short and too heart-rending for real happiness.

To save the ideal religion came such saints as Teresa of Avila who, inflamed as a young girl by reading the lives of the saints, conspired with her brother to do battle against the infidels, and when the children were convinced of the unfeasibility of such an undertaking, they decided to become hermits. This is divine knight-errantry, for as the knight seeks immortality in the memory of men, the saint seeks it in the bosom of the Lord. In contrast, Antonia Quijana, Don Quixote's niece, has the impudence to deny knight-errantry. How can such a woman—a pecking hen, a house cat, a simpleton, Unamuno calls her—inspire men to glorious deeds? The Antonias who cook chickpeas, do the mending, and mumble prayers with sugar-paste piety, will never become Dulcineas or St. Teresas.

Antonia's counterpart is Sansón Carrasco, the man of common sense, the "crafty, routinized university graduate," who extends himself to bring the knight back to his village. Sansón Carrasco takes it upon himself to defeat Don Quixote for the same reason the Scribes and Pharisees could not countenance the Son of Man. And among the latter-day Pharisees stands the "grave ecclesiastic" who called Don Quixote "Don Fool" (*Don Tonto*). Were Jesus Christ to return to earth today, such priests would denounce him as a mad or dangerous agitator and seek to execute him. Thus do the twisted of heart mistreat those whom they call the twisted in mind, but in so doing—how cruel are the despicable jokes the duke and duchess perpetrate on their guest—they reduce their own stature and heighten that of their victims. Even when Don Quixote is finally overcome by Sansón Carrasco in the disguise of the Knight of the White Moon, he proclaims the beauty of his lady Dulcinea and prefers death to retraction. And Unamuno advises that we follow the example of the knight even when we are most abjectly defeated; let us have the courage to proclaim a faith beyond despair, to assert our Divine Idea in which name we commit the great "folly" or offense of denying all denial so that we may say with the Good Thief: "Lord, remember Thou me."

Only with such an élan can the Phoenix rise from its ashes: the Spain that once discovered an entire New World may well, by striving towards a glory that it generates through sheer creative will, discover a spiritual world reserved for it by God. Only when Don Quixote refuses to die after defeat, and when he takes up the introspective pastoral life, becomes Don Quijotiz and sings his shepherd's song, will the giants who pretended to be windmills fall to the ground, the galley slaves will be chastened, Roque Guinart will dismiss his bandits, the canons and priests will fall silent, and the rural guard will recognize that basins are helmets. Then will the Master Peters give up their puppet shows, the cave of Montesinos will yield up its secrets, whores will become maidens, wrongs will be righted, and the Golden Age of Don Quixote's discourse will become flesh. This is Spanish philosophy and this its message to Spain and to the world.

*    *    *    *    *    *    *

In his headstrong rush to revive and make contemporary the figure of Don Quixote, Unamuno was impelled by the desire to provide for his countrymen a broad-spectrum myth around which to rally in their abjectness. In the process, it has been seen, he makes short shrift of everything that stands in his way and his text bristles with irreverences and incongruities. He even brushes Cervantes aside as the author of only one significant work the full import of which he himself did not fathom. For Cervantes was the father to Don Quixote, while Spain was its mother and the book favors the latter more than the former. Indeed if Cervantes were to return to earth, he would be not a quixotist, but a Cervantist, one of those scholar-locusts who would strip the work of its contemporaneity, just as in religion theologians turn theological studies into pure routine.[29]

With regard to Cervantine studies as well as to religion, Unamuno is indeed a fool who steps in where angels fear to tread, debating carefully elaborated concept with bold supposition. He is undaunted by the authoritative word of scholarship as he is by theology: both are stepping-off points for a restless, extravagant fantasy that would outstrip even possibility. Not only is Spain Unamuno's oyster but also this world and the next, for he sees the problem of his country as overlapping the problems of all others and he provides an antidote forged out of native materials that would radiate to the four corners of the planet. The economic question, he had said many times, hinges on the spiritual, and his aim was to excite his countrymen to such a pitch of awareness that their foreign counterparts could not but become infected. Unamuno was not only haunted by the emaciated, blood-spattered Spanish Christ presiding over the churches and cloisters of the peninsula, but by the Christlike spirit incarnate in that most Spanish of myths, Don

Quixote, whose message, if apprehended and fervently embraced, is nothing less than ecumenical.

Literature inspired by a nationalistic messianism is no novel phenomenon in modern Europe. Berdyaev has shown that the nineteenth-century Germany of Idealism and Romanticism considered itself a spiritual dike against the high tide of materialism in the rest of Europe, while the Russians felt themselves preserved by their less advanced state from the corrupting influence of Western commercialism. The picture of a "redeemed" Spain envisaged by Unamuno is, however, closer to Dostoevski's hopes for Russia than to German transcendentalism. Both Russian and Spaniard were suspicious of radical reform because they feared and distrusted the selfish, demonic motives of reformers who either deny or have no time for the spirit and proceed by conspiracy and brutality. Each was convinced that the New Crusade needed not bridges of iron and steel for the cunning in mind, but bridges of faith for the pure in heart. Decades before Unamuno advocated the Hispanization of Europe, Dostoevski had fought the partisans of the Europeanization of Russia with the argument that Western Europe was demoralized, despiritualized, and on the verge of collapse, that "material well-being was hiding Heaven," and that "the Russians had been saved from it by their backwardness." [30]

Like the Russian, Unamuno condemned the invidious comparisons made between strong and weak nations, for the weak of today may be storing up the strength necessary for survival. Unamuno's friend and admirer, Antonio Machado, as if supporting the former's point of view, holds Don Quixote up as the antithesis of the pragmatist who makes of success the measuring rod of virtue and truth: "It is possible that a nation resembling Don Quixote in some ways will not always be what we call prosperous. But that such a nation is inferior, that I will never admit." Nor is such a nation without a mission to fulfill, "For one day it will be necessary to challenge the lions with weapons totally inadequate for battling with them. And we shall need a madman to attempt such a venture. An exemplary madman." [31]

Shatov, in *The Possessed,* said that a great nation is one that thinks itself in possession of the truth and is therefore called upon to save the world through that truth. [32] The truth that Unamuno drummed into his people was that only the religious view could sensitize man into that true peace which comes from acceptance of the agony of belief. Like Dostoevski he was repelled by man's attempt to be his own savior, and his concept of intrahistory sustains comparison with the Russian's distrust of the enlightened elements of his time. When Dostoevski asked himself in what figure of Western civilization the spirit of Christ was best embodied, he found it was in Don Quixote.[33] And it is significant that the two countries in which Rainer Maria Rilke sought primordial religious values were Russia and Spain.

*   *   *   *   *   *   *

If we laugh at Don Quixote, it is not in derision, for laughter, Unamuno explains in a theory surprisingly close to Bergson's *Le Rire,* expresses our exhilaration at being free, if only momentarily, of "that ferocious tyrant [logic], of that lugubrious *fatum,* of that incoercible power that is deaf to the appeals of the heart."[34] Because Unamuno interprets Don Quixote's challenge to the lions as obedience to a sign from God who wished to test his faith, he can say apocalyptically to his compatriots that "our reason for being and our destiny among nations is to see to it that the truth of the heart illuminates minds against the darkness of logic and ratio- cination and consoles the hearts of those condemned to the dream of life . . . " It is a supreme comfort to know that each one of us is unique and irreplaceable in a scientific world that emphasizes our insignificance in the immense structure of facts, figures, and classifications, and Unamuno asks us to return to the roots of Christianity, to dissolve away all accretions and reveal in all its splendor the religious principle that each soul is worth a universe.

Towards that end, Unamuno has, without a care for verisimili- tude, hammered out totally new significances—personal, ethical, and religious—from a text taken too frequently as the exclusive province of the scholar. Unimpeded by established opinion of any order, Unamuno, as free as Don Quixote himself on his nag to go in any direction he desired, strikes new sparks from the friction of his decisive personality and abrasive talent against old thoughts, intuitions, dogmas, and prejudices. The reader is not unaware of the gratuitousness of Unamuno's conclusions, his verbal and spiritual headsprings, the presence of Kierkegaard's *Fear and Trembling,* but he is willy-nilly drawn into the orbit of the *vate* who, because his feelings are thoughts and thoughts feelings, and because he is unashamed to identify his personal anguish with the

most significant character and deeds of a sacrosanct text, carries
through an unusual work of renewal.

In his *Life of Don Quixote and Sancho,* Unamuno lifts the reader
to a new level of understanding. It is a summons to interiorization
or the holy madness which Kierkegaard called the "teleological
suspension of the ethical," [35] and is therefore a magnificent effort
to negate defeat and death. Unamuno suggests new realms of
spirit for those who, at the end of the horizontal line which dips
down to skepticism, mechanization, and impersonality, would
swerve the will into an ascending direction through the introduction
of a new set of plausibilities. Unamuno's lyric terms provide the
proper accent for renewed debate with those whose God has become so institutionalized that He has been depressed into a guaran-
tor of vested interests and with those whose indifference to or
denial of the divine spark has deprived men of the sense of their
own sacredness.

Perhaps the soul that is stirred by Don Quixote is one already
prone to Christ. Nevertheless, Unamuno is convincing when he
points out how foolish man is in his allegiance to finite things
which, even if brought to a point of perfection, are still subject to
the imperfection of death. And death, which is a part of history,
can only be overcome by faith, the transhistorical offense to the
intellect, just as the "hideous centuries" of history are made bear-
able by the uninterrupted flow of intrahistory. Unamuno, who
intuited intrahistory by plunging himself into the eternal physical
and moral landscape of his peninsula, found in Don Quixote
another savior crucified and risen from the dead, and with all the
intellectual and poetic powers at his disposal, put before Spain,
and through Spain before all men who would listen, the religion
of Quixotism, a loyalty to eternity which does not abandon history
but categorically refuses to be confined by it.

## CHAPTER 4

# History and Eternity—II

FROM 1914 on, Unamuno found himself enmeshed in a series of historical circumstances that demanded nothing less than the taking of sides. The wrath he felt at his unexplained dismissal as rector that very year, plus his unequivocal pro-Ally sympathies brought him squarely into the field of political debate, aimed primarily at the Germanophile king and his various governments. World War I, the costly defeat of the Spaniards in Morocco, Italian Fascism, Russian Communism, the Salazar régime in Portugal, the Primo de Rivera dictatorship in Spain, Nazism, the Spanish Republic, and the beginning of the Civil War, all tore him from his dream of eternity.

These were developments that would not allow for that precious intellectual independence he had passionately defended; each change was so severe an emergency that Unamuno's hand was forced. History was proceeding so rapidly and implacably that intrahistory was forcibly submerged; faction faced faction across lines that Unamuno mistrusted; necessity came to grips with freedom and men of good will had to suspend their nonpartisan roles in order to aid and abet what they considered the least corrupt of the antagonists.

Since his preoccupations were of the longest range, trailing off into a nebulous infinity, where could Unamuno find a political philosophy? He had won his right to anticlericalism through personal sacrifice and anguish, but he could not align himself with the superficial anticlericalism of the radical elements of his country; nor could the solitary of Salamanca approve of the arbitrary rule of a military clique or the majority rule of democracy. True welfare, the only welfare, was to him eternal, and all patterns in life tentative, yet he could not deny that life in this valley of tears is a chain of many specific situations, in which, willy-nilly, one is engaged.

Like so many before and after him, more specifically like "his" Kierkegaard, and like his own compatriots, Azorín, Baroja, Maeztu, Ortega y Gasset, Unamuno viewed with distaste the leveling processes of democracy, its tendency to middle-class uniformity, the socialization of religion, the reduction of charity to philanthropy, the plentiful opportunities afforded to the wily and aggressive. Free competition in peace and democracy, he held, engenders envy: had there been a people more envious than the Athenians who invented ostracism?[1] Democracies lean on the opinion of the majority without opinions and appeal to the social consciousness of masses concerned only with their narrow interests.[2] Equality cannot be legislated into existence by universal suffrage, nor can superior representatives be elected by a majority that favors those who most resemble them.[3] Kierkegaard had put it clearly: ". . . wherever there is a crowd, there is untruth . . ."[4]

Unamuno's reverence for the masses, it may be said, alternated with fear and contempt: so long as the people were content to remain a moving poetic image, they excited his sympathy and love, but when they expressed themselves through their elected representatives, they became to him capable of monstrous error. The sleeping giant elicited reactions ranging from reverie and nostalgia to optimistic expectation, but when it bestirred itself, it brought down on its head his wrath and fustigation. For all their appeal, Unamuno's concepts of intrahistory and quixotic Messianism remain enigmatic, and when confronted by the precipitate of concrete political action on the part of the less inspired, Unamuno's indignation is akin to that of the poet whose song has been paraphrased into pedestrian prose.

He could not for a moment lend-lease the grandeur of his view of the total individual man to the status of "elector" or "tax payer," and his contempt for Parliamentarianism cannot be overemphasized. Parliament is a theater "full of snares and verbiage, with almost prehistoric formulas,"[5] and since public opinion is "variable, fluctuating, passion-driven and superficial,"[6] Parliament cannot represent it. It represents "at most a passive, given opinion which the newspapers with the greatest circulation—an extension and result of Parliament and of its factions—give to their readers, not the active opinion of the latter." The Spanish Parliament is made up of the rich, the servants of the rich, the lawyers of the rich, in descending moral order. Thus the powers that would rule in a nonrepresentative system are the very powers that rule in Parliament.[7] "The way a nation has for expressing itself collectively is a sort of braying . . ." for it too often happens that when rational or semirational men get together, they form a donkey nation (*un pueblo asno*).[8] The collective spirit is the spirit of the anthill or beehive in contradistinction to the radical principle of Western civilization which "is the absolute value of the individual, the persistence of individual awareness, in short, the immortality of the soul."[9]

Unamuno might have said with Kierkegaard: "The misfortune of our time is just this, that it has become simply nothing else but 'time,' the temporal which is impatient of hearing anything about eternity; and so . . . would make eternity quite superfluous by means of a cunningly devised counterfeit which, however, in all eternity will not succeed . . ."[10] And Unamuno himself would say that "When political preoccupations take hold of a nation, it seems that all other spiritual activities, especially the loftiest ones, suffer a sort of stoppage and stagnation."[11] In politics as in metaphysics, Unamuno was at odds with himself, torn between his guardian angel and guardian demon. Obsessively bent over the ephemeral quality of any human endeavor, his conclusions were often as mystifying as those of the Delphic priestess intoxicated by her fumes.

In the First World War, Unamuno's attitude was vehemently anti-German. From the early eighteen-nineties on he had expressed nothing but scornful disapproval of the Kaiser (Emperor Heliogabolus he called him in his letters to Pedro de Mugica),[12] of the growing military agressiveness, anti-Semitism, and martinet discipline of a Germany which he later called a "nation of fakirs who spend their lives regarding the German imperial navel . . ."[13] The nation was predatory and carnivorous[14] with a language that was a "heavy, difficult, extremely complicated instrument."[15] In *The Tragic Sense of Life* he had damned their *Kultur* as totally alien to the quixotic spirit which, by willing it, brings into being a world that science cannot ratify. Addicted to soulless research, the Germans produced methodologies, manuals, encyclopedias, and monographs like cannons of various calibers designed to "shoot off knowledge."[16]

In December, 1914, three months after being dismissed from the rectorship and fully aware of the pro-Axis sympathies of Alfonso

XIII, he wrote that "it is well known that the Germans have no other political criterion than the ones they are commanded to have by their authorities . . ." and that it was the German High Command that had hurled Germany into the war "without any previous provocation from their enemies, and has invented to that end all sorts of deceits in order to be able to invoke necessity." [17] Not only did Nietzsche strike him as a symptom of the anti-Christian spirit of the German people, but he accepted *in toto* the myth of Goethe's Olympian serenity and indicted it as hardness of heart. In no uncertain terms he proclaimed that he preferred Bouvard and Pécuchet, and even the Don Juan Tenorio he had always abhorred, to Faust. [18]

He was just as forceful in his condemnation of the "compulsory," "shameful" Spanish neutrality in a war brought on by a nation whose principal national industry was war, a nation that had savagely violated the neutrality of small countries, that had sunk the "Lusitania," executed Miss Cavell and subscribed to the "Jesuitical" principle that the end justifies the means. [19] Invited in September, 1917, along with other writers (Santiago Rusiñol, Américo Castro, Manuel Azaña, Luis Bello) by the Italian government to visit the military front, his feeling of national shame was intensified. Spain, despite its iron and coal, was said to be unprepared for war, while Italy without such resources, was able to improvise an army, warships, and locomotives. [20] Shortly after his return, he even confessed publicly his mistake in approving the execution of the anarchist and anticlerical Francisco Ferrer for his presumed role in the Barcelona riots of 1909. [21]

Such pronouncements all point to a dissatisfaction not only with the general stagnation of the country, but with the monarchical régime responsible for its continuation: now he vividly recalled the mistakes made by the rulers of Spain from the 1875 Restoration on, the execution of Martí and Rizal, the ignominious or ill-advised officialdom of a "Habsburgian," "Jesuitical," "trogloditic," "quartermaster's" Spain, and extolled the revolution of 1868 which had dethroned Isabel II, grandmother of the reigning king. [22]

## I  *Exile*

After the war, Unamuno's bitterness towards the régime did not abate. Spain was still a cloister and suffered from the monk's

disease of *acedia* or hopelessness. He recalled the words of Don
Francisco Silvela that Spain had no pulse, that all effort to spur
it on was useless, and that like Cervantes' Glass Licentiate, a
Spaniard of intelligence and goodness could do nothing but go
mad.[23] Wormwood was the soul of Spain and only a strong purga-
tive would carry away the excess of bile.[24] The references to the
monarchy and more specifically to the king's personal power and
to the pro-German activities of the Queen Mother involved him in
a lawsuit: he was sentenced to sixteen years in prison for *lèse-
majesté* and then pardoned. Although favored by prominent politicians and appointed vice-rector of his university, he could not
forgive the king his *lèse-Unamuno* and claimed that he was condemned so that he could be pardoned.

In 1921, General Fernández Silvestre decided to attack the
eastern sector of Melilla in North Africa, an undertaking approved
by the king without prior consultation with his ministers, and on
July 23, Abd-el-Krim, the Riff leader, attacked the Spanish forces
at Annual and defeated them, killing and imprisoning many
thousands. Public opinion was aroused and responsibilities had to
be fixed. A speech given by Unamuno at the Ateneo of Madrid in
which he blamed the king for the disasters, was followed by an
invitation to an audience with the monarch, which he accepted and
which earned him harsh criticism. But Unamuno came away from
the interview with renewed conviction that the monarchy was
rotten and crumbling, that the Moroccan war had been a venture
of frenzied imperialism, and that the errors of the past were of such
a nature that the thinking public could never again feel confidence
in the old ways.[25]

It was indeed that fear on the part of the king and the army
which motivated them to support the Captain General of Catalonia,
Miguel Primo de Rivera, who, on September 13, 1923, perpetrated
his coup d'état: constitutional rights were suppressed and the dictatorship was instituted.

Unamuno was scathing in his open criticism of Primo de Rivera.
Yet despite violent attacks against the régime made in Valladolid
and at the "El Sitio" club of Bilbao, it was a private letter written
to a Spanish professor in Buenos Aires and heedlessly communi-
cated to the Argentine magazine *Nosotros* that was the immediate
cause of Unamuno's banishment. In this letter Unamuno referred
to the king as "the royal goose . . . with less sense than a cricket,"

and to the Carlist "leprosy" of 1820, 1840, and 1876 which was again emerging: priests and the priest-ridden (*curoides*), quartermasters, sextons and their assistants, *ratés,* these were on the side of the "filth" that was responsible for the suspension of the Constitution.[26] On February 21, 1924, Unamuno was advised of the decree exiling him to the island of Fuerteventura in the Canaries. The day of his departure Unamuno gave his last Greek class,[27] and carried away with him three books only: the New Testament in Greek, the *Divine Comedy,* and the poetry of Leopardi.

In Fuerteventura he made close friends, took long walks through the barren island—an oasis in the desert of civilization—read, wrote verse, and came to know and love the sea. On July 9, a few days after the authorities decided to rescind the order of exile, a M. Dumay, director of the leftist paper *Le Quotidien,* engineered Unamuno's escape from the island in a small schooner, and on July 11 Unamuno arrived at Las Palmas where he was joined by his eldest son and the latter's wife; ten days later he boarded a Dutch ship for Cherbourg where he landed the end of August and proceeded to Paris.

In the French capital he occupied a small sparsely-furnished room, his "cage," in a small *pension.* Away from his beloved Salamanca, his classes, and above all separated from his family, he was in wretched spirits. Despite the many admirers who gathered around him, Paris represented the worst type of sophistication, worldliness, false *politesse,* and *savoir faire.* The Eiffel Tower evoked nostalgia for the Gredos Mountains, he contrasted the endless automobiles with the camels of Fuerteventura, and the boulevards lost by comparison with his own Zamora road. The subways, the "artiness," the vaunted cosmopolitanism of the "capital of the world," the museums which appeared to him "cemeteries of art," all depressed and exhausted him. He preferred only those spots that reminded him of Salamanca—the Place des Vosges brought back memories of the Plaza Mayor, the Place des Etats-Unis near his hotel reminded him of the countryside of Salamanca. Like Don Quixote in the palace of the duke and duchess, he felt mainly out of place in the French capital, "where it is impossible to find refuge in any corner previous to History . . ."[28]

A more congenial place was Hendaye to which he moved after thirteen months in Paris. Here he was on the Spanish border, on

Basque soil, here he was again in contact with the eternity of mountain and sea, and here, above all, he could, despite his loneliness, fear, and doubts, meditate on the meaning or effect of his exile, and he could again work more easily. He turned down invitations to lecture or teach in Germany, Switzerland, the United States, and the Spanish-American countries, and despite several efforts on the part of the French—pressed by the Spanish government—to remove him from the border, he would not budge. Yet he kept up his attacks on the king and Primo de Rivera, especially the latter, whom he called a woman-chaser and gambler, a reckless, guilty soldier, and an opportunistic politician. In Paris he had written weekly articles for *España con honra* (*Spain with Honor*), founded by Blasco Ibáñez, and during his stay in Hendaye he contributed to the *Hojas Libres* (*Free Papers*) edited by Eduardo Ortega y Gasset in Bayonne. Articles flew across the seas to Buenos Aires, while his invective found poetic outlet in the verse he kept writing throughout his exile.

## II Cómo se hace una novela (How a Novel is Made)

The story goes that when Unamuno was taken to task for having been a "bad son of Spain" he retorted that he was not her son, but her father.[29] As a father in exile, he was certainly tormented by a sense of having surrendered his true task in a useless gesture of defiance. Not only was he overwhelmed by loneliness, not only did he feel abandoned by God, but he also felt that these were punishments meted out to him for having abandoned his post within the battle for the sake of comparative safety outside. Although he could identify himself with such great exiles as Dante, Mazzini, Lamartine, Victor Hugo, and the Ecuadorian Juan Montalvo, with the prisoners Columbus, Cervantes, Fray Luis de León, and Quevedo, his mission as exile in France was not consonant with his deepest instincts, since his politics was metapolitics, the consideration of events *sub specie aeterni.*

The role of watchdog and censor he had always played had now snowballed into that of martyr in a specific cause, the epicycle of an infinitely larger question. An ambiguous heroism had been thrust upon him and he had caught it; now the question was whether his stubbornness was a sort of self-discovery or an act of vanity. Was he not now indulging the penchant for self-display that had tortured him at every turning point of his life, for even as far back as the crisis of 1897 he had feared making capital of his conversion, and had prayed for simplicity.[30] Now he suspected that he was "playing" the role of exile, right to the slovenliness of his person.[31] Even after his return home, he confessed: "Really—the truth must be said— I was not very much persecuted. It was I who did the persecuting."[32]

Would he not have been a real hero if he had accepted the pardon offered him, had returned to Spain, and faced the possibility of assassination? Had he simply taken advantage of the existence of a concrete enemy to discharge the ire that was his temperamental mainstay? Had his deep-rooted inclination to self-righteousness found a convenient historical justification? Such plaguing thoughts of cowardice, the suspicion of having betrayed his true mission, and fear of death in a strange land, are all implicit in his quasi-novel *Cómo se hace una novela.* The title is as ambiguous as Unamuno's political motivations, for although it means *How a Novel is Made,* it also suggests how one makes oneself into a novel or legend.

This confession-fantasy was begun in Paris in December, 1924, was translated into French by Jean Cassou as *Comment on fait un roman* and published in the May 15, 1926 issue of the *Mercure de France,* preceded by a *"Portrait d'Unamuno"* written by the translator. When Unamuno moved to Hendaye, he left the Spanish manscript behind and when in 1927 an Argentine publishing house expressed the desire to publish it, Unamuno had to retranslate the French text, made additions in brackets, wrote a commentary to Cassou's *Portrait,* and composed a "Continuation" which ends the book. More disjointed and freewheeling than his other works, this hybrid creation was written to capture—like the Proust to whom he was to refer later—the inexorable passage of time during an exile which might end in annihilation far from home.

In the grip of self-righteous anger and self-pity, Unamuno could scarcely control his emotions to the point of transmuting them into some artistic form, and he tells us that although he had considered writing a novel into which to pour the most intimate feelings of his exile and loneliness, he chose instead to tell how such a novel comes into existence. Thus he invents a character whose name not only includes Unamuno's but is extended to encompass his nation: U. Jugo de la Raza. U. stands, of course, for Unamuno;

·Jugo was the name of his mother and his maternal grandfather and of an ancient hamlet in Vizcaya; Larraza was the name of his paternal grandmother, but with the "de" also means "of the race," while Jugo de la Raza means "the juice (or quintessence) of the race."

The significance of the "hero" lies not only in the resonances of his name but in the fact that he embodies a possibility of Unamuno's ultimate destiny in exile. For Jugo de la Raza picks up a book on one of the stalls along the Seine and reads: "When the reader finishes reading this tragic story, he will die along with me." Jugo de la Raza burns the book but is tempted to find it again and resume his reading of it. Thus the story becomes the novel about the reading of a fatal novel, with personal interpolations of the author on his solitude and boredom, blasts directed at the Directorate of Primo de Rivera, at the stupid nation that tolerates it, reflections on history, commentaries on passages from the exiled Mazzini's correspondence, execrations hurled at those poets who dared celebrate the tercentenary of Góngora's death under the dictatorship, and above all, variations on the inescapable theme of death.

When the hero acquires another copy of the book, Unamuno refuses to tell us what happened—whether Jugo de la Raza finished it and died, or gave it up and lived. In the "Continuation," however, after recounting attempts made by government officials to get him to leave the frontier, Unamuno declares that he would send his creation back to his place of birth where he would find his "inner" self, and goes on to elaborate on precognitive belief, on vague memories of his father, on the role of the reader, on his own readings.

An inability to control the raw materials of his work led him once again to the conviction that the frontiers between fiction and life were artificial, and that if his book was a commentary on how a novel comes to be, all great works were in essence commentaries: the *Iliad* a commentary on an episode of the Trojan War, the *Divine Comedy* a commentary on the eschatological doctrines of medieval Catholic theology and the stormy history of thirteenth-century Florence. What Unamuno overlooks is that in great works of art, the simple facts are carefully arranged, integrated, and potentiated, and not cast at the reader formlessly.

As inadequate as the book may be artistically, it is nevertheless

another important document underlining Unamuno's agony in any
situation: even when certain of the moral inferiority of his opponents, he was not certain of the integrity of his opposition. If any
novel represented the construct of the author behind it, was not the
picture of the exiled Unamuno a fiction devised by himself and his
sympathizers? Was he not sacrificing his true intimate self to an
historic self? Was he not making, in short, a legend or novel of
himself by indulging in that herostratism which drives men to the
most extravagant acts for the sake of fame?

He was already well acquainted with the terror of staring at
himself in the mirror for a period of time and finally seeing himself
as someone else, the terrible sensation of the split personality, of
becoming the spectator of himself. Now again, in his exile, he
found it painful to gaze in the mirror, for as he looked at his own
reflection, he felt emptied of himself and experienced the vertigo of
nothingness. For if he had initially chosen a given political position, he feared it was now his master; it was as if he were caught
forever in one posture or dimension, as in a snapshot or statue.
His real opposition to the dictatorship had perhaps hardened
into attitudinizing; he feared that the vicissitudes of history had
created for him a role that was completely overtaking him. The
concern with the all-encompassing eternal had broken down into a
discrete situation which he had to inhabit but which, in a sense,
was trivial in comparison with the matrix from which all *engagement* comes. "And that is how religion and politics become one in
the novel of contemporary life." [33]

### III   *The Republic*

By the beginning of 1930, sentiment against the dictatorship was
running so high that the king, fearing for his crown, prevailed
upon Primo de Rivera to resign; this he did on January 28, and
General Berenguer took his place as head of a provisional government. The Republican movement, aided by the Socialists, gained
momentum: insurrectionists proclaimed the establishment of the
Republic at Jaca on December 15, 1930, but were put down, and
their leaders Galán and García Hernández were executed. Berenguer stepped down from his post, a new government was organized
under Admiral Juan Aznar on February 14, 1931, but Republican
agitation continued and finally municipal elections took place on

April 12. In all the important cities of Spain, the Republicans and Socialists won a resounding victory, and on April 14, 1931 the Republic was declared and the king left the country.

On February 9, 1930, barely two weeks after the fall of Primo de Rivera, Unamuno crossed the frontier and was acclaimed at Irún and Bilbao where he uttered the motto, *Dios, Patria y Ley* ("God, Country, and Law") instead of the traditionalist *Dios, Patria y Rey* ("God, Country, and King"), thus emphasizing his animus towards the monarchy rather than any pro-Republican sentiments. On February 13 he was received in Salamanca with enormous enthusiasm and when on May 1 he came to Madrid, he was wildly hailed. He did not let up on his campaign against the king, especially in the lecture at the Ateneo of Madrid on May 2 and the cinema Europa two days later.[34]

He himself proclaimed the new Spanish Republic from the balcony of the Town Hall (*Casa Consistorial*) of Salamanca, overlooking the vast Plaza Mayor, and shortly after, in a statement to the foreign press, he announced: "I know of no other case in history where a political revolution . . . has come about through a more sincere plebiscite and without recourse to arms. This means that the Spanish people who have given to other nations the word *pronunciamiento* have a much higher culture than has been admitted up to now." [35] He expressed his pride in the absence of all praetorianism and was confident that all difficulties would be solved democratically.

The Republic showered Unamuno with honors: he was again made rector of the university, member of the Spanish Academy he had always denigrated, deputy to the *Cortes Constituyentes* (Constituent Assembly). He was given the title of *Ciudadano de Honor* (Honored Citizen), a chair was created at the university in his name, and in 1935 the Ministry of Public Instruction supported his candidacy for the Nobel Prize. Yet not long after the triumph of the new régime Unamuno began retreating into the position he had held earlier in the century when he declared that he believed neither in revolution from above, below, or the middle, but in an inner revolution, and that only an "epileptic" nation believes in doing things by jolts or shocks (*a golpes*).[36]

His attitude towards the Republic, its innovations, its flounderings, the furious certainties that provide the afflatus for any radical change, became increasingly inimical. Certainly the coalitions, the realignments, oppositions, and personal antagonisms that marked the growing pains of an extremely heterogeneous party system were anything but edifying to one who had concurred with Renan's words: "What is politics today? . . . Agitation without principle or law; a struggle of rival ambitions; a vast theater of cabals and personal conflicts." [37] As he stood back to survey the political panorama, he was convinced once again that to pledge one's allegiance to any party, was to lose sight of the whole man and to become a "part." In addition, there is no doubt that as the Republic proceeded with its work and its dissensions and splits, Unamuno felt personally anachronistic, hemmed in by a new generation of leaders, of necessity impatient and aggressive. He felt relegated to an inferior rank among party members battling towards specific ends and to whom his constant meditations on the survival of each man through his elongation into perpetuity, were superfluous and obfuscating considerations. "Is there anyone in this country of ours," he asked, "who wishes to examine his conscience? Doesn't anyone see that all these convictions and all these disciplinary fervors are only theatrical lies?" [38]

His Kierkegaard had said that "none has more contempt for what it is to be a man than they who make it their profession to lead the crowd." [39] Now again Unamuno heard debates aimed not at truth but at victory, and all around him he saw "external" men, as external as those who had clung to the monarchy: citizens, voters, politicians, but no "cosmic" men. [40] If the aristocracy had betrayed both the "national, popular, lay" fatherland and the "national, popular, lay" church by seeking their own ends behind a screen of piety, [41] the Republic was now in the hands of lawyers and position-seekers, and the din they made with their parties, their prognoses, their elections, their programmes and dogmas bored and irritated the aging writer. Perhaps, in the last analysis, the masses were at fault because they allowed themselves to be yoked to unworthy leaders; it is the sheep who make the shepherd and the frogs who begged Jupiter for a ruler. [42] For the people were again accepting on faith not the religion of Father Astete's catechism, but a new creed grounded in the vanity of things and elbowing out all political heresy exactly as the catechism circumvented the free examination which generates religious disquietude and liberty.

The articles of the new Constitution which he himself had

voted in were a series of laborious deceits (*afanosos camelos*): the declaration that Spain was a democratic Republic of workers of all kinds; that Spain solemnly renounced war as an instrument of national policy; that the Republic would assure all workers the means of dignified existence. Especially infuriating to Unamuno was the decree dissolving all religious orders which, aside from the three canonical vows, also imposed the obligations of obedience to any authority apart from the State. And since very little came of it, the "enraged madmen of the revolution," made uneasy by public expectation and eager to play the role of conquerors, burned defenseless churches and convents. Then, fearing monarchical reaction, and suffering from the illness of all persecutors—paranoia— they promulgated what he called the "shameful" *Ley de la Defensa de la República* (Law for the Defense of the Republic) making anything like sedition illegal.[43]

Such strictures on Unamuno's part are not easy to reconcile with the attitudes he had expressed on other occasions when he argued that the separation of Church and State and the prohibition of religious teaching in the schools would force the Spanish clergy to administer religious instruction where it belonged, in church, and that in order to teach doctrine, the priests, especially the torpid rural clergy, would first have to learn it.[44] And before the declaration of the Republic, he had categorically stated that a Republican government should be ruled by laymen even when the country is Catholic, since in such a country most Catholics are laymen. And when a certain archbishop had claimed that monarchy was consubstantial with religion, Unamuno pointed out that such a position, when sustained by the French *Action Française,* was condemned as heresy by the Pope.[45]

As for the danger that monarchist elements posed for the Republic, it could not have slipped Unamuno's mind when in an open letter written in 1934 to Don Alfonso de Borbón y Hapsburgo-Lorena, "once the king of Spain" (*rey que fué de España*), he warned the ex-ruler that he was no longer wanted in Spain, not even by monarchists, that the people could not forget that he might have prevented the execution of the patriots Galán and García Hernández, and that he had not faced the street revolt of April 12, 1931, but had fled, leaving his family behind. "In order to avoid Civil War? No, rather to prepare it more deceitfully, as we now see." He tells Alfonso to discard all illusions, not to depend on a monarchical tradition to restore him,[46] yet when on his way to Oxford in the spring of 1936 to receive the degree of doctor *honoris causa,* he visited Mathilde Pomès in Paris, and his eye alighted on the portrait of Alfonso XIII, he said, "I fought him so strongly because I loved him." [47]

The skepticism and revulsion he evinced for the new laws were also directed at one of the most undeniable achievements of the Republic: the spread of literacy through the establishment of thousands of badly-needed schools. In this ready accessibility of learning, Unamuno detected another sign of the vulgarization of knowledge and its degeneration.[48] Article 48 of the Constitution, which decreed that all teaching would be purely secular, he called meaningless; "neutral" instruction is a contradiction in terms, since no teacher exists without beliefs or disbeliefs and his special vision of the world.[49] Purely lay education would set up a new idolatry that already manifested itself in the prohibition of crucifixes in the classroom. In its recoil from the miracles, fetishes, and amulets— the witchcraft—of religion,[50] the antireligious climate of the period was going to the other extreme of burning monasteries and convents.[51] And he deemed it unjust to prohibit the religions orders from teaching if they possessed the qualifications required by the State and accepted governmental inspection.[52]

Equally unjust was the dissolution of the Order of the Jesuits. Despite his repeated condemnation of the Jesuitical discipline as the stronghold of authoritarian belief, he could do an about-face to strengthen his anti-Republican arguments. By 1932 the Republic was already looming as a champion of free thought as rigid and inelastic as the orthodoxy the Jesuits had fought to maintain, and Unamuno's sympathies shifted to the underdog. "Spanish Jesuitism, the school of Molinist free-will [which] opposed Lutheran enslaved will (*siervo arbitrio*) and Calvinist predestination, what was it but another root of liberalism? It was Spanish will, our enormous irrational will that opposed rationalism; it was our fire against light." [53] Yet around this time he again took Menéndez y Pelayo to task for not understanding that the clerical, Jesuitical Counter-Reformation had been a police force rather than a source of religious consolation." [54]

Above all, he feared the rashness of the new leaders in promulgating a constitution before public opinion had sufficiently matured.[55] The very intellectual "overproduction" which he had once hoped would create further demands and a much-needed upheaval, he now feared would produce thoughts and actions faster than they could be digested.[56] In proceeding too quickly and too heedlessly, the leaders were forgetting the national weaknesses of hyperaesthesia and hysteria, the propensity to thoughtless epileptic action which he had analyzed in *On Authentic Tradition*: most Spaniards neither know what they want nor what they do not want.[57] What did the ordinary Spaniard, deeply personalistic, born and bred in an atmosphere of bossism (*caciquismo*), know of party programmes and ideological abstractions?[58] The leaders had forgotten Miguel Servetus' judgment of Spaniards: *inquietus est et magna moliens hispanorum animus.*[59]

He feared that those who shouted "Down with Fascism!" would become Fascists,[60] and foresaw the inevitability of a struggle between "the madmen of one pole and the madmen of another," in which intelligence and free examination, the essence of liberalism, would suffer.[61] In an article titled "Class and Fasces" ("La clase y el fajo"), written in 1933, he was most specific: Fascism would be the inevitable outcome of the Republic, for each movement engenders its opposite, the sistole must be followed by the diastole. The collective instinct for self-preservation would lead the people to surrender to a régime in which a small minority would establish a totalitarian system, an antiliberal state that would abolish class distinctions, level all differences, and impose an existence of material, intellectual, and even moral privation. Who would lead this movement? The answer was "anybody," a "nobody," a "busybody" or "good-for-nothing," any photogenic, demagogical blusterer. And when this happens, he added: "I shall keep on meditating on history and hoping . . ."[62]

\* \* \* \* \* \* \*

Throughout the period of the Republic, Unamuno floundered in a sea of independence. The "liberalism" which he claimed had always been his was not the atheistic Jacobinism "which persecutes all Christian feeling, which conspires to tear faith in another life from the soul of the people,"[63] nor was it a compromise between extremist positions; it was a total freedom of political conscience, a freedom that takes to task any entrenched code, a position above opinions. He coined the word "alterutrality" (*alterutralidad*) as against neutrality to qualify his position as being, not so much detached from any side, but with one side and another, as they appealed to him or repelled him.[64] He was neither of the left, right, or center, but of the *inside (entraña)*,[65] for the "fertile principle of relativity of all knowledge"[66] is the basis of toleration, and Unamuno's liberalism was a cognate of his religious openness, a disposition offering no solutions.

But in the turmoil around him, Unamuno saw the principle of infallibility transferred from the religious to the political sphere. Such mad strife, he warned, could lead only to disaster since *Quos Deus vult perdere dementat prius.*[67] The rebellions of 1934 in Catalonia and in the Asturias called forth a fury directed at both sides: he condemned the "unfathomable stupidity of the Asturian Communist propaganda leaflets" on the one hand, and on the other the repressive measures taken against the insurrections by those in the government "who laid claim to a monopoly of decency and patriotism."[68] "On principle," Kierkegaard had said, "a man can do anything, take part in anything, and himself remain inhuman . . ."[69]

It is, however, of paramount importance to emphasize that despite his disgust with the confusions and troubles of the Republic, at no time did Unamuno join forces or even sympathize with Fascist causes. Every form of totalitarian régime—Portuguese, Italian, German—was anathema to him.

> Not a bundle but a herd
> is the sheaf of fascism;
> behind the salute, nothing,
> behind the nothing, abyss.
> (*No un manojo, una manada*
> *es el fajo del fascismo;*
> *detrás del saludo, nada,*
> *detrás de la nada, abismo.*)[70]

Professional militarism, much more than professional pedagogy or professional religiosity, was the ignoble consequence of man's diabolical aptitude for organization. The rigid discipline and *esprit de corps* of the military—even among the boy scouts—repress independent judgment, and not even in the name of one's country does one have the right to lie, for truth must not be sacrificed to patriotism, and the army must be prevented from becoming the arbiter of patriotic feelings.

In exile he had sounded the warning against those Fascist leaders who professed to be saving their countries from Communism: "I cannot tolerate it when an aggrieved and cowardly bourgeoisie, [caught up] in a panic of unreflecting fear of the Communist conflagration . . . hand over their homes and possessions to firefighters who destroy more than the fire itself."[71] The country Mussolini ruled with an iron hand was "that perturbed Italy of Fascism where they are trying to throttle all free spontaneity of the spirit in the name of action."[72] As for Italian "Caesarian" Catholicity, it was nationalistic, Fascistic, that is, antiuniversal, anti-Catholic, even though the pagan unbeliever Mussolini had signed the Lateran Pact. Along with papal infallibility, Italy was being treated to the infallibility of the executive power; Guelf paganism was being matched by Ghibelline paganism.[73]

From the first, Unamuno had looked upon the Salazar régime in Portugal as a wretched little thing (*una pequeña mezquindad*),[74] and on his last trip to Portugal in 1935, when his travelling companions requested an audience with Salazar, Unamuno dissented.[75] When passing through customs on that occasion, the visitors' periodicals had been examined in the event they were carrying anything prohibited by the "Portuguese State Inquisition." Thinking back on the Primo de Rivera dictatorship, which was neither violent nor bloody, but simply petty and stupid, Unamuno saw it reproduced in Portugal where the dignity of the individual was sacrificed to so-called national security, where in order to be a loyal citizen, one had to give up being a complete and true man. To what avail is the balanced budget when there is a spiritual deficit? he asked.[76]

The face of Europe was pockmarked with absurd individuals— not personalities—in a period increasingly anti-individualistic and antiliberal. Was there anything more contemptible than the poor Führer, deficient mentally and spiritually? He wondered how such a scandalously vulgar fellow could fascinate any mass of people— he dared not call them a nation.[77] The swastika was a parody of the Cross, an Asiatic solar hieroglyph, neither Christian nor human, zoological, not anthropological.[78] The racism that was making of Germany a hideous charnelhouse was unqualifiedly denounced by Unamuno as "barbarian and ignorant," xenophobic, a denial of a Christianity which is as Semitic as it is Aryan. The notion of the superiority of the so-called Caucasian race was nothing less than ridiculous and presumptuous.[79]

Fascism was a fashionable illness that was catching on everywhere, and Unamuno was appalled by the signs of incipient Fascism in Spain. From the young men of the *Juventud de Falange Española* with their parades, their uniforms and emblems he expected not so much madness as stupidity.[80] Yet, on the occasion of the visit of José Antonio Primo de Rivera—the moving spirit behind the Falange—to Salamanca on February 10, 1935, Unamuno attended a Falangist meeting and was the object of complimentary remarks.[81] He himself justified his attendance by affirming that he was being faithful to his independent stand.[82]

Even though the Fascist trend was a noxious epidemic, it was perhaps an inevitable consequence of the disappearance of the larger transtemporal sense of the triviality of all causes, the sense of "historic eternization and universal community." [83] For the pace and temper of the times were informed by the anxiety to live—not to die—better; the pressure of immediate material goods was displacing or ignoring the larger, universal metaphysical problem. Since he had always held the essence of Spain to be the dilemmatic or dialectical condition and not the pull to assuagement, he could not reconcile himself to the fact that, short of relinquishing power to a dictator, factions and concessions, buttonholing and bargaining within the legislative framework were the only convenient working tools society had. Recoiling from the "caverns of Parliament" into the "divine and eternal Spain," he forgot that while the latter was a metaphor, the problems of his day were all too concrete and that one cannot live by metaphysics alone. The "average" Spaniard of the future, he feared, would be a Spaniard not of flesh and blood, but of cement—reinforced or waiting to be reinforced—unable to do without party labels,[84] and Unamuno would not concede that a new régime, with all its false starts, short-range plans, its compromises, and even its absurdities, was in the throes of making up for a régime that he himself had declared hopelessly outmoded, ineffectual, and corrupt.

So far did Unamuno fear the laicization of the national spirit, that he expressed his nostalgia for the "good old days" when baptism, marriage, and burial were the three crucial ceremonies sustaining the religious life, and in a characteristic *boutade* foretold the possibility when "to christen" would be called "to Spanishize" (*españolizar*).[85] If one may again use the vocabulary of Tillich, Unamuno's fear was that the "theonomous" or ultimate meaning that shines through finite forms of thought and action would be converted to "autonomy" or pure secularism which "cuts the ties of a civilization with its ultimate ground and aim, whereby, in the measure in which it succeeds, a civilization becomes exhausted and spiritually empty." [86] It was not curialism Unamuno wished to resurrect—although in some of his more exasperated moments he seemed to react in that direction—nor "civil disobedience" that he advocated, but a religious resistance to a relativity that threatened to enthrone itself as an absolute.

The nation that he had interpreted as the vessel of the spirit was again being led, he feared, to the worship of worldly glories, this time of the future, rather than of the past. The Pascal he loved had warned (*Thought 88*) that "All that is made perfect by progress perishes also by progress." And Kierkegaard was convinced that God "does not have the least shred of a cause in the human sense." [87] All worldly attempts at ascension were doomed to death within the history of man, Unamuno was convinced, and history was consequently by definition tragical in contrast to that subhistory which is serene and the superhistory which embodies within itself the hope of the everlasting. History, despite moments of glory or success, was earth-bound and evanescent; unless hedged in by the recognition of something unchangeable, all positive accomplishments were incomplete, contingent, and culpable. "Instead of showing us daily events *sub specie aeternitatis* . . . they show us the most permanent things *sub specie momenti,* as mere events. And thus we lose the notion of the moral perspective of life." [88]

Man needs to connect with an unconditional essence, rather than with the shifting climates of opinion created by himself; unless he does so, the conditions that dominate recede eventually, leaving him stranded on the sands of time. Unamuno's inevitable reaction to the great political shifts was sounded even at the end of the Spanish-American War: ". . . the truth is that these national dramas interest me much less than those developing in each man's consciousness. . . . The fate of each man is the most universal theme there is." [89] And although during the First World War his sympathies were unequivocally with the Allies, he hoped for the defeat of techniques and even of science, in short the defeat of the Europe of engineers, druggists, professors, scholars, travelling salesmen, soldiers, pedants, monist philosophers, extollers of life, and ". . . any ideal limited to the increase of wealth, worldly prosperity and territorial and mercantile aggrandizement."[90] And so, in 1934, exasperated by grandiloquent speeches calling for loyalty to a "sacred" cause, he asked, "Can we take seriously the nonsense . . . about republican essences and the sacred mysteries of transubstantiation of sovereignty and the consubstantiality of the nation with this or the other régime?" [91]

One other extremely important factor must be taken into account: namely, that at the height of the Republican troubles, Unamuno's loneliness was no longer a matter of temperament, but one of fact. In 1932 his sister María, who had lived with his family from 1908 on, died; on March 3, 1934, his sister Susana, the nun, died. And with the death of his wife on May 15, 1934 ("I never really believed in life and she . . . never believed in death"),[92] after an illness of two years, followed by the death of his only married daughter Salomé on July 14 of that year, with his official retirement at the age of seventy in the Fall of 1934 and the erection of a bust in his honor, the impression of living posthumously grew stronger. As the face of Spain kept drastically changing, friends and relatives were dying; as the question of life and death became again a here-and-now agony, political panaceas were even more abhorrent than they had been. In many ways he repeated what he had said at the beginning of the century: "No, I do not love this world. It bewilders me, makes me ill, confuses me. Its men and its things hover about, buzz around my spirit and prevent me from dreaming; they are like clouds of locusts blocking off my stars. Their longings, their pleasures, their laughter and tears, their fortune hunting, their bookish or worldly enlightenment, their frivolous fashions, the seriousness of their calculations, everything about them embitters and poisons my heart." [93]

## IV   The Civil War

By the time the Nationalist revolt against the Republic started in mid-1936, Unamuno was convinced that Spain "was close to death," that Marxism had succeeded in dividing the citizenry, that the class struggle had bred a "reign of hatred and envy . . ." Spain was in need of profound reforms, but the Republic was not capable of effecting them and "this has decided me to join those whom I had not ceased fighting up to now." [94]

According to one report, Unamuno expressed to a representative of the United Press his disgust with the [Republican] government made up of "armed gangs committing all sorts of abominations," while Azaña was a "monster of frivolity" unequal to his position, thinking only of the Popular Front, but not of the farmers, workers, and middle class; he was a man lost in dreams and taking notes for his memoirs. Only the army had the experience required to save Spain, although as he praised Franco's former accomplishments, he confessed surprise at himself, since he had never had confidence in the military and while in France had said, "I prefer a cannon to a lieutenant colonel." [95] But now he was convinced that only the army could at this time provide stability. So plain did he make his pro-rebel position that the Republican government withdrew his lifetime rectorship from him while the *Junta Nacional* at Burgos published a decree keeping him in his post.

However, several of his friends who opposed Franco were dismissed from their posts, others arrested, and some—among them the only Protestant minister in Salamanca—shot. Moreover, shortly after the Nationalist rebellion, German and Italian reinforcements started pouring into Spain to help the insurgents, and they were concentrated in Salamanca where the bishop had provided headquarters for the Franco government. The misgivings and doubts concerning the desperate remedy he was supporting against a desperate national illness and the growing realization that he was backing a revolt instigated by the military aided by foreign régimes he had loudly denounced, turned Unamuno sharply against the men whom he had for a short while considered as possible saviors of his country.

The opportunity to denounce them came on October 12, the *Día de la Raza,* i.e., Columbus Day, one of the great days in Spanish history. As rector, Unamuno opened the ceremonies in the Great Hall of the University. After several important personages had spoken, it was the turn of General Millán Astray who had organized the Spanish Foreign Legion and had lost one eye and one arm in the Moroccan campaigns where his battle cry had been, *"Long Live Death!"* (*¡Viva la muerte!*). In his speech the general denounced one half of all Spaniards as guilty of high treason, referred to the federalist and pro-Republican Catalonia and Basque provinces as two cancers to be exterminated, and praised not only the totalitarian states for helping the revolt, but the "gallant Moors" who were fighting against the "bad Spaniards." There were shouts of *¡Viva la muerte!*, *¡Arriba España!* and the audience chanted, "¡Franco, Franco, Franco!"

Then Don Miguel rose to speak: how could he remain still, he asked, after the wild and insolent remarks of the mutilated general, after the condemnation of the Basque country where he had been born and which he had so passionately loved, or the Catalonia whose literature he had so carefully studied and whose language he had urged all Spaniards to learn? If Unamuno was still prompted by the histrionic element in his temperament to see how far he, a living classic, could go, it nevertheless took an inordinate amount of courage to face a battery of military men and a cowed public, to remind them that he was a Basque and that the Bishop of Salamanca, Plá y Deniel, present at the ceremonies, was a Catalan from Barcelona. He, an experienced weaver of paradoxes, expressed his disgust with the cry "Long live Death!" for it was the equivalent of "Down with Life!" (*¡Muera la Vida!*) and could only mean that the previous speaker to whom it had been addressed was a symbol of death. The crippled Millán Astray, Unamuno continued, was indeed a symbol, not of death, but of the many Spaniards mutilated by a mass psychology dictated by a general who, lacking the loftiness of that other "cripple," Cervantes, could only experience relief at observing the mutilation around him.

A cry from Millán Astray rang out: "Death to the intelligentsia!" (*¡Muera la inteligencia!*), and after the confusion had died down, Don Miguel declared: "I have always been, contrary to the proverb, a prophet in my own land. You will win, but you will not convince (*Venceréis, pero no convenceréis*). You will win, because you possess more than enough brute force, but you will not convince, since to convince means to persuade. And in order to persuade you would need what you lack—reason and right in the struggle. I consider it futile to exhort you to think of Spain. I have finished." Accompanied by Señora de Franco among others, Unamuno was led from the hall.[96]

That same afternoon, as was his custom, Unamuno went to the Casino where loud insults forced him to withdraw. He was forthwith dismissed from the rectorship bestowed upon him by the Nationalists, and retired to his house, never again to leave. If he was watched by the police, a few foreign journalists were yet allowed access to him. To one, the French author Jean Tharaud, Unamuno explained that the frightful civil war was the consequence of the primitive, inhuman, antisocial propensities of his countrymen. From the religious point of view, the civil war was the result of a profound despair, characteristic of the Spanish soul which cannot discover what its faith is and deriving also from a certain hatred for intelligence married to a cult of violence for its own sake. Spain was split between those who, on the one hand, believed, but were pagans and worshipped the Virgin and the saints as local divinities, and on the other hand, the desperados (Unamuno emphasized on this occasion, as he had done frequently in the past that the original word, *desesperado,* is Spanish) who kill those who have faith because they are jealous of their certainties.

More important than this metaphysicising of the appalling situation whirling around him, is the fact that in this interview Unamuno reveals his hope that the Burgos Junta would stay clean of Fascist totalitarianism. He had denounced the militaristic spirit and Millán Astray, but still refused to identify the Franco revolt with Fascism and made it clear that "It is to be hoped that the Burgos government will have the courage and authority to oppose those who wish to establish another régime of terror." In the beginning, he had been convinced that the revolt was at bottom a popular movement of anti-Marxists willing to forget their differences; now he feared that the Falangists, who smacked of Italian Fascism, would absorb all other elements and dictate the course of the future.

The sight of Italian and German troops on Spanish soil had increased his fear that the two Spains fighting in mortal combat would surrender national sovereignty to foreigners, and he warned against the tendencies of "reactionaries" to go beyond justice and humanity, "as they usually do." He deplored the efforts of the Falangists to frighten others into joining their ranks. "What a sad thing it would be if the Bolshevik régime were replaced by the Fascistic, a régime of social slavery. . . . Neither one nor the other, for at bottom they are the same." He was even more temperate towards the unfortunate Azaña whom he now gave credit for good intentions but bad timing: "Azaña and his friends thought they could impose very advanced ideas on Spain. Events stood in their way." [97]

\*　\*　\*　\*　\*　\*　\*

It becomes clear from this account that at the beginning Unamuno had considered the revolt against the legally constituted Republic as a salutary expression of opposition to a government leaning dangerously to the extreme left. It is clear, also, that even after the crucial event of October 12, he distinguished firmly between the Burgos government and Falangism, between the reaction against a weak, even bad, government on the one side, and the proto-Fascist reactionaries he despised. Convinced that Spain was not ready for democratic government, he was deluded into thinking that Franco had little sympathy for Falangism and was prompted only by the ideals of saving Western civilization on home soil.

By mid-November 1936, Germany and Italy had recognized the "Nationalist Spanish Government" and established embassies and missions in Salamanca. "The Germans behave on Spanish soil as if they were on their own . . ." Unamuno lamented.[98] Terrified over the mounting storm in which he was condemned to quasi-silence, he confided to his notebook:

| | |
|---|---|
| Empty hours of waiting; | (*Horas de espera, vacías;* |
| the days pass slowly | *se van pasando los días* |
| without value, | *sin valor,* |
| and terror | *y va cuajando en mi pecho,* |
| curdles in my breast, | *frío, cerrado y deshecho,* |
| cold, closed, destroyed. | *el terror.*)[99] |

The day of December 31, 1936, was spent much as usual since he had confined himself to his home. He had lunch with his family, and at four in the afternoon received a visit from Bartolomé Aragón, a young teacher and now a Nationalist soldier on leave. Unamuno thanked his guest for not coming in his blue shirt even though he did wear the insignia of the yoke and arrows. When offered a Falangist periodical, Unamuno refused it, for "How can one go against intelligence?" The two men sat at the table beneath which the brazier gave warmth. When, during the conversation, the young visitor remarked that sometimes he wondered whether God had not turned His back on Spain, Unamuno retorted: "That is not possible, Aragón. God cannot turn His back on Spain. Spain will be saved because it has to be saved." Suddenly the old man lowered his head and turned very pale. The brazier began to smoke and Aragón perceived that one of Unamuno's slippers was burning.

He drew the foot out of the fire and ran out, crying for help. But Unamuno was already dead.[100]

Miguel de Unamuno was given a Falangist funeral: a man dressed in blue with his arm raised, stood before the open tomb and cried: "Miguel de Unamuno y Jugo!" and the Falangists in attendance answered "Present!" [101]

## V   *Against This and That*

Early in the century, Ortega y Gasset took Unamuno to task for participating in the tendency of his period to be "against someone" or "against something," [102] and at Unamuno's death he published a eulogy in which he felt constrained to draw the contrast between Unamuno whose claim to being a poet impelled him to avoid all doctrine, and those who came after Unamuno's generation: "Because we intellectuals are not on this planet to do juggling tricks with ideas and show people the biceps of our talent, but rather to find ideas with which other men can live. We are not jugglers: we are artisans, like the carpenter, like the mason." [103] Some years later, Camus was to affirm that it is the first duty of the intellectual to create, but that "in certain exceptional circumstances . . . he should permit no ambiguity about which side he has chosen. He should refuse above all to dilute the effectiveness of his choice by shrewd hairsplittings or prudent reservations, and should leave no doubt as to his personal intention to defend freedom." [104]

Such statements, if applied to Unamuno's fluctuating attitudes towards the Spanish Civil War, would condemn him out of hand. But we have seen that Unamuno was not fully aware (although he was assailed by dire presentiments) of the totalitarian leanings of the Nationalist movement, and secondly, that he had so concentrated his authority on analyzing the weaknesses of the Republic that he blinded himself to its virtues. His special brand of liberalism made of him a "conservative and revolutionary, anarchist and socialist, believer and non-believer, pessimist and optimist." [105] He was therefore always at loggerheads with officialdom and took up the cudgels against any form of government which lay claim to being the embodiment of Spanish "tradition." Always true to his role of seer and censor, he fought the monarchy and its Praetorian guard, the Republic, Falangism; intent always on divinizing human activity to reinforce his dream of metapolitics, Unamuno was a latter-day Ecclesiasticus who looked upon power as impotence. Earthly progress was a sorry thing if contingent only on itself; ease was baneful and pointed to decadence; sociology, psychology, political partisanship, all dealt with specious categories removed from the vital center.

"He whom God has touched will always be a being apart; whatever he does, he is disconnected from other men . . ." [106] he quotes Renan, and then recalls how during the Franco-Prussian War, the Frenchman had wondered whether Bismarck understood the vanity of everything he labored for so ardently. The *prêtre manqué* in Unamuno was, whatever the political situation, always in the forefront to preach that "for a true Christian . . . any question political or otherwise, had to be conceived, treated, and resolved in its relation to individual interest in eternal salvation, in eternity. And suppose the country perished? The country of the Christian is not of this world." [107] In so many of his political pronouncements, the voice of his master Kierkegaard is only too evident, for the latter had said that the difference between politics and the religious view "is heaven-wide (*toto caelo*) . . . since politics begins on earth and remains on earth, whereas religion, deriving its beginning from above, seeks to explain and transfigure and thereby exalt the earthly to heaven." [108]

The immediate practical disadvantages implicit in such an exclusive attachment to the spiritual are acted out in Unamuno's own shifting positions and deadlocks. In any positive position, Unamuno was what Gide said of Dostoevski: "a man of whom there is no way to make use!" [109] since he could never suspend his antihumanism sufficiently to join with man-made forces. The tragic sense was, to him, irreconcilable with any party platform; he could not foreshorten his views long enough to accept the inevitable admixture of venality present in all human enterprise working for the greatest good of the greatest number. The Church, for all its imperfections, he might on occasion condone as a distorted interpretation of the Divine Idea, but the shortcomings of social, political, or economic man he regarded as unmitigatedly ignoble or foolish.

If he had any ideal for worldly governance, it was that of a modified theism, permissive of all thought, provided it was chastened by a sense of the unknown. His work sometimes echoes the spirit of reformers like Luther and Calvin, who defied establishment but sternly punished laxity, and carries us back to the mystics whose contempt for the world was so deep and broad that it aroused the mistrust even of the Church. The qualities commonly associated with enlightenment are scarcely discernible in him: rational control, utilitarianism, deemphasis of the dark, unforeseeable and submerged, and above all, buoyant hope in the human potential. It is no wonder that the romanticists who melancholically dispelled this basic optimism exercised a strong pull on his imagination—Wordsworth, Leopardi, the Portuguese poets—since Unamuno considered all optimism blind, all *joie de vivre* superficial, and the next step merely a step nearer the grave.

H. Richard Niebuhr has pointed out the value of such men as Unamuno: they recall society to its "transpolitical destiny" and its "suprapolitical" loyalty.[110] Yet, at the same time, they themselves are caught in the culture through which they have met Christ and must, within that culture, cast their lot with that design which leaves them most free to worship Him. "Though the whole world lies in darkness, yet distinctions must be made between relative rights and wrongs in that world, and in Christian relations to it."[111] Unamuno, however, saw the issue mainly as one between divine righteousness and human self-righteousness; if he felt infinitely removed from holiness, how much farther removed were those embroiled in creaturely pursuits! Holding high his position of intransigent independence for all to see and, presumably, to imitate, he refused to admit that a nation of independents was a nation in anarchy, and that condemnation of all codes is as injurious as uncritical fidelity to any single one. It was impossible for him to concede that certain systems, albeit imperfect, are the best available, that the world's business rolls on the wheels of compromise, and that for the sake of stability, we are constrained to agree that the barber's basin is both basin and helmet.

It must, however, be admitted that Unamuno speaks to the unhappy company of those for whom the reasonable patterns of behavior and acceptance are not enough, and who must worry themselves and unsettle others in a search for deeper, more comprehensive answers. He appeals to those "outsiders" who, tormented by the insufficiency of day-to-day movement, must inveigh against the multitudes functioning within such a rhythm. For he held on, under the most pressing of circumstances, to the conviction that the philosopher must fend off the objectification or "thingification" of man into what Gabriel Marcel calls the *l'on* and Heidegger labels the colorless, odorless, and tasteless *man* ("one" says, "one" does).

Thus, Unamuno sounds the warning for those who, pledged to desk, laboratory, pulpit, or forum, forget that the premises on which they labor are forever questionable. Unamuno provides a metaphor for those who, hoping for the best, are ever aware of the abyss; for those who, on either side of any question, are afraid of their convictions; for those who fear they believe too blindly and for those who fear they disbelieve too obdurately. Unamuno warns that allegiance to the natural as well as to the supernatural is open to endless corrigibility and that righteousness in either camp is partial and Pharisaical. He himself said that "If the Unamunist party is ever established in Spain, I shall be the first anti-Unamunist." [112] As outlandish as his quixotism may sound when dealt with out of context, the creed of noble folly, of error and dissent as inalienable privileges of living personality, is a grandiose defense against uniformity, cowardice, and regimentation.

## CHAPTER 5

# *Fiction as Philosophy*

THE philosopher who avails himself of the devices of literature is not an uncommon phenomenon in the last century. Nietzsche had recourse to epigram and dithyramb, Sartre incorporates his thought in novel and play, some of Gabriel Marcel's concepts are expounded in the form of drama, while Heidegger seeks the affinity between *Denken* and *Dichten* through Hölderlin and Rilke. With the Kierkegaardian equation of truth-subjectivity as the inescapable ground of modern existential thought, the variety of specific human situations that can be acted out in imaginative literature attracts the professional philosopher as much as truth arrived at through impersonal proposition.

Unamuno, the philosopher interested above all in the contradictions and paradoxes of the concrete man of flesh and bone, was not intimidated by the requirements and restrictions of the various genres, for if his essays were a strange compound of confession, poetry, description, and sermon, he could equally refashion the drama or novel to fit his own needs or deficiencies. If he could confuse desire and reason, emotion and logic, need and reality, he could also repudiate the boundaries distinguishing fiction from straight discourse, verse from lecture, short story from moral lesson. Repeatedly he pointed out that if the *Iliad, Odyssey, Divine Comedy,* and *Paradise Lost* were officially epics, Hegel's *Logic* and Spinoza's *Ethics* could be considered poems or tragedies.

## I   *The Plays*

If, for Unamuno, the summit of the Spanish classical theater was represented by Lope de Vega,[1] the best of modern theater was represented by Ibsen.[2] The influence of the Norwegian's concept of the theater as a forum of ideas on Unamuno's plays is evident, especially in certain scenes and characters, but Unamuno was sorely lacking in Ibsen's rich sense of plot and variety, his power of characterization, his poetry and range of expression. The Spaniard's characters are hieratic, his vocabulary strangely repetitive and impoverished, and except for the division of his plays into acts and scenes, and the division of the author into characters that do not bear his name, the plays may be confused with some of his more strident essays. They are, in short, *druma*,[3] not drama, and are meant to be read as complements to his other, more compelling work.

The original title Unamuno had intended to give his first significant drama, *The Sphinx* (*La esfinge*), was *Glory or Peace* (*Gloria o paz*). Like his *Nicodemus,* it was written shortly after the crisis of 1897 and is of interest because it points to the development of the thinker along several unbroken lines. Briefly, the play concerns the early success of Angel who allows himself to be enticed into political life by his childless wife Eufemia, then withdraws in the hope of finding true spiritual meaning within himself, and is killed as a traitor by a revolutionary mob. The language is stilted and declamatory, the political whirlwind supposedly raging about Angel trickles into the drama only through the flattery of a few friends, Eufemia is the merest outline of the childless woman who will take several other forms in Unamuno's fiction.

Unequal to the demands of dramaturgy, Unamuno has nevertheless created in Angel a counterpart of himself, an indecisive, difficult creature forced into playing a role at variance with his deepest self. Unamuno had just passed through a crucial period in his life when, in the midst of a growing reputation, he had experienced the sensation of the futility of all accomplishment if made void by total death. In Act I, Scene III, Angel looks at himself in the mirror and finds himself overpowered by the split in his own personality and the fear of becoming a spectator of himself. The call to action had come from without, from wife, friends, and admirers, and he exclaims: "How shall I give solace to others when I have none for myself?" While shouts of political contention come from without, his mind turns back to the episode when, as a child, and curious about the future, he had opened the Gospel and read: "Go ye therefore, and teach all nations . . . ," and then again ". . . I have told you already, and ye did not hear: wherefore would ye hear it again?" At this late date, he realizes, however, that his desire to return to simple faith, his aspirations to purity, are all irredeemably impure, and as he surrenders his position as leader and faces the mob, he also faces the terrors of religious uncertainty. Angel's final understanding of his self-deception is, of course, the obverse of Brand's realization that he had confined the Christian pattern to gloomy Puritanism, but Unamuno's character does not have the impact of Ibsen's since we have not witnessed, except through Angel's words, the trials and tribulations that tortured Brand's soul. In short, the concept of Angel is not set within the framework of some meaningful realism through which the metamorphosis of the character may be followed.

Faith that will not survive confrontation with facts is given the most obvious and categorical treatment in *The Blindfold* (*La Venda*) of 1899, adapted one year later as a short story of the same name. A drama in one act and four tableaux, it concerns a young woman who, blind all her life, marries, bears a child, and is miraculously restored to sight through medical intervention. When she is informed that her father is dying, she wishes to go to him, but is warned that the shock might prove fatal to the old man. She insists, but finds that in order to trace her way back to the house of her youth, she must blindfold her eyes and use a cane. It need scarcely be pointed out that the restored light, so unwelcome to the girl, is the loss of faith, that the blindfold and cane represent the childlike faith which is the only path back to God, and that Unamuno treats the theme of the pain of enlightenment versus consoling innocence far better in terms of himself than when he hangs it on a talking mannequin such as the protagonist of this puppet show.

*The Past Returns* (*El pasado que vuelve*), 1910, is a skeletal family chronicle in three acts, and traces the alternation of idealism and materialism over four generations to show that both sides can adduce rationales in a dialectic that seems to offer no chance of resolution.

In *Soledad,* 1921, the woman whose name provides the title of the play is married to the playwright Agustín. They have lost their child and she, grieving over her bereavement and jealous of the actress Gloria, urges her husband into politics. There he fails ignominiously and is driven into hiding. For two tiresome acts his mind wanders over the mysteries of life and dreams, theater and reality, while Soledad is reduced to the role of sur- rogate mother. Characters step in and out almost symmetrically,

make inconclusive remarks or sibylline commentaries on the
meanness of politics, the futility of action, on sleep, God, eternity,
madness, and sanity.

In *Rachel in Chains* (*Raquel encadenada*), 1921, the roles of
the main characters are reversed, for this time it is the wife who
is a famous violinist and her husband Simón who is her manager
and to whose craze for money the heroine attributes the sterility
of their marriage. Raquel finally leaves her husband to take care
of the illegitimate child of her first lover. Vaguely reminiscent of
Ibsen's Norah, Raquel is yet another one of a long line of Una-
munesque women driven to frenzy by childlessness; Simón is a
caricature of a miser; and the endlessly repeated obsessions of
the author make for monotony and shapelessness.

*Dream Shadows* (*Sombras de sueño*), 1926, written during the
author's exile and based on his earlier novelette *Tulio Montalbán
y Julio Macedo,* again reflects Unamuno's preoccupation with
self-fidelity and with reality as an ignominious reproduction of
the quixotic ideal. Elvira Solórzano and her father are the last
scions of an ancient family that had conquered the still, sad
island they inhabit. The girl is in love with the subject of a biography she reads over and over: Tulio Montalbán who had liber-
ated a small American republic and then disappeared. Her love
for this unknown man is the love of Don Quixote for Dulcinea in
reverse, since when she meets Julio Macedo who is Tulio seeking
a new authentic life totally independent from his historical past,
she cannot love the tangible human being and causes his suicide.

A far more interesting treatment of the subject of the personality split into antagonistic roles, uppermost in Unamuno's mind
from 1924 to 1930, is the play *The Other One* (*El otro*), also
completed in 1926. As we have seen in *How a Novel is Made,*
Unamuno was plagued by the ambivalence of his position outside
of Spain. Righteous in his defiance of tyranny, but suspicious of
his self-righteousness, he justified his position by every objective
criterion but the implacable inquisition he practiced on himself,
and his thought again ran to the Cain and Abel theme not only as
the paradigm of the inevitable friction uniting all men, but of that
inner friction suffered by all men of good faith. Like Everyman,
Unamuno contained within himself both the seven virtues and the
seven cardinal sins: he was "proud and humble, gluttonous and
temperate, sensual and chaste, envious and charitable, avaricious

and generous, indolent and industrious, wrathful and long-suffering. And from the same person comes the tyrant and slave, the criminal and the saint, Cain and Abel . . ." [4]

He had already written his novel on fratricide, *Abel Sánchez* (1917), in which one friend causes the other's death, and as he wrote the prologue for the second edition of the tale during his period of deep self-questioning, he put himself to the task of dramatizing a short story of 1908 called "He Who Buried Himself" ("El que se enterró"). The story, a variant of the *doppelgänger* theme that had so impressed him in *Dr. Jekyll and Mr. Hyde,* treats of a man who comes face to face with his other self, as if his reflection in a mirror had come to life. He dies, comes to life, kills the "other one," and buries him; although things go on as before, their "tone" and "timbre" have changed, but even when the protagonist himself finally dies, there is no solution to the mystery of who killed whom.

The play that grew from this macabre tale is significantly called a mystery in three acts and an epilogue. It is a claustrophobic charade about identical twins, Cosme and Damián, who both fall in love with Laura. She marries Cosme, Damián goes away, and years later, when Laura leaves home on a visit and then returns, she finds *The Other* half-mad: he has killed his brother but refuses to reveal whether he, the survivor, is Laura's husband or brother-in-law. He sleeps alone, talks in riddles, and torments himself with unanswerable questions.

Damiana, Damián's wife, arrives looking for her husband who had, a month earlier, left his home to visit his brother Cosme. Ernesto, Laura's brother, has seen the corpse but cannot tell which of the two brothers it is. Who is Cain and who Abel, who the assassin and who the victim, who the wife and who the widow? And whoever the dead man is, he slowly becomes the executioner as well as the victim, for remorse, like a Fury, drives the surviving brother to madness and suicide, and not even the brothers' former nurse can distinguish between the two bodies. "I do not know who I am," she says, "you do not know who you are [nor] does the author know who he is."

The comparison between *The Other One* and Pirandello's *Right You Are, if You Think You Are* comes to mind immediately. Although the Italian play is richer in texture, both plays are fundamentally debates over the hidden character of truth and identity, and both leave the reader baffled and frustrated. Since it is totally lacking in action and character development, *The Other One* is perhaps more appropriate to a dramatic reading than to a conventional theatrical production, but it does sum up once again Unamuno's dilemma over man's inextricably triad nature: as others think he is, as he thinks he is, as he really is. Cast by exile into a part made for him and later voluntarily chosen, Unamuno could not evade the riddle of being and the contradictory forms it had taken in his own life, and evolved this dramatic metaphor which is more compelling for its philosophical than for its theatrical value.

In 1929, towards the end of his exile, Unamuno wrote the play *Brother Juan, or The World is a Stage* (*El Hermano Juan o El mundo es teatro*) to demonstrate that the fame associated with even so universally recognized a seducer as Don Juan is actually a legend foisted upon him. The concept is much like that of Shaw in *Man and Superman*—to show that Don Juan is more sinned against than sinner—but the execution is completely different, for it is dour, totally lacking in wit or verbal agility, weak and confused in development, in short more noteworthy for its intention than for the technique through which the purpose is worked out.

The Don Juan figure had always been the object of Unamuno's withering contempt, for it was his conviction that chastity was one of the most cogent signs of true virility, and he roundly condemned promiscuity as debilitating to the intelligence.[5] Indeed, unlike Shaw's buoyantly intellectual and resourceful John Tanner, Unamuno's Don Juan is a listless character, haunted by the shadow of death, given to morbid introspection and meditation on the indistinguishability between shadow and substance, reality and the imagination. Frightened rather than enticed by women, he pleads with his "victims" to marry men who can give them children; when he quarrels with Benito, one of his "rivals," he does not strangle him but begs to be beaten and punished. He can take no pride in the women who throw themselves at his feet since to them he is "Juanito" (Johnny) and *niño* (child). His is the shame of the mountebank, since he entertains and excites the senses—or the compassion—of women, but it is the non-Juans who marry these women, and become fathers.

And Don Juan ends his life as a friar, caring for little children, and awaiting the only marriage possible for him—with Death! But like Ahasuerus, he cannot die, for he is not a man but a legend existing in the collective imagination, and is doomed to be re-incarnated in various theatrical dress. His is the fate of the talking effigy so horrifying to one who, like Unamuno, was obsessed by the desire for actual, personal immortality. Thus does the author strip Don Juan of all qualities connected with the tempestuous, fickle lover, and if Shaw vindicates his hero, Unamuno gathers him into the fold of his other Hamlet-like protagonists, creatures who doubt their existence, who do not know, like the Segismundo of Calderón's *Life is a Dream* (*La vida es sueño*), whether they are dreaming or living their lives.

Mention should also be made of Unamuno's *Fedra,* 1910, a modern version of Euripides and Racine, in which Hippolytus is saved, and his translation of Seneca's *Medea,* 1933. He also tried his hand at two one-act farces, *Princess Lambra* (*La Princesa Doña Lambra*), 1909, and *The Late Lamented* (*La difunta*), the same year.

In sum, Unamuno's theater is little more than the perfunctory insertion of his ideas into dramatic outline. In almost every one of the plays, the exposition is made at the beginning in long, awkward sentences put into the mouth of some one or more characters. And the rest is atemporal conversation between people addicted to Unamuno's interrogatory or declamatory form, and who play with notions, words, and literary allusions that trail off into suspension points. Because dramatic literature was to Una-muno primarily word and not spectacle, the absolutely indispens-able dramatic machinery he found himself forced to use is of the most creaky, primitive kind, while the word is prolix and un-adorned, alternating between harangue and truncated ejaculation. Since the affections, hatreds, and obsessions of his characters are outlined by themselves or others near the beginning of the play, there is no need for them to unfold slowly through action and reaction; in short, the shadings of suspense, ambiguity, surprise, and novelty are missing. Not the play, but the theme is the thing, incarnated into talking machines: Fedra, despite her writhings, is an unfortunate *bourgeoise;* Victor of *The Past Returns* the merest excuse for a rebel; Tulio Montalbán is a bare phantom. Raquel starts full-blown and cannot work herself out, as does Ibsen's Norah, from doll-child to independent woman, while Agustín, reverting to childhood at the end of *Soledad* to find refuge in the lap of his wife-mother, is an attenuated echo of Oswald Alving.

The themes of the plays are reiterations of those found insistently throughout Unamuno's other work: dream vs. reality, blind faith vs. reason, the vanity of human wishes, individual integrity, surrogate immortality to be found in fame, children, and work, but they remain in conceptual orbit, disembodied, meagerly orchestrated, monochromatic. Unamuno was as much in revolt against the operatic flamboyance of a Zorrilla or the well-made play of Echegaray, as Shaw was against the theater of Scribe, Sardou, Pinero, or Jones; but while Shaw made drama out of concept through brilliant discourse, sharp wit, antithesis, and playfulness, Unamuno's language is staccato and circumscribed, and the style of his characters interchangeable rather than sharply differentiated. Shaw's superb introductions are sparkling adjuncts to many plays that stand robustly on their own merits, while Unamuno's dramas are justified only as complements to his other work. As one critic has said, it is unfortunate that one cannot affix to the programs of Unamuno's dramas the words: "In order to understand thoroughly what you are going to see on the stage, first read Unamuno's entire work."[6]

## II  *The Short Stories*

Nineteenth-century Spain produced short story writers of some consequence: Fernán Caballero, Alarcón, even the benign Palacio Valdés, were adept at the genre. Leopoldo Alas (Clarín) wrote tales of moving simplicity, some oversentimentalized, others of delicate fancifulness; the regional tales of Emilia Pardo Bazán and of Blasco Ibáñez, however, stand out for their stark, cruel realism which win them a place alongside the best of Giovanni Verga.

Although Unamuno's first short story dates back to 1886, and his last may be dated 1934,[7] in no way does he earn a distinguished place among the great practitioners of the genre. Some of his tales are mere literary jottings, products of a spare moment; others are excuses to hammer away at his favorite concepts and are barely distinguishable from his less successful essays. Yet quite a number, although lacking in the adroitness and irony of a Maupassant or a Chekhov, strike the reader as containing the kernel of a finished work.

Some are unashamedly romantic: "The Mirror of Death" ("El espejo de la muerte") is the story of an unhappy, tubercular girl; "In the Cook's Hands" ("En manos de la cocinera") tells of how the hero marries the simple servant girl who looked after him during an illness when his affected fiancée considered it unseemly to visit him as he lay in bed; "Godfather Antonio" ("El padrino Antonio") is the story of an old man who marries his dishonored ward; "Soledad" is the tragedy of the old maid who turns disappointed love into a fount of understanding.

But "As the Years Go by" ("Al correr de los años") averts the trap of mawkishness and becomes a moving tribute to conjugal love; "The Simple Don Rafael, Hunter and Cardplayer" ("El sencillo don Rafael, cazador y tresillista") is a straightforward account of a bachelor who adopts a foundling, engages as its nurse the simple Emilia whose breasts are full of milk for an illegitimate child that had died, marries her, and has ten children more. "The Teacher of Carrasqueda" ("El maestro de Carrasqueda") tells of a humble schoolmaster in a backward town who, despite unresponsive classes, realizes that something must come of dedication, while in "Mr. Milquetoast" ("Juan Manso"), the protagonist who avoided doing either good or evil in life, is refused admission to Heaven, Purgatory, and Hell.

"A Visit to the Old Poet" ("Una visita al viejo poeta") and "Don Martín, or On Glory" ("Don Martín, o de la gloria") both illustrate Unamuno's preoccupation with the coating which fame puts upon self-knowledge. The first story, written significantly in 1899, concerns an old poet who retires to the simple life of the country to disentangle the pure "I" from the personality given to him by his fame, "the reflection of ourselves which we receive back from the world where we are surrounded by a thousand mirrors." In the second, dated one year later, the author Don Martín, now a classic and "statuefied," repents of his thirst for glory which he recognizes as vainglory since at bottom, all of life is a failure.

Unamuno was also capable of short macabre pieces such as "Children of the Mind" ("Hijos espirituales") which treats of an aspirant to literary fame, Federico, spoiled by an overindulgent mother. He marries Eulalia who, as she finds she is denied children, goes mad, buys baby dolls with which she displaces her husband's beloved books. The tragedy explodes one day when he throws her dolls into the street and she matches him by doing the same with his books. In "The Attack of Love" ("El amor que asalta"), Anastasio finds the love he has vainly sought, at a railroad station in the person of Eleuteria; they retire to a dingy hotel room where several days later they are found in bed naked, both dead of heart attacks. "Justina" is the pathetic story of a simple girl whose mistreatment at the hands of relatives aggravates her natural awkwardness and culminates in the unintentional death of her nephew, and when she drops her own child, she goes mad.

In "The Madness of Doctor Montarco" ("La locura del doctor Montarco"), the author dramatizes one of his ex-futures, since it is the story of one of the "possible" but circumvented directions Unamuno's own life might have taken. The protagonist, an exemplary father and husband, and a conscientious physician, writes fantastic and aggressive stories which he refuses to explain to his suspicious patients. He resists the pressure of a society where only the middle path or *aurea mediocritas* is acceptable, and is finally removed to a nursing home where he spends his time reading *Don Quixote*.

"Susin's Tribulations" ("Las tribulaciones de Susín") is a lyrico-fantastic piece on the wondrous world of children's imaginations. "From Eagle to Duck" ("De águila a pato") is an apologue of the eagle who accepts the challenge of the lion to fight on equal terms; he cuts off his wings and is slowly turned into a duck. A stronger point is made in "Ignorant John" ("El lego Juan"), in which the humility of the saintly John serves only to excite his victimizers to greater cruelty, while "The Chant of the Eternal Waters" ("El canto de las aguas eternas") is a finely wrought parable, suggestive of Kafka, about the man who attempts to reach a mysterious castle by climbing a narrow winding road while the invisible torrent below continues singing always.

A somber satire, suggested possibly by Butler's *Erewhon,* is "Mecanopolis," an hallucinatory tale of a perfectly mechanized and uninhabited city; "Don Bernardino and doña Etelvina" is, on the other hand, a hilarious farce-satire concerning two sociologists: one a male, who is the champion of women's rights, and the other, a female, who champions men's rights. "Batracophiles and Batracophobes," a wry commentary on the causes of war and reminiscent of the braying episode in *Don Quixote,* tells of a city split down the center over the frogs in the pool of the club garden.

### III   *The Novels*

The modern novel in Spain was born in the early part of the nineteenth century under the aegis of the *costumbrista* essay, an amalgam of picturesque description, slight story line, jest, and satire. The marriage of *costumbrismo* and the extended tale produced the regional novel which flourished with such writers as Fernán Caballero, Alarcón, Pereda, and Palacio Valdés. These were competent novelists who, because of the emphasis they put on quaint local customs, moralizing and sentimental effusions, produced works now of slight interest to anyone but students of Spanish literature and perhaps social anthropologists. The Countess Emilia Pardo Bazán, in the literary vanguard of the late nineteenth century, through her interest in French and Russian writers, produced two novels that might lay claim to more than national importance—*The Manor-Houses of Ulloa* (*Los pazos de Ulloa*) and its sequel *Mother Nature* (*La Madre Naturaleza*), while Leopoldo Alas (Clarín) wrote *La Regenta,* an enormous thousand-page documented novel of provincial life and adultery which may indeed be the greatest single work of fiction out of nineteenth-century Spain.

But the Titan of the modern Spanish novel was Benito Pérez Galdós, who in addition to bringing the historical novel to a climax in over forty volumes of the *National Episodes* (*Episodios nacionales*), wrote a series of novels on contemporary life that combine the compassion and humor of Dickens, the scope of Balzac, and an insight into the dark impulses and the self-destructive psyche reminiscent of Dostoevski. Pérez Galdós' production is powerful in impact and monumental in range: his enormous gallery of characters includes aristocrat and bureaucrat, drunkard and scholar, rogue and priest, usurer and fanatic, politician and schizophrenic. He created a comprehensive world made up of an infinite variety of situations, and described it in wry, ironic, witty, angry, and benevolent tones.

When Unamuno was writing his first novel, then, Galdós was the master of Spanish fiction, while Flaubert and Zola exercised perhaps the greatest influence from abroad. But neither the sweep of Pérez Galdós, nor the technique of Flaubert, nor the scientific pretentions of Zola impressed Unamuno. It was not Flaubert

the craftsman, the author of *Madame Bovary,* who interested
Unamuno so much as the Flaubert of *Bouvard et Pécuchet* and
the *Correspondance,* the writer who prefigured his own detestation
of common sense.[8] Disregarding the epic strength of the Rougon-
Macquart series, Unamuno dismissed Zola as one with a puerile
faith in the science of his time which he did not understand.[9] As
for Galdós, he took him to task for the mediocrity of his characters, his milieu, and his personal vision. The Spanish master's
work, he felt, reflected the appalling hollowness of the middle
class of his time, since the author, for all the enormous breadth
of his fiction, had not created a single powerful personality struggling with destiny, not a single desperado. As for Galdós' style, he
judged it to be slow, vast, compact, like a placid river without
storm or quake.[10]

Except for his first novel, *Peace in War* (*Paz en la guerra*),
completed in 1897, Unamuno's fiction represents a complete break
with traditional realistic techniques and an attempt to devise a new
genre that would replace breadth by depth, documentation by
religiously-charged symbolism, variety by concentration. The large-
scale background, the slow accretion of fact and physical detail,
the interplay of a broad cast of characters with historical determi-
nants, all these he considered as nonessentials obstructing the ultimate realism of each man standing alone in his agony. Consequently, most of Unamuno's characters have little or no relation
to the world at large, but agonize in a small, circumscribed area.
Each protagonist is the equivalent of a *passion maîtresse* with few
or no secondary characteristics to make for verisimilitude, and as
their envy, virile pride, *idées fixes,* or maternal longings deepen
into abysses, they seem to sever connection with any frame of
reference other than themselves.

These characters who struggle with themselves more than with
their circumambience, Unamuno calls *agonists* (*agonistas*), while
for most of his novels he prefers the word *nivola* rather than
*novela,* to suggest not only a repudiation of accepted standards of
fictional composition, but the mist that erases environmental contours. Further, Unamuno insists upon the distinction between the
"oviparous" novel, a consequence of long incubation during which
the work receives consistency and body, and the "viviparous"
creation which springs alive fully formed and recognizable by a
cry, a gesture, a raw passion, all unsupported by artificial ma-

chinery. In the first case, the author conceives an idea and expands on it with notes, observations, qualifications, research, additions, and subtractions. In the second, the writer bears it all in his head where it gestates, and when he feels "true labor pains" he takes up his pen and "gives birth." In the viviparous novel, there is no turning back, no rethinking, no revising, for the embryo is completely formed and therefore must be born.[11]

*Peace in War,* 1897, is Unamuno's one oviparous novel since he spent about a dozen years accumulating information and developing it. The germ lies in a short story, "Solitaña," [12] published in a Bilbao newspaper in 1888, and which may be assigned the prominent place in Unamuno's work which "A Simple Heart" occupies in Flaubert's. This touching piece describes the commonplace life of an undistinguished man who, despite ironic and even caricaturish elements introduced by the author, approaches archetypal stature. After writing the story, it occurred to Unamuno to write a novel by increasing the number of *dramatis personae,* expanding the action, and developing the historical circumstances of the Carlist Wars of 1874-1876. Thus began the real hatching of the egg, the oviparous accumulation of deeds and words, the note-taking on day-to-day living, contemporaneous language and references to military actions, and the bombardment of Bilbao which Unamuno had witnessed as a child.

The title may have been suggested by Proudhon's *La guerre et la paix,* by Tolstoy's *War and Peace,* by the line from Alfieri's *Saul* (Act II, Scene I): *Bramo in pace far guerra, in guerra pace* ("I yearn to make war in peace, and peace in war").[13] With Galdós' novels on Spanish history in mind, Unamuno read Zola's *Débâcle* which he did not like, and Tolstoy's epic novel which he found "unforgettable," [14] especially since the Russian novel stressed a point which Unamuno was to work out fully in his own way in *On Authentic Tradition:* namely, the difference between what occurs and what history records, the contrast between the " 'real' texture of life, both of individuals and communities [and] the 'unreal' picture presented by historians." [15] Compared, however, with the gigantic historical canvas of Tolstoy's work, *Peace in War* shrinks to insignificance, for alongside the epic sweep of the battle-scenes of the Russian work, the burning of Moscow, the retreat of Napoleon, the massive reverberations of the military, political, social, and philosophical upheavals, the Spanish Carlist Wars are like local skirmishes. Lacking also in the Spanish work are the fullness and diversity of Tolstoy's characters who evolve, learn, and enrich their humanity through vast and highly-charged experiences. Instead of the titanic leaders such as Napoleon and Alexander, the enigmatic yet appealing Kutuzov, the saturnine restless Prince Andrey, we are given the shadowy figures of the Carlist Pretender or the inept, pious General Lizárraga. In contrast with the multifaceted Pierre who grows in stature with the novel, there is Ignacio, a minor if serious Basque Candide who only on rare occasions is able consciously to identify his human situation.

In addition, but on a much smaller scale than in Tolstoy, *Peace in War* is also a family chronicle, of humble, earthbound people: the modest shopkeeper Pedro Antonio, his devoted pious wife, their only son Ignacio, along with the priest, their other friends, the businessmen and inhabitants of Bilbao, simple people fulfilling their civic and religious obligations, enveloped in a routine that neither inspires them to greatness nor displeases them into rebellion. If the novel has a focal figure, it is the young Ignacio whose authenticity lies in the peaceful pursuit of those instinctive life processes that make up the course of unrecorded history. Obedient to parents and priest, entranced by the stalwart country girls, remorseful over the weakness that leads him to the brothel, he is most alive in the familiar daily pattern.

In the army, however, he is bewildered; finding military life to be more servitude than grandeur, his enthusiasm for the Carlist cause in which he is enrolled simmers down to apathy and resentment. Truth for Ignacio does not lie in causes, but in birth, copulation, and death; wider meanings are imposed from without by his father's memories of the First Carlist War (1833-1840), the Bishop's pastoral letter, the sight of the Pretender. Although he is told that by fighting on the Carlist side, he is defending old-fashioned regional virtues against the "depravity" of centralist Castile, in reality the war is for Ignacio one of blurred distinctions and confused issues, and his eventual death is an inglorious one in a war that peters out. If Ignacio's death is useless, the victims of the siege of Bilbao also seem to be suffering for nothing. Doña Micaela, terrified by the bombardment which brings back memories of similar miseries suffered in the First Carlist War, languishes and dies. The pale liberal, Don Juan Arana, frets over his business despite the disasters. Pedro Antonio, Ignacio's father, worries over the money he had contributed to the Carlist cause, and Josefa Ignacia, Ignacio's mother, dies, leaving a poor declining husband.

It is during the bombardment, however, that the novel really acquires a collective hero—the town, reduced to eating cats and rats, swayed by rumors, holding on to hopes soon shattered, caught in endless discussions about taking sides against a mysterious brotherhood of masons, freethinkers, and anti-Christs. Enmities and jealousies are exacerbated, hiding and cringing alternate with scenes of military disorganization, waste, listless and bewildered defenders, and bungling generals in what amounts to a burlesque of a campaign. With the inevitable failure of such an undertaking comes the resumption of the quiet plodding lives of the survivors.

There is one, however, who must take stock of the entire cataclysm, of its meaning for himself, for the town he loves, for the world. This is Pachico Zabalbide who in 1866, at the age of 18, had gone to Madrid to study and there lost his faith. At the close of the book, Pachico, hitherto a secondary character but now the *raisonneur,* sits on a hill overlooking the countryside and finds temporary subsidence for his inner tumult, just as the civil war had subsided, leaving in its wake a sense of lost lives but surviving humanity. In the relaxation of twilight, this provincial intellectual is no longer driven by the Luciferian pride of demanding everything or nothing; there is a suspension of war in him, or more exactly, a deep if temporary peace abstracted from the ceaseless war of antinomies which will be his fate. Looking about him, he has his moment of truth as he grasps the essential unity underlying all antagonisms, from cosmic wars of the elements to man-made struggles. With the understanding that the true history of man is his ability to survive generically in the *durchhalten* of the still, small processes, Pachico, clearly the alter ego of the author, finally pronounces his "Yea." Since war is to peace what time is to eternity, simply a passing form, there shall always be war, and happiness will be for those who can draw a deep personal tranquillity from the unending conflict.

*Peace in War* not only bespeaks Unamuno's love of his native city and the unsophisticated, hard-working, deeply pious people who inhabited it in his childhood and youth, but dramatizes his memories of the "two Spains" foolishly pitted against each other, and on the whole may be considered the fictional counterpart of his

*On Authentic Tradition.* But notwithstanding the obeisance he pays to circumstance in his novel, despite the sociological and historical framework he provides and the occasional success he achieves in conveying the rhythm of masses in emergency, the chords sounded are in a minor key, the secondary characters are sketchy, and Pachico's final lofty meditations do not grow organically out of the fabric of the novel. In short, *Peace in War* is already, like much of Unamuno's subsequent fiction, an imperfect attempt to translate beloved concepts into fiction with a minimum of artistic requirement.

With *Love and Education* (*Amor y Pedagogía*), 1902, Unamuno enters his viviparous period, and eschews all historical or sociological approach in order to concentrate on fictionalizing another of his favorite notions through the many words and few acts of a small core of characters. Reason, he argues in this novel, is valid only if applied to abstractions, but sadly inadequate when dealing with the concrete and the unpredictable. The attempt to impose an ideological straitjacket on the mercury of life, to force instinct and impulse into preconceived molds, is a ridiculous effort which may end, as in this case, in tragedy. Thus, *Love and Education* is a satire of the religion of science (one of the manifestations of what Flaubert called *la bêtise humaine*) embodied in Don Avito Carrascal who "walks by mechanics, digests by chemistry, and has his suits cut by projective geometry."

Don Avito's supreme desire is to sire and mold a genius, and towards that end he must choose a mate for eugenic rather than sentimental reasons; yet instinct is stronger than ratiocination, and instead of deductively marrying Leoncia the "dolico-blonde" with wide hips, solid breasts, and healthy color, he is carried away by the sight of a "brachi-Plutonian brunette" and "inductively" marries the Marina who clings to her prayers, her church, and even her superstitions. The son born to them is called Apolodoro, although in secret he is baptized Luis by his mother (Matter) who sinks into a torpor of resigned perplexity over the complex pedagogical ambitions of her husband (Form).

Don Avito's companion is the foolish theorist, Don Fulgencio Entrambosmares, and together they form a pair reminiscent of the Bouvard and Pécuchet who tried all the latest fads leading to the inevitable *cul-de-sac.* Proud of his intellectual accomplishments, Fulgencio is embarrassed by the need he has for his wife (the philosopher is but a man in the marriage bed) who henpecks him, and he lives most of his time in his study with the grotesquely attired skeleton of a gorilla called *Simia sapiens*. In addition he concocts strange systems, juggles paradoxes, and drops cryptic hints to higher truths which puzzle even his admirer and consultant, Don Avito. The latter is in dire need of help since his system for educating his son is thwarted at every turn by Fulgencio's vague, contradictory counsel, by Marina's soporific, passive resistance, and most distressingly, by Apolodoro's disconcerting sluggishness.

Marina gives birth to a girl who is another obstacle in Avito's way and whom he shamefully neglects, since the omniscient Don Fulgencio, who in private reads to his wife and even sews for her, tells Avito that women cannot be conditioned: they are instinct, tradition, memory, nature, while man is reflection, progress, understanding, and reason. The supreme defeat, however, comes when Apolodoro cannot withstand his love for Clarita. Reason has given way completely in the son as it had once done in the father; the older man, however, had reduced his wife to a sort of mental helotism, while Clarita holds Apolodoro in agonizing abeyance as she inclines more and more to his rival, the full-blooded Federico. Apolodoro, very much like Galdós's scholarly Máximo Manso (from the novel *El amigo Manso*), lacks the initiative and agressive masculinity which would force Clarita's decision, and in despair he goes to Don Fulgencio who, true to his oblique character, skirts the issue with all sorts of erudite irrelevancies and disquisitions on how to cheat death, but finally exclaims with the anguish of the thinker who has thought himself out of all hope: "Have children, have children, Apolodoro!"

Apolodoro is even more melancholy after such an inconclusive interview; he has sorely disappointed his father with his mediocrity, and does not even have the talent to woo a woman successfully. His love is now an abscess festering beyond cure, and no one can help him, certainly not the father who, at the bedside of his dead daughter, makes clinical comments on the physiology of death. Apolodoro finds fleeting consolation in a perfunctory affair with the serving-girl Petra, but such a relationship leaves him even more despondent, and he ends by hanging himself. Avito, coming upon the body of his dead son, cuts him down and begins to pull the dead boy's tongue rhythmically in a vain attempt to revive him, as the mother intones, "My son, my son, my son!" Suddenly face to face with his despair, Avito echoes her cry, and Marina, turning to her husband, welcomes him. "My son!" she cries to him and he answers, "Mother!" Feeling has become all.

*Love and Education* is an object lesson in fictional form, a cautionary tale woefully lacking in novelistic substance, more noteworthy for clever details than for its total effect. Unamuno has already taken the decisive step in the direction of the "naked" novel (*novela escueta*) where the one obsession of the principal character inevitably narrows down the scale and structure of the entire work. The characters are too vague and one-dimensional to come alive long enough to convince the reader that they live in the great lags we must suppose between episodes. Marina is submerged in so helpless an apathy that she frees the author from any further development of her potential; Avito is a monomaniacal follower of that pedagogy and sociology which Unamuno considered to be, along with psychology, the most meretricious of all "sciences," and his pretentions are so preposterous that he elicits neither sympathy nor hatred, but a minor sort of scorn. Apolodoro, as much a guinea pig of his father's "system" as the J. S. Mill of the *Autobiography* and George Meredith's Richard Feverel, is yet too much of a mannequin to earn the compassion his suicide should excite. As in *Peace in War,* it is a secondary character, this time Don Fulgencio, who, in a bravura piece of self-analysis, is given the opportunity to take on truly moving psychological proportions. For Don Fulgencio is a caricature and buffoon only until, in one "big" scene, he becomes a quivering, anguished creature grappling with the enigma of death which may totally annihilate the over-specific personality he had been at such pains to construct.

In order to provide the proper length required by the publisher of the book, *Love and Education* is followed by *Notes for a Treatise on Cocotology* (*Apuntes para un tratado de cocotología*), presumably written by Don Fulgencio, a *reductio ad absurdum* of all scientific treatises, methodology, and jargon. The name of the new science "cocotology" derives from *cocotte,* the French for paper bird, and *logia* from *logos* or treatise, and is no more hybrid than the word sociology, a compound of Greek and Latin. From there, Unamuno proceeds in mock-erudite style, bristling with word derivations and literary and biblical allusions, to demonstrate the relations between cocotology and chemistry, physics, psychology, even embryology and anatomy, in a delightful attempt to disprove the neo-Comtean contention that the social sciences are the capstone of all studies. Reason, the author again tells us, falls by its own weight into error unless checked by a force greater than itself, and in Chapter XIII of Unamuno's next novel, *Mist*, Don Avito is found in church praying to a God in whose existence he neither believes nor disbelieves, although he does understand that neither learning nor philosophy can take care of the affective needs.

*Mist* (*Niebla*), 1914, like *Love and Education,* combines playfulness with melancholy overtones, but is distinguished by the absence of any obvious didactic intent. It begins as Augusto Pérez appears at the door of his house, puts out his right hand palm down, to ascertain whether it is raining or not, and wonders, *à la* Prufrock, whether to mar the elegance of his tightly-rolled umbrella by opening it. The tone is established: bewilderment will prevail over action, indeterminateness over boldness, a morbid addiction to minute self-analysis will thwart resolute choice.

Life presents itself to Augusto empty of content as he stands there on the threshold of his home and on the threshold of the adventure of independence. The only son of a widowed and over-devoted mother, he has been pampered and insulated from the shocks of life; with her death, he has awakened from a deep dream of uneasy peace, but is unprepared for self-reliance. He hesitates over the choice of substance with which to fill the outlines of a mode of existence now entirely up to him, and he wanders in a mist of indecision which will not lift or precipitate.

To decide which direction his walk will take, Augusto waits for a dog to give him his cue, but instead of a dog, there passes the beautiful Eugenia, a piano teacher who hates music. Now content has started to seep into the empty spaces, and Augusto can begin to direct his own life; yet so absorbed is he in self-congratulation over having met a girl that he passes her twice without noticing her. To the stray dog Orfeo whom he has taken in, he confides the subtle play of ideas which every chance event stirs in him, and when he is not confiding in the animal, he indulges in long monologues, juggles whimsical and macabre notions, and finds himself in general absorbed in ideological computations abstracted from the active life whose pull he enjoys and fears.

Augusto is now enchanted by every woman he sees, not excluding the double-chinned married cook of fifty whom he employs; but the sight of Eugenia herself brings trepidation and an overpowering sense of inadequacy. Instead of winning her away from the ne'er-do-well Mauricio, he begs her to allow him to buy the mortgage on her house. For refuge and consolation, he makes love to the frightened little laundress Rosario who is, in turn, willing to sacrifice herself to him, but even there he is unable to take what is offered him: like Buridan's ass, he starves between Eugenia and Rosario, one a treacherous Eve repaying kindness with contempt, the second a virgin Mater Dolorosa, pouring maternal compassion over a man who inspires both love and fear. One speaks to his imagination, the other to his heart, while Liduvina the cook speaks to his stomach.

Eugenia promises to marry him if he secures Mauricio a position in some distant place, ostensibly to be rid of him, but when this is done, Augusto receives a letter from her telling him that now that her house is hers and Mauricio has work, she is eloping with her lover. The easy deception perpetrated on Augusto aggravates the doubts he entertains about his own substantiality, and despite his friend Goti's mysterious advice to forge life out of suffering, his decision is to commit suicide. But first he must consult Miguel de Unamuno whose comments on suicide he has read. He goes to Salamanca only to come up against an Unamuno who forbids him to take his life, for in order to do so, he would first have to be alive, and in truth he is only a figment of Unamuno's imagination. Creator and creature clash, and the former can give free rein to his fancies once more: he can play verbal volleyball with reality and fiction, cast aside all ballast of common sense and freely ride the waves of poetic truth.

When Augusto suggests that Unamuno himself may be a fictional entity created by an even higher power, the debate becomes heated and eventually Augusto delivers a telling blow: he, Unamuno, may have no existence aside from Augusto and the other fictional characters he has created, since any author is the sum of his characters, and if Unamuno does not understand that suicide for Augusto is the inevitable outcome of a sorry predicament, he does not know his own character very well. Enraged at such insolence, Unamuno retorts that not only will he deny suicide to Augusto, he will kill him himself! Now Augusto is terrified; now that death threatens him from the outside, he wants desperately to live. He falls at the author's feet, begging for mercy, but he must die, since Unamuno cannot carry him about indefinitely. Augusto turns on him: "You too, my lord and creator, you too will die and return to nothingness. God will run out of ideas for you, too— He will cease dreaming you! You will die, those who read about me will die, everyone will die."

Augusto returns home in anguish, not only over his imminent death but over the question of who it is that will die. How can one die if one has never existed; or how can he, Augusto, affirm his own concrete existence in defiance of Unamuno's revelations? He orders a slight meal but as his appetite grows, he orders eggs, steak, ham, pâté. Man's supreme battle against death is reduced to the absurd *Edo, ergo sum,* and Augusto, stripped of all power to support himself against annihilation, catches on to his voracious appetite as a last line of defense. But after ordering cheese, pastry, and fruit, he sends a telegram to Unamuno: "You have had your way. I have died." And the doctor declares Augusto dead of a heart attack.

Unamuno's oft-repeated concept of the reversibility of author and work antedates by several years the popularity of Pirandello in Europe. An author, Unamuno had made plain as far back as *The Life of Don Quixote and Sancho,* may create in so dynamic a fashion that his creatures acquire a life independent from him, and may even bestow their honors upon their creator: Shakespeare is the sum total of his Hamlet, Macbeth, and Othello, while Cervantes lives primarily in terms of Don Quixote. The idea of the fictional character who is aware he lives in literature goes back to Cervantes, Carlyle, Pérez Galdós's *El amigo Manso,* and Kierkegaard, but in Unamuno it grows from the author's own perspectives.[16] Just as it may be said that the father derives his paternity from his child and is therefore in a sense his child's creation, and just as we have no knowledge of God divorced from the existence of the men He has created, so also are we in no position to understand the novelist or playwright except as we interpret the beings he has projected from himself. The public performances of Unamuno himself—whether prepared at his desk or acted out on the podium—created the figure of Unamuno just as truly as Unamuno created his Avito Carrascal or his Augusto Pérez.

The dialogue between character and author in *Mist* is, then, a natural consequence not only of Unamuno's reading, but of his lifelong dialogue with the God who may not exist, and his preoccupations with the nature of personality which struggles with the inconsistencies contained within itself and is also in a constant state of war with others. If man is the "heautontimoroumenos" or self-devourer, he is, in addition, challenged, confused, exasperated, or maddened by those who differ from him. And while Unamuno maintained that friction among people or civil war was one of the most fertile ways of *rapprochement,* he understood that a basic cause of contention was envy, the hatred of qualities which one does not possess.

The biblical story of Cain and Abel was one of Unamuno's lifelong obsessions, not only for its broad-spectrum connotations, but because it also seemed particularly pertinent to Spain where envy, he alleged, is one of the congenital vices, and as a counterpart of his personal friction with his brother Félix.[17] Jealousy and hatred are therefore endemic to every level of existence. The passion to survive at least in the memory of the race is the metaphysical basis for envying those who stand a better chance.[18] Among Spaniards, envy is already manifest in the early *Poem of the Cid;* Gracián had called it the "Hispanic cancer";[19] and Unamuno had in his childhood lived through the experience of a civil war in which brother fought brother and in which neither side was completely right nor wrong, a fact which no doubt led him to condemn Abel for finding unmerited grace in the eyes of God and to condemn Cain for murder. On the personal level, Unamuno himself confessed that "It is my envy, my pride, my arrogance, my covetousness, which make me hate the pride, envy, arrogance, and covetousness of others." [20]

These metaphysical, national, and psychological implications of the Cain-Abel story are woven into the texture of the novel *Abel Sánchez,* 1917. The duel between the friends Joaquín and Abel (Cain and Abel) which forms the core of the book had been summed up, perhaps not coincidentally, by William James years earlier: "Some men . . . are so naturally cool-hearted that the moralistic hypothesis never has for them any pungent life, and in their supercilious presence the hot young moralist always feels strangely ill at ease. The appearance of knowingness is on their side, of *naïveté* and gullibility on his. Yet, in the inarticulate heart of him, he clings to it that he is not a dupe, and there is a realm in which . . . all their wit and intellectual superiority is not better than the cunning of a fox." [21] In short, the hatred falls upon the hater, for the object of his venom is indifferent to him and secure in his *Anziehungskraft.*

Envy and its inevitable cognate, hatred, are not aspects of Joaquín's life, they are the very substance of it. His friend from infancy, Abel Sánchez, is the easy-going charmer, the untroubled victor who carries off all the prizes and even wins the love of Joaquín's cousin Helena. Abel's is the power and the glory while Joaquín's is the travail: to the former success as an artist comes without effort while Joaquín becomes a doctor only through perseverance. Abel achieves fame with his portrait of Helena; Joaquín can never find the peace of mind necessary to pursue the medical research that would make him Abel's equal in his own eyes.

Despite marriage to the pious, compassionate, maternal Antonia, Joaquín's motive force is his loathing of Abel, a loathing so necessary that he prevents its disappearance. When the opportunity comes to denounce the superficiality that parades as talent in Abel's case, he turns the occasion to Abel's benefit and bestows a glowing tribute upon him; later he saves Abel's life as he had his reputation. Joaquín no longer feels any desire for Helena, only the sting of the original offense of having been rejected, yet he cannot overcome the conviction that Antonia had married him out of pity. If he refuses the comfort held out to him by his wife who takes him on her knees and cries, "My poor child!," he derives satisfaction from Abel's son, Abelín, who, neglected by his father, turns to Joaquín and decides to be a doctor. His own daughter, Joaquina, is attracted to the convent in her desire to expiate the sinful torment of her father, but he begs her to save him by marrying Abelín, for then he will have something belonging to his enemy, or even more, he will have part of the enemy himself.

In Byron's *Cain*, Joaquín had found the suggestion that if Abel had left children, their marriage to Cain's children might have alleviated the hatred Cain bore in his soul. With his grandchild, Joaquín feels he will perhaps have another opportunity to prove that the world was not so stupid for rejecting him as it was for not recognizing his talents and deep sensibilities, but the child turns from him to his painter grandfather who can draw sketches for him. In despair Joaquín runs to Abel to beg him to release his hold on the child, and in a scene of anger and vituperation Abel shouts that the child shies away from Joaquín out of instinctive fear of the contagion of his evil blood. Joaquín rushes at Abel, seizes him by the throat, and Abel, long a cardiac, dies of the shock. Abel has been killed, he has paid for his easy good fortune, but Cain is also marked for death and in full realization that had he loved Antonia, he would have been redeemed, he dies.

Except for Joaquín, the characters in the novel are shadowy and undeveloped. Abel lives only as a thorn to Joaquín, his challenge, his target. Helena is the temptress in the abstract, another Eugenia preferring the difficult male to the cloying, deferential one; and Antonia is another one of Unamuno's wife-mothers, long-suffering, hurt, and bewildered, holding out her arms in supplication to a man who deliberately shuts his heart to the healing power of love. The black shadow that dominates the novel is Joaquín who plays a sinister game of solitaire; he is the underground man who derives his energy from his festering resentments and is therefore the author of his own damnation.

Technically Unamuno finds it difficult to hold his ground: time in his novel is discontinuous and discrete, coexistential only with the crucial episodes that make of the plot a series of *tableaux vivants*. Nor could Unamuno handle the passion in any form but the most strident; the effects of suggestion, indirection, understatement were beyond his ken, and it is almost as if he were saying to his reader: "Is not the subject itself shattering enough, why do you require the bothersome contrivances of art?" Nevertheless, the pain of the branded protagonist is so strong, his self-condemnation so pitiful that, for all its awkwardness, its bombast, and its lamentations, *Abel Sánchez* is a curiously moving confession of a man bound to his own rack, and its nakedness may be accepted as the proper counterpart of the rawness of Joaquín's wounds.

The havoc wrought by sensuality is a subject Unamuno never treated in his novels, for erotic love *per se*, independent of its function in procreation, aroused in him only impatience and wrath. When he came to dramatize Don Juan, he conceived of him only as a marionette; his seductresses are vague and of little consequence, while the wives he created in his fiction are motivated more by their maternal than their sexual instincts. The essential fulfillment of woman comes with motherhood, for the urge to protect and comfort the weak and suffering is so deeply ingrained in her nature that she becomes the mother of her lover or husband as naturally as of her children. "Love in woman, it seems, is compassion while in men it is pride, but on closer examination, it appears that in the latter it is the need to be sheltered and protected and in the former the need to shelter and protect." [22]

When, however, woman is cheated of self-realization through children of her body, she is capable of unhealthy compensation by every means at her disposal. The name Raquel which Unamuno gave to the protagonist of his *Two Mothers* (*Dos Madres*), the first of three short novels grouped as *Three Exemplary Novels and a Prologue* (*Tres novelas ejemplares y un prólogo*), 1920, was suggested by the biblical Rachel who, during her long period of sterility, gave her husband Jacob her handmaiden Bilhah by whom he had two sons. Don Juan is Raquel's lover, a parody of his famous name, a "kitten" whom she fondles on her knee, whom she has indeed saved from the clutches of former mistresses. Since she is unable to have children, she uses Don Juan as an instrument for the fulfillment of her maternal desires, and manipulates him as one would a puppet into marrying Berta who will have the child that she, Raquel, will appropriate. When Berta gives birth to a little girl, named for Raquel, the latter immediately assumes care of the child during the mother's prolonged convalescence.

The two mothers of the Solomon story are now in battle for the control of Don Juan: one has unmanned him craftily, dispossessed him of his fortune and thus forced him into allowing her to raise his child; the other, his wife, is full of pity which, in its own way, relegates the husband to the status of a child. Too disoriented and humiliated to fight his way out of the impasse, Don Juan commits suicide, leaving a pregnant wife who, this time, can have her baby. Raquel advises her to remarry: it is no good to live without a mate, she says, and she will give Berta a dowry.

Even more single-minded and invincible than Raquel is the Carolina of *The Marquess of Lumbría* (*El Marqués de Lumbría*), the elder of the eponymous nobleman's two daughters. When Tristán—the name is again not devoid of irony—comes to court the younger sister, Luisa, and is about to marry her and assume her father's title, it is Carolina who takes matters in her own hand and seduces him. Pregnant, she is spirited away by her father to avoid the inevitable scandal her condition would provoke in the sleepy town where they, the sad remnants of an ancient aristocracy, live. Tristán and Luisa marry and have a son, but she dies and Tristán brings Carolina back and marries her.

Now Carolina is mistress of a fate that almost overcame her, and she brings back the son she had had by Tristán, the boy who is the firstborn child of the new marquess, but illegitimate and therefore deprived of the title which the "other one"—legitimate but born later—will inherit. It is now the task of the latter-day Rebecca to further the interests of Jacob to the detriment of Esau. Instinctive hostility sets the boys against each other, for the young sickly legitimate heir senses the danger to his person and his position, while the other is protected by a scheming mother. Tristán is now *de trop,* and slips back into hopeless silence, and finally Carolina's decisions prevail. Her husband declares the illegitimate boy to be his own, the "other" is superseded by the lioness's cub who will succeed to the title.

In *Aunt Gertrude* (*La Tía Tula*), published separately as a novel in 1921, Unamuno delineated the third of his triad of obsessed women. If Raquel is forced into cheating others because of having been cheated by nature, and if Carolina must make up for having been outdone by her younger sister, Tula is driven by an asexual hunger for children whom she would rear and teach, but not conceive. Since she is repelled by men yet driven by a hunger for children, she must wait for the opportunity to care for the progeny of others, preferably those close to her.

When Ramiro comes to court the lovely Rosa, it is her sister Gertrudis (Tula) who exercises the stronger fascination upon him. He hesitates to propose to Rosa, but Gertrudis urges him to do so and he marries his original choice in a daze of passivity. Gertrudis awaits her "family" impatiently. Rosa's confinements are difficult, and when her third causes her death, Gertrudis has no time for mourning, for she has now become mother to her sister's children. Her strange life-force has been fulfilled for her by others of her blood, leaving her untainted. She rejects all suitors, especially the brother-in-law who now languishes for her, for if she married him she might adopt the hateful role of stepmother instead of the actual role of mother she now plays. Rather than be second in Ramiro's life, she prefers to be first in the lives of her sister's children who now scarcely remember the woman who gave them birth.

When the priest tells her to marry Ramiro to save him from the sin of sensuality, she objects to the concept of marriage as a solution for the needs of the flesh: marriage is meant only for the begetting of children. And when the servant-girl Manuela becomes the victim of Ramiro's needs, Gertrudis is almost relieved, and against his will, she urges Ramiro to marry the girl. There is no danger of Manuela's being a stepmother; she, Gertrudis, will be there to protect Rosa's children, and if need be, Manuela's. Powerless to fight the monumental will of the only woman he loves, Ramiro sinks again into a state of resigned despair. "You are a saint, Gertrudis," he tells her, "but a saint who has made sinners."

By avoiding marriage, and yet infusing her being into the children of others, Gertrudis had wished to experience totally nonegoistic love, only to find eventually that there is no such thing. She had sought to avoid the despair of disappointment and surfeit attendant on carnal love, but had discovered that by avoiding such suffering, she had avoided one of the essences of life. Such a confession comes from her when she admits that perhaps her idea of virtue was inhuman, but behind that stood her fear of men. Even Christianity is a man's religion, for Father, Son, and Holy Ghost are masculine, she complains.

Because she realizes that the children of Ramiro and Manuela are children of her sin, she is as devoted to them as to Rosa's children, and especially tender to the timid, sickly Manuelita whose birth causes Manuela's death. Ramiro dies, and Gertrudis is the mainstay of the family, her virginal maternity enveloping them all. Her passion for purity is so overwhelming that, even as she supervises the children's studies, she discloses her love for geometry and her aversion to anatomy and physiology. She arranges for her nephew's early marriage to save him from the usual young man's wild oats, and although she is overcome by illness, she rallies to save Manuelita's life, and then collapses. On her death bed she repents of not having done violence to her nature in order to make Ramiro happy; her wings, she finally understands, had been those of the hen since she had not transcended but merely escaped. Her last injunction to her "children" is not to fear rottenness, for in Purgatory those who had refused to be washed in mud here on earth, would burn in manure. After her death she is known as *La Tía,* The Aunt, a sort of domestic saint whose vestal virgin will be Manuelita.

The author's attitude towards Tula is ambivalent: he admires her greater-than-life strength, but disapproves of her determination not to "soil" herself. Unamuno fervently admired the great celibates, Don Quixote and the saints who either sublimated the instincts of the flesh or did not feel their sting, yet he understood that many of the "immortal mortals" would have sacrificed their eternal fame for the kiss they had dreamed of all their lives.[23] And he himself had felt the attraction of the priesthood, but had decided on the role of husband and father, and had combined it with the role of preacher.

The idea of the novel is indeed extraordinary, a fictional variation of another pair of antinomies constituting Unamuno's agonic thought, yet the artistic impact would have been far stronger if the outside world had impinged more on the paradigm of the domestic drama. There is no question of work, play, the integration of the drama into a self-sustaining cosmos; the entrances and exits, appearances and disappearances, are too mechanical and contrived, the conversation too fitful to be artistically satisfying. The secondary characters are unfortunately mere mannequins who represent no challenge whatsoever to the strange complexities of Tula's neurosis. They are as dim as the atmosphere in which they live is dingy, as vague as the physical atmosphere surrounding the "plot." To raise the work from the level of a psychological parable to that of a substantial prose narrative, the novelist would have had to provide Tula with counterforces worthy of her strength. As it is, Tula stands as a lone, if fascinating, character study with nothing else in the novel to measure up to her stature.

With the tales of Raquel, Carolina, and Tula, Unamuno exploited strange, off-center, erratic themes in which the larger category of motherhood is turned inside out. To compensate for the mother-wives who in his other novels exist in a sentimental nimbus (Josefa Ignacia, Marina, Antonia), Raquel and Carolina are virile women endowed with the powers of sorceresses vis-à-vis their men, while Tula is an inverted saint whose devotion to her charges involves no real self-sacrifice. These women care little for the men whom they reduce to the status of instruments, and the men they use and discard are indeed mockeries of their sex, pitiful abulic creatures, hypnotized into obedience in a matriarchal world, superfluous ornaments after being joyless procreators.

If failure, abdication, and social impotence are the lot of Don Juan, Tristán, and Ramiro, there are others of their sex who appear to be supermen, who are proud, astute, even cruel, and who will yield no ground to the women they use solely for their purposes. In *Every Inch a Man* (*Nada menos que todo un hombre*), the third of the *Three Exemplary Novels,* the protagonist Alejandro Gómez (Alejandro suggests the conqueror Alexander, Gómez the robust man of the people), is an *indiano* who, after a mysterious career in the New World, has come back to Spain wealthy, to force men and women by sheer might to respect him and defer to him. Although he takes pride in his slovenly appearance and crude speech, he surrounds himself with luxury and marries the unhappy Julia, the "official" beauty of her town, whom her father has been trying to marry off to the highest bidder. Twice abandoned by lovers she had chosen in defiance of her father, Julia regards Alejandro both as an escape and a possible salvation.

But Alejandro will not give up an iota of his independence to a woman who, once she becomes aware of her power over him, may try to possess him. He cannot even evince jealousy, since how can he admit that a woman who has tasted of his love can take second best elsewhere? Julia, however, feels that she has simply changed masters: instead of being used by a father who had wished to acquire a rich son-in-law, she is now being dominated by a husband who provides for her sumptuously but will not recognize her individuality. In a fury of frustration at being unable to arouse her husband's jealousy, she admits that the Conde de Bordaviella is her lover, and Alejandro summons two psychiatrists who immediately realize they must declare her insane to save her from being murdered.

Julia is committed but cannot live in confinement and, in order to regain her freedom, confesses she has lied. In a sudden paroxysm, Alejandro avows his love for her, admits she is indispensable to him, and then, in violent reaction to his outburst, tells her to put his words out of her mind. Julia enters a decline, and as a vague, unidentified illness undermines her health, Alejandro offers his fortune to doctors if they will save her; she must not die, since what is his cannot be taken away so arbitrarily. But Alejandro's titanic pride is punished, for as he warms his wife's waning body with his own, he feels her breath leave her. Coldly, deliberately, he bids their little son farewell, locks himself up with

Julia's corpse, and is later found with her, his blood all over their marriage bed. Even the superman, calculating, masterful, apparently ruthless, is in some way dependent on woman, and in her death, Julia triumphs over the hypertrophied pride of her "master."

Self-sacrifice, Alejandro had seen too late, is the price for happiness. This is the unhappy lesson learned, also too late, by the two main characters of *A Love Story* (*Una historia de amor*), which appeared in 1911, and was reissued in book form as the last of the series *St. Manuel Bueno, Martyr, and Three Other Stories* (*San Manuel Bueno, mártir, y tres historias más*), 1933. Ricardo, surely one of Unamuno's ex-futures, courts Liduvina out of sheer apathy, cognizant of the fact that he loves her no more than she loves him. To bring the tedious situation to a head one way or another, he proposes they elope, and Liduvina, bored with her home, her paralyzed mother, and envious tight-lipped sister, consents. But their adventure makes clear to them that they are essentially indifferent to each other. They part, and Ricardo can now heed the biblical injunction that had weighed on his conscience, the passage in Matthew that read, "Go ye therefore, and teach all nations . . ."

But as his theology teachers see, it is really Ricardo's ambition to achieve eminence which goads him on, while Liduvina, who enters a convent, sinks into the melancholy of unfulfilled motherhood. Only when Ricardo, now a friar and celebrated preacher, comes to her convent to deliver an impassioned sermon on love, do they reach out to each other spiritually and understand their failure to forge a happiness which, despite the absence of the ideal, might have been.

The comforts of wife and home and children are priceless, Unamuno again asserts in the charming, ironic novelette *A Poor Rich Man, or the Comic Sense of Life* (*Un pobre hombre rico o El sentimiento cómico de la vida*), 1930. Emeterio, methodical and thrifty, wary and hypochondriacal, avoids the blandishments of Rosita, the daughter of the widow who keeps the boardinghouse where he lives. It is only after the girl accepts another suitor that he fully realizes his loss, yet he continues to avoid entanglements by spying on pairs of lovers as substitutes for the relationship he will not risk. A good deal of the story is taken up in dialogue with his friend Celedonio, a disciple of the Don Fulgencio Entrambosmares of *Love and Education,* who quotes the Bible and

*Don Quixote* and indulges in Unamuno's favorite etymological games.

The old bachelor plods, saves, becomes rich. And one day he comes across Rosita's daughter, Clotilde, and through her again meets her mother, now a plump, appetizing widow. About to retire from his work at the bank, Emeterio assumes a new position, that of husband to the middle-aged but enticing widow and Maecenas to her daughter and the latter's impecunious fiancé. The tale is rounded out with a long dialogue on the satisfactions of even a belated marriage, the indispensable comic sense of life (despite what Unamuno says, declares Emeterio) which is the enjoyment of creaturely pleasures. Emeterio is even presented with a step-grandchild who will be his heir, and with this turn of events comes the full realization that anything is preferable to solitude: even being taken in.

*The Novel of Don Sandalio, Chess Player* (*La novela de Don Sandalio, jugador de ajedrez*), dated 1930, and included as the second in the collection headed by *St. Manuel Bueno,* is one of Unamuno's most interesting experiments, the ultimate of the unadorned novel, for even the character of the protagonist is missing. The germ of this novelette goes back to a story dated 1889 and called "The Scissors" ("Las tijeras") [24] in which two old men, both retired, meet every day in a café to exchange complaints and platitudes. One is a bachelor devoted to his poodle; the other, a widower, is obsessively attached to his married daughter. They are friends and rivals, attracted to each other through loneliness and yet separated by the profound impenetrability of each man's essence, and it is only when the widower dies that his "friend" realizes how little he knew of him. The lesson, not only for the Spaniard who spends so much of his time outdoors or in his favorite café, but for Everyman, is that the exchange of commonplaces, gossip, even political commentary, is not communication, but a way of hiding from others; it is, at bottom, spiritual avarice. "I shall die," said Unamuno, "without knowing most of the people I speak with and deal with every day, and if I know anything about them, it is in spite of them . . ." [25]

To Unamuno, an avid player in his early days, the game of chess was the symbol par excellence of how far a man can live "socially" without surrendering anything of himself, and is the axis around which the tale of Don Sandalio revolves. In form, the novelette is a series of letters from a misanthrope who has fled *la bêtise humaine* to a coastal mountain resort where he joins a club and plays chess with Don Sandalio. The latter becomes an obsession with the author of the letters as he realizes that just as every man is seen only from the angle we are given to study him, so Sandalio simply projects the image of the silent chess player whenever the raconteur meets him at the club.

Later, after Don Sandalio has disappeared, news comes from afar of his having lost a son, of having been in prison and died there. In the end, his son-in-law comes to recount his father-in-law's history to the writer, to endow him with a specific profile, but such light in darkness is rejected, for the narrator prefers to keep his former chess partner in his mind as an eternal potential instead of adding another dossier to those already choked with futile information.

Thus Unamuno has gone the entire way in stripping the novel: not only has he minimized description of background and décor, but he has eliminated even that human psychology which is considered the *sine qua non* of the novel. If, in his other novels, the crisis arises from an excess of personality and friction, or an excess of lucidity and self-examination, in this story the personality of the central character is conspicuous by its absence. Resolution is forever held in suspension in *Don Sandalio,* and possibility remains in its pristine state. Since man's personality can be defined only in part through his actions which do not cover his secret dreams, his silent remorse, his repressed impulses, his oscillating desires, it follows that even the best fiction writers cannot create complete and authentic entities. They can only extend themselves to give us novelized autobiographies which, in the case of Don Sandalio, Unamuno refuses to do, since he would merely be creating another self. If our true selves are known only to God, Don Sandalio's true self must be left a mystery.


IV　*The Best Novel:* St. Manuel Bueno, Martyr

*San Manuel Bueno, mártir,* first published in March of 1931, may be considered, by Unamuno's own suggestion, the third of the trilogy begun in *The Tragic Sense of Life* and continued in *The Agony of Christianity,*[26] and is deservedly his most widely admired work of fiction. In our age, when men of good will are promoting the humanistic ideal of supreme virtue formerly held to be possible mainly within the framework of some supernatural belief, Don Manuel Bueno, the priest who could not believe in the fundamental doctrines of the Catholic Church and yet devoted his life to the welfare of his humble parishioners, stands as the tragic embodiment of a modern ethos still longing for the old securities.

The story is told by Angela Carballino who is writing the biography of the dead priest of her parish, now being considered for beatification by the bishop of the diocese that includes the town of Valverde de Lucerna. Her memories of the priest who was her spiritual father and to whom she, in turn, was helper, conscience, lay confessor, and "mother," go back to her childhood. His name had been on everyone's lips at the nuns' school where she was supposed to learn to be a schoolteacher and where "pedagogy" earned her revulsion. At fifteen, she returned to her Valverde de Lucerna, the town where the mountain of eternity was reflected in the lake of mystery, where life was dreamed away in simple routine, temporal and religious, and where simple people placed their hopes in the reality of everlasting life. The leader in all areas was the priest Don Manuel who in action and word gave comfort and meaning—height and depth, like the mountain and the lake—to lives which, if left to their own resources, might have been unleavened, directionless, animalistic.

Don Manuel had rejected offers of a brilliant ecclesiastical career to remain with his charges and protect them from the realization that, as St. Paul wrote in I Corinthians, XV, 19, "If only in this life we hope in Christ, we are the most wretched of all men" (the epigraph of the novel), or as Kierkegaard put it, "If an eternal oblivion were always lurking hungrily for its prey and there was no power strong enough to wrest it from its maw—how empty then and comfortless life would be!" [27]

But although the priest's tragic secret is that he has lost his belief in immortality, his life is neither empty nor comfortless, for by consoling his parishioners in their sorrows, he consoles himself. He helps to patch up marital difficulties, reconciles parents and children, finds fathers for blameless children born out of wedlock, but adamantly refuses to be used by the secular authorities for their own ends. For although religion cannot avoid worldly commitments, if Catholicism is to be more than a vast organization, it must be primarily eschatological and only secondarily ethical.

The priest's favorite is Blasillo *el bobo,* the town simpleton, who wanders about echoing the priest's hidden despair as he cries, "My God, my God, why hast Thou forsaken me?" Blasillo not only represents the injunction to "become as little children" (Matthew 18:3), but also Pascal's *abêtissement,* the simplicity which Don Manuel had abandoned. And if the "fool" holds on to Don Manuel's hand for safety, Don Manuel holds on to his hand for strength.

Angela plays the part of recorder, but is also a significant participant in a complex of events that is almost exclusively spiritual. She stands between the townspeople whose faith is anchored in custom, and her brother Lazarus, the atheist. She adds to the priest's torment since she not only requires the reassurance of his presence and impeccable conduct, but also doctrinal enlightenment:

"Is there a Hell, Don Manuel?"
"For you, my daughter? No."
"Does Hell exist for others?"
"What does that matter since you will not go to Hell?"
"I am concerned about others. Is there a Hell?"
"Believe in Heaven, in the Heaven we see. Look at it . . ."
"But one must believe in Hell, just as in Heaven."
"Yes, one must believe in everything the Holy Mother Catholic Apostolic Roman Church believes and teaches. Enough."

But he is so remorseful over the anxieties his equivocations stir in Angela, that after one particularly agonizing scene with her in the confessional, the priest asks her: "Now, Angela, in the name of the people, do you absolve me?" And her answer is: "In the name of God the Father, the Son, and Holy Ghost, I absolve you, Father."

Lazarus returns from the New World, and is determined to remove his mother and sister from the "rural, feudal, priest-ridden town." Instead he is attracted to the priest, and during their long walks by the lake the latter convinces him to take communion and reenter the bosom of the Church. He complies, the townspeople are elated, but to Angela her brother must confess the truth, just as Don Manuel had confessed his truth to Lazarus: he tells her that there had been no conversion, but that the contagion of Don Manuel's sincerity had won him over to feigning belief in order to set a good example. "I shall never forget," Lazarus continues to disclose, "that day when I said to him: 'But Don Manuel, what about truth, what about truth?' and he whispered in my ear, even though we were alone in the midst of the fields, 'The truth? The truth, Lazarus, may be something terrible, something insufferable, something mortal: simple people could not live with it. There is no one true religion; any religion is true in so far as it allows its adherents to live spiritually and consoles them for having had to be born in order to die . . .' And his religion is to console himself by consoling others although the consolation he gives them is not his own."

Where once Unamuno had declared war on all "sanctioned fictions" and had advocated perpetual anguish, now his priest takes this suffering upon himself in order to perpetrate the pious fraud of orthodox belief upon his people. Since we are all victims of the painful illness that ends in death—or as Pascal had said, we are all in prison awaiting execution—the very "opiate" of religion which the Marxists turn to scorn is defended by Don Manuel against all logical refutation. And when his death draws near, the priest celebrates his last Holy Week; when he comes to administer communion to Lazarus, he whispers, "There is no eternal life apart from this one, but let them dream of eternity . . ." And he begs Angela to pray for them and "pray also for Our Lord Jesus Christ . . ." For perhaps He, the greatest of all martyrs, had welcomed death to create the illusion of the God-man identity and consequently of immortality for perishable creatures.

After Don Manuel's death, the Lazarus who had been resuscitated from the death of nonbelief to the life of compassionate deception, falls into the decline that will lead to everlasting death. In her attempt to keep her languishing brother alive, Angela reminds him that he had always concentrated his efforts on extolling life and its dreams, but Lazarus retorts sadly that happiness here on earth is for others, not for those who had looked upon the truth, those who had figuratively but nonetheless terribly, looked upon the face of God. He enjoins the new parish priest to give his congregation religion and not theology, security and not free examination, and begs Angela, the last of the three repositories of the awful secret, never to reveal it to the people.

With the death of her flesh-and-blood brother, following the death of her spiritual father, the aging Angela is left to wonder whether these two "holy" men had died in the conviction that they had not believed, and yet had truly believed. In any case, Don Manuel had converted Lazarus to the cause of life through the truth about death. And Angela too had been his epigone since she had persisted in believing in the saintliness of a nonbeliever who had never departed from the true spirit of Christianity. Perhaps for inscrutable reasons, she ponders, God had caused them to believe themselves unbelievers.

When Unamuno was writing *St. Manuel Bueno, Martyr* in the Fall of 1930, he again heard the voice that said, "And after this, what is the purpose of everything? What for?" [28] The attitude he manifests towards social change in this little book is clearly anti-liberal, conservative, even reactionary, and his Don Manuel asks Lazarus: "And suppose social and economic change is achieved, will not *taedium vitae* grow stronger with general material well-being?" In an article written after the novelette, Unamuno de-clared himself in sympathy with Pope Pius X who, in his encyclical *Pascendi dominici gregis* (1907), had condemned modernism in his desire to protect the implicit faith of the "charcoal-burner." [29] Once Unamuno had exclaimed, "Anyone who says: 'One must keep illusions alive' must be considered lost; for who is he to keep them alive if he knows they are illusory?" [30] Now, after six years of exile and facing the prospect of radical change on every level, his heart went out to the millions who might be stripped of spiritual comforts in exchange for bewildering innovations and strange, dis-quieting ideas. The old traditions which he had alternately—even simultaneously—attacked and extolled, now took on a new warmth, and he realized that if in so many cases they had been maintained by selfish exploiters and an ignorant clergy, in some cases they had been kept alive by intelligent, altruistic men who wished to spare the great body of the people the mental and spiritual torments they themselves had experienced.

It was in this mood that his mind no doubt turned back to his childhood friend, the priest Francisco de Iturribarría, with whom he had resumed relations in 1901 and whom he had seen periodi-cally thereafter until his death in 1916, for the similarities between Don Manuel and Father Iturribarría are remarkable. Like Don Manuel, the Basque priest had attended the seminary in Vitoria only to return to the Bilbao which he never again left, and where

he lived in "desperate resignation," [31] just as his fictional counterpart had lived and died in Valverde de Lucerna in "active, resigned desolation." And it was to Unamuno that the priest had
confided his dark secret, just as Don Manuel was to whisper it into
the ear of his friend and disciple Lazarus.

The idea of the clergyman whose lost belief only strengthens his
sense of obligation had also come to Unamuno from the story
"Karl" contained in the book *German Reminiscences, First Series*
(*Reminiscencias tudescas, Primera serie*) by the Colombian writer
Santiago Pérez Triana, 1902, which Unamuno had reviewed; from
Mrs. Humphrey Ward's *Robert Elsmere* (1888); or perhaps even
from Manuel Ciges Aparicio's *The Vicar* (*El vicario*), 1905.[32]
But Unamuno's priest is a far greater creation than these, and com-
mands a prominent place in the gallery of tormented priests de-
lineated by Mauriac, Bernanos, or Graham Greene. For in Unamuno's hands, Don Manuel, like Don Quixote, is assimilated to the
Christ figure: his name is Manuel (Immanuel) or "God with us,"
he has curative powers for body and mind, he is responsible for
Lazarus' "resurrection," and, perhaps like Jesus, established a myth
to hide from men the great horror of existing only in history.

Furthermore, he conjures up remembrances of the Grand Inquisitor, for both Dostoevski's Prince of the Church and Unamuno's parish priest are martyrs to a great secret, their nonbelief
in God. Both belie their thoughts by their actions, in order to
keep their spiritual charges out of the bewildering range of free
choice. In exchange for that heavy burden, the Grand Inquisitor
gives his people material and spiritual safety while Don Manuel
isolates his flock from the onslaught of modern thinking. Men
must worship something incontestable, says the Inquisitor; and they
must do that all together, Unamuno's priest knows, as he introduces
the type of worship that affords his parishioners the added comfort
of unanimity in exchange for individual free examination. The
Inquisitor holds up the three forces that captivate the consciences
of feeble mortals: miracle, mystery, and authority. Don Manuel
gives them the miracle of saintliness, the mystery of prayer, and
the authority of kindness.

There are, of course, enormous differences between the two
men. The Inquisitor cannot insist too much that man is weak and
base; Don Manuel sees man only as weak. To the Inquisitor the
Church is authoritarian, to the priest it is a pool of healing. Both

know that man is a rebel, and a rebel cannot be content, but while
the Inquisitor is made harsh and implacable by this knowledge,
the saint is forgiving and compassionate. The Inquisitor forbids, the
saint pleads; the Inquisitor rules, the saint persuades. Yet with such
variant procedures they achieve an almost identical purpose:
the Inquisitor receives Christ's kiss, the saint leaves behind him a
serene, undisturbed parish.

*Avant la lettre,* Don Manuel Bueno exemplifies Camus's dictum
that there are examples of Christians who do not believe in the
future life.[33] The erection of positive action on a negative theological basis is dramatized in Don Manuel Bueno and in Camus's
Dr. Rieux of *The Plague.* If Dr. Rieux is Camus's most successful
statement of human purpose on earth, the rural priest is Unamuno's
most poignant dramatization of his own lifelong conflict between
sincerity and necessity. In *The Plague,* Tarrou asks, "Can one be
a saint without God? That is the only concrete problem I know
of today." [34] Dr. Rieux provides his answer in the Journal towards
the end of the novel: men cannot be saints, but they can refuse to
bend to the scourge of life by exerting themselves as physicians.
Rieux has discarded the religious pieties for a purely human
morality which, although it contains all the traditional features of
self-sacrifice and disinterestedness, is independent of metaphysics.
As a physician, Rieux offers his patients ministrations which he
suspects are of little avail, while Don Manuel keeps his parishioners
safe in their belief in a God who, for him, does not exist. The
doctor's crusade aims at the attenuation of the tangible evils of
existence, the priest offers consolation for inevitable pain and death.
In short, each character, the humanist Rieux who labors to heal
the sick in body, and the atheistic priest Don Manuel who wishes
to protect the poor in spirit, is a bold, dramatic refutation of Ivan
Karamazov's assertion that if there is no God, then everything is
permitted. It is significant that the quotation from *Obermann,* so
admired and repeated by Unamuno, prefaces the fourth letter of
Camus's *Letters to a German Friend* (*Lettres à un ami allemand*):
"Man is mortal. That may be; but let us die resisting; and if our
lot is complete annihilation, let us not behave in such a way that it
seems justice!"

Since *San Manuel Bueno* stands as a final and major statement
of all of Unamuno's antinomies—the interaction of holy living and
doubt, the pull to active participation in life and the nostalgia for
serenity and silence, the need for progress and the charms of

quiescence, the obligation to speak out and guilt generated by self-assertion—attention should also be paid to the supporting cast of the work. The people of Valverde de Lucerna represent intra-history, not only the continuity of collective humanity, but of eternal Spain, for the setting of the story was suggested by the lake of San Martín de Castañeda in Sanabria, at the foot of the ruins of a Bernardine monastery, and containing, according to legend, the submerged city of Villaverde de Lucerna. The six planks Don Manuel had cut from the "matriarchal" oak under which he had played as a child and which were there to be made into his coffin, were suggested to Unamuno by the planks he had gazed upon, during his visit to Yuste, which had been cut from the trees of the eternal sierra and had contained the remains of the great Charles V a dozen years before they were transferred to the Escorial.[35]

As for the triad of characters surrounding Don Manuel himself, if they are lacking in relief, they convey the credibility of symbols in a morality play. Angela is the priest's harrowing conscience, and suggests all the questions dogma poses to the far-reaching mind. Lazarus is not only the atheist brought back to the life of faith in faith, but as his name further indicates, he is the crutch on which the master leans as he makes his way through the dark night of his soul. And Blasillo (little Blas, suggesting the Blaise Pascal of the *abêtissement*) is at once the pathetic simpleton deprived of autonomy and the blind follower relieved of the crushing re-sponsibility of independence.

But if Don Manuel labors and suffers in the midst of these people, he is at one and the same time the aggregate of them all. In the past he had partaken of the simple life of the townspeople and had enjoyed the bliss of Blasillo's *idiotism;* through contact with the new currents of ideas he had become, like Lazarus in the New World, an atheist; but with a conscience as urgent as Angela's, he had reached the conviction that personal despair must be transcended and converted into an instrument for good. Thus, through a combination of direct exposition, implication, descrip-tion, sermon, prayer, and dramatic dialogue, Unamuno has created not only the most vigorous, unified, and moving of his narratives, but within the confines of its subtly wrought fabric, he has molded a character of such broad stature that he synthesizes the principal polarities of all the author's other work.

V   *Concluding Unscientific Postscript to Unamuno's Fiction*

To arrive at a fair evaluation of Unamuno's novels one should perhaps keep in mind Kierkegaard's affirmation that the subjective thinker does not have the leisure to create imaginatively nor to give aesthetic form to his writings. "He is essentially an existing individual in the existential medium, and does not have at his disposal the imaginative medium which would permit him to create the illusion characteristic of all aesthetic production." [36] This, better than any other commentary on Unamuno the novelist, is a concise résumé of the lack of that virtuosity which might have helped him create the anti-selves that endow fiction with a mysterious autonomy.

Since Unamuno's novels were primarily a complement to his philosophy, and since philosophy to him was inextricably linked to his own problems, it is of value to note that several, at least, of his fictional works can be construed as answers to the question "What might have been . . ." (1) had he not been reared as a Christian—*Love and Education;* (2) had he not found his proper mate—*Mist;* (3) had he concentrated on his envy of others—*Abel Sánchez;* (4) had he extended his intransigency to his relations with his wife and children—*Every Inch a Man;* (5) had he resolved his doubt into total disbelief—*St. Manuel Bueno, Martyr.*

It is difficult to refute Unamuno's oft-repeated contention that all writing is in some way autobiographical, but it is equally true that artistic fiction is confession transmuted through projection and artistic distance. It is self-revelation distributed, ordered, and refined. But Unamuno was niggardly with fable, the span of his inventiveness was too limited, and his exposition too rough to make of him a first-rate teller of tales. In the main, Unamuno's characters are built about major ideas from which they are rarely separated, while his plots do not unfold organically, but rather take the form of a series of explosive scenes or dialogues, like quantum leaps, without conjunctive tissue. Since the apocalyptic moralist is not resilient enough to objectify, control, and round out his material, he claims to have avoided description of background or the concretization of time and place—stage directions—in order to give his novels "the greatest intensity and dramatic value possible . . ." [37]

Julián Marías would therefore credit Unamuno with being an

extreme exponent of that existential novel in which the problems of personality replace all other conflicts, in which the "essentialities" of hate, love, sadness, envy are not states of mind, but ways of being.[38] The twentieth century can boast of many attempts to break the stolid mold of the nineteenth-century novel, but while these are "deliberate transgressions of the established rules of the game . . . ,"[39] in Unamuno's case the reader is aware of the discrepancy between the power of the theme and the weakness of its handling. Consequently, when Julián Marías holds up such qualities in Unamuno's fiction as brevity, narrative nudity, multiplicity of perspective, opaqueness of character, he is reminded by another critic that he forgets to tell us whether such a technique follows given aesthetic principles or is simply the result of certain inabilities on the part of the novelist.[40] In favoring the viviparous form of novel, it was Unamuno's purpose to make us feel that verisimilitude is at best a specious approximation to reality while seemingly uncontrolled creation is the most sincere kind. This was making a virtue of necessity, since if artificiality is indeed bad art, it does not follow that unhampered outbursts are necessarily admirable. Forthrightness is often forensic and clumsy, and "intimate" or "noumenical" reality is thin and one-dimensional, while apparential apparatus, subtly drawn about the core of a novel, lends breadth, height, and solidity.

The need to sacrifice spatial and temporal dimensions for the purpose of more deeply penetrating "the fetid abysses of the soul"[41] was not felt by the major novelists of Unamuno's time. Psychopathy, Proust showed, moves within the closely-knit fabric of a given world, not utopically or "ucronically."[42] The secret corners of the soul, we know, can be precipitated out of middle-class Lübeck or twenty-four hours in Dublin. Complete subjectivity, alienated from larger palpable associations, and used too often as a springboard for speculation more proper to the essay, makes, in the case of Unamuno's fiction, for the claustrophobic, dematerialized *nivola,* a minor genre. For all his dissatisfaction with the novelistic tradition that he inherited and which he deemed external, anecdotal, and cortical, Unamuno was unable to devise an adequate replacement. The very power of some of the ideas he sought to dramatize required the forging of a more resourceful instrument to contain them than he could supply, and the strangeness of Unamuno's novels falls short of the level of innovation.

## CHAPTER 6

# *Philosophy and Poetry*

UNAMUNO made it quite clear on more than one occasion that he wished to be considered, above all things, a poet: "I have never been anything but a poet," he wrote Federico de Onís,[1] "that is, nothing less than a poet." Rubén Darío went further and declared that Unamuno was perhaps "only a poet . . ."[2] and others, such as Professor Ferrater Mora, have felt that Unamuno's work in verse form was simply one phase of a "single poem" within which varying "accents" distinguish his poetry from his novels, essays, and tales.[3]

We might suggest that if Kierkegaard objected to the bifurcation of human ontology into being and intellection, Unamuno had recourse to poetic license to heal the breach. The poet, in Heidegger's opinion, deals with the holy task of reconciliation, the unification of dispersed completeness.[4] Elaborating on Heidegger's notion of "the essential and initial connection between poetic and philosophical discourse,"[5] Antonio Machado's Juan de Mairena, an apocryphal teacher speaking to his students, foresees the day when poets and philosophers will exchange roles, since philosophers, pondering the *fugit irreparabile tempus,* will arrive at an existentalist metaphysics, "something, in truth, more poematic than philosophical. . . . And poet and philosopher will stand face to face—never hostile—each one working on what the other leaves."[6] Machado was referring to a poet like Valéry and a philosopher like Heidegger, but he could just as well have had in mind the Unamuno who wrote to the Catalan poet Maragall that "because we wish to separate passion from idea, fire from fuel, we convert passion into idea. Our passion becomes metaphysics. But there is a world of poetry in which everything is harmonized."[7]

If, as Heidegger avers, "The poet speaks Being,"[8] it is not surprising that Unamuno should have found his way irresistibly to verse form as a natural correlative to those essays which are as much confession and rhapsody as they are exposition. The defender, in all things, of the alogical mode, he mingled thought and feeling in such heightened fashion that the bonds of prose opened into poetry, the world of pure heterodoxy, or better yet, of pure heresy, since the true poet is a heretic concerned not with precepts, but with "postcepts," not with premises but with effects.[9] Poetry he considered the unmediated outpouring of fears, memories, and hopes since it tends to be freer of the dross of lies and concessions required by a prose that purports to convince. In the "Go with God!" from his first volume *Poems (Poesías)*, he says to his verse:

> you reveal my true feelings,
> children of freedom! and not my deeds
> in which I am slave to a strange fate . . .
> (*vosotros reveláis mi sentimiento*
> *¡hijos de libertad! y no mis obras*
> *en las que soy de extraño sino siervo . . .*)

In the "seeking" mood of poetry Unamuno could most legitimately abandon the declarative elements of prose and indulge in that maximum tension of thought that both uses and abuses logic.[10]

## I  Poesías (Poems)

When Unamuno published his first volume of *Poems* (1907), he was already going on his forty-third year, but most of the verse included in this book was the product of the three years or so preceding publication. Utterly at variance with Spanish poetry as it had developed in the nineteenth century, he was an ardent admirer of Leopardi, Carducci, Wordsworth, Coleridge, Tennyson, Browning, and Keats. Only scorn was what he felt for the "sonorous vacuities" of a Zorrilla whose verse, he said, yielded the least amount of poetry that could be obtained from the greatest rhythmical harmony,[11] or even for the "virtuosity and technical tricks (*tecniquerías*)" of the more fashionable modernist Rubén Darío.[12] The sweet sincere verse of Bécquer, although small in range and muted in tone, appealed to him more than the bombast of a Núñez de Arce and the wry, frequently charming dramatic scenes and cryptic pseudo-Voltairean verses of a Campoamor.

With Darío had come new sensuous rhythms and exotic themes, too often patterned after the French decadentism of princesses, parks, and eighteenth-century pseudo-Hellenism. "I am tired," Unamuno exclaimed, "of swans, satyrs, chrysanthemums, Pan, Aphrodite, centaurs . . ."[13] and was especially proud of never having made reference to such platitudes in his Greek classes. His purpose was not to be a melodious bird like Verlaine, but to create verses that were a natural overflow of philosophic rumination in the mode of Leopardi or in the meditative mood of English *musings* which he defined as "sort of expanded and diluted meditations, at the same time a bit somnolent, somewhat vaporous, without any solid connection, which pass like a dream, while one seems to hear an organ from afar; meditations composed rather negligently, like domestic conversation . . ."[14] Above all, he was proud of the psalm-like quality of his poems, and the absolute lack of the erotic which he identified with the sensuality of sweet music. Confident of the impact of the raw idea on his readers' nerves, he did not apply himself to giving it wing, for his poetic creed (*"Credo poético"*) was a deliberate refutation of Verlaine's *Art Poétique* which Darío and his epigones had so admired:

> something that is not music is poetry
> only the heavy remains.
> (*algo que no es música es la poesía
> la pesada sólo queda.*)

And later in the volume, in "Music," he reiterates:

> Music? No! Not thus in a balmy sea
> will you lull my soul to sleep;
> No, I do not want that;
> do not shut my wounds—my senses—
> open to infinity,
> bleeding with desire.
> I wish the raw light . . .
> (*¿Música? ¡No! No así en el mar de bálsamo
> me adormezcas el alma;
> no, no la quiero;
> no cierres mis heridas—mis sentidos—
> al infinito abiertas,
> sangrando anhelo.
> Quiero la cruda luz . . .*)

Music is light, fluid, indistinct; it puts the soul to sleep, like a drug, and throws the veil of forgetfulness over the hope alive in every fiber in his being.

Although in many of the *Poems* the sentimentalist is in greater evidence than the poet, although flat statement alternates with swollen shapelessness, the volume boasts of some of Unamuno's most impressive production: his hymn to Castile, the vast "altar" to which he dedicates his canticles, the land which suggests permanence, the cradle of the past and of future rebirth ("The Tower of Monterrey"); the stately processional poem to "Salamanca," part of which provided the libretto for Joaquín Rodrigo's Cantata written on the occasion of the seven-hundredth anniversary of the university; or the solemn "In the Lap of the City" in which the city of his mature years is a

> lap of serenity
> gravid with anguish,
> calm sea of stormy depths.
> Your lap, my golden city,
> is a lap of love all bitterness,
> of peace full of battle
> and tranquillity built on anxiety.
> (*regazo de sosiego*
> *preñado de inquietudes*
> *sereno mar de abismos tormentosos.*
> *Es, mi ciudad dorada, tu regazo*
> *un regazo de amor todo amargura,*
> *de paz todo combate*
> *y de sosiego en inquietud basado.*)

The theme of the tranquillity that permits deep civil war of the spirit is again developed in "In the Old Cathedral" written on the occasion of a visit to the deserted cathedral, the more ancient of the two in Salamanca: if the silence within tells him that the house is empty of faith, the tumult without seems to have no center, no dwelling place, and if the people and traditional religion are poles apart, there must yet be some way of reconciling the secular and the religious, for the greater glory of both. In "Beauty" the poet is so transported by the loveliness of sleeping waters, the dense greenery, the golden-tinted stones of Salamanca's towers and the silver sky above them, that his will is absorbed into ecstasy, yet pain returns with awareness and the eternal question is posed:

> And now tell me, Lord, whisper in my ear:
> will so much beauty
> kill our death?
> (*Y ahora dime, Señor, dime al oído:*
> *tanta hermosura*
> *¿matará nuestra muerte?*)

"The Cathedral of Barcelona" is a heavy-lined poem that captures the gravity of worship with a slow beat reminiscent of incense, vestments, and laden hearts. Another poem inspired by a place of worship is "In the Basilica of St. James of Bilbao": as he enters the church in his beloved native city, his lacerated breast is like a stormy lake and memories of childhood prayers descend upon him; he recalls his early faith, his religious impressions, and how much Bilbao is part of him. Begging the temple to allay his pain, he promises in return to build another basilica, in the form of his own fame, which will also adorn his city.

If there is any connecting link among the emphatic statements of the poetry, the interrogations and exclamations unleavened by acoustical variations or newly-minted language, it is the suffering of the God-hungry doubter, and in three *Psalms* he pours out his anguish over not comprehending the God he believes in and his bewilderment over the paradox of the Man-God. The vulture at his vitals is thought ("The Vulture of Prometheus") but such torment is welcome since it keeps alive the desire for surcease and is infinitely superior to the sleep that is free of grief, the endless sleep without illusion to which he nevertheless addresses a long dithyrambic poem, "To Sleep." In "Lord, Set Thyself Free!" he pounds at the gates of mystery in short staccato breathless lines ending in a wail:

> Set Thyself free,                     (*¡Liberta-te*
> set Thyself free, Lord!                *liberta-te, Señor!*
> Set Thyself free!                      *¡Liberta-te!*)

The unresolved dialectic of desire and impotence is expressed with great technical skill in "The Seven Words and Two More." The poem is constructed of sharp transitions and swift antinomies:

a reverential tone is struck at the beginning of each stanza through a quotation from the Gospels, then followed by the sharp contrast of words betrayed, hope abandoned, redemption forgotten. "Within" and "Clouds of Mystery" both lament the distortion suffered by feeling or thought when forced into words, while in "Forgive!" the poet holds that the inner anguish he so often advocates is pride and stubbornness. In "Do not Seek Light, my Heart, but Water," he laments the individuation that left him vulnerable, for enlightenment was a deflection from the deep waters of eternal love, just as "the bird who flew away from the ship dies in the sea" of the poem of that name. The soul of the ascetic is at constant grips with the intellectual, for as Unamuno shows in "The Eternal Elegy," he could not reconcile the value of the moment with its transiency.

When the poet can suspend some of his florid oratory and his wide gestures, his thumping, oft inept rhythms for shorter, sweeter periods, he can write verses such as those making up the monologue of the abandoned wife ("The Wife's Lament") who prays with her son for the return of her unfaithful husband (an amalgam of the serious Campoamor and the manner of Browning's dramatic monologues), or the lovely traditional ballad (*romance*) of "The Cypress Tree and the Girl." Especially moving is the poem of consolation to his wife and himself called "On a Son's Death," or the unpretentious tributes he pays his wife in "Your Hand is my Fate" and especially in "To Her Eyes":

| | |
|---|---|
| And if you, my mate, | (*Y si a ti, mi compañera* |
| were fated | *te cumpliera* |
| to depart | *de este mundo antes partir,* |
| this world first, | *la luz toda de mis ojos,* |
| the light of my eyes | *luego rojos,* |
| red with tears, | *con los tuyos se ha de ir.* |
| will depart with yours. | *Llevarás a la otra vida* |
| You will bear into the beyond | *derretida* |
| the faded flower of my heart | *de mis entrañas la flor* |
| and to the kind bosom of the Lord | *y de Dios al seno amigo* |
| my love, imprisoned in yours | *va contigo* |
| will go. | *de tu amor preso mi amor.*) |

More important than the ten sonnets included towards the end of *Poems* are Unamuno's admirable translations from Carducci,

Coleridge, Maragall, and especially "The Broom Plant" of his beloved and inseparable Leopardi.

II   Rosario de Sonetos Líricos (Rosary of Lyrical Sonnets), *1911*

The 128 sonnets which were written in five or six months and make up this collection again reveal the intimate griefs and disenchantments of the poet. "Fortunately I am married and have children!" he wrote, for he was again worried about his heart, was suffering from insomnia, nerves, and hypertension. Although he wrote these sonnets in the spirit of Louis Veuillot's "Oh, my God, take away my despair and leave me pain!" [15] he imposed on his feelings an exact compressed form, with salutary results. Concision was a much-needed counterweight to his sprawling bathos for it forced on his wordiness an effective minimum.

Some of the most famous of these poems are reminiscent of the Portuguese poet Antero de Quental whose sonnets Unamuno described as "frequently bony and dry: the conceptual, abstract element seems very fleshless, not always well covered over by fancy." [16] Unamuno's sonnets are equally angular, notched, and granitic, yet a large number will pay rereading.

In Number XXI he tells us of the stabilizing effect of domestic ties:

> . . . for man does not enjoy
> liberty if he is not in bondage to the ties
> of love, his companion on the road of life.
> (. . . *que el hombre no disfruta*
> *de libertad si no es preso en los lazos*
> *del amor, compañero de la ruta.*)

"Sweet silent thought" inspired by Shakespeare's sonnet XXX, is a lovely domestic evocation, a still-life grouping of wife, children, and poet reading, as sweet silent thought makes its way through him "like a quiet ox across the field" (*como un manso buey la tierra*). More excited are sonnets like "Non Serviam," a defiance hurled by enslaved mortals at annihilation, or those reflecting the poet's angry reaction to the battle between the Spanish bishops, backed by King and Vatican, and the Prime Minister José Canalejas who wished to check the growth of religious orders both in number and wealth. Unamuno had always felt that the alliance of Altar and Throne was "in the long run, fatal to both," [17] and in his fiery "Numantia" he recalls the resistance of that city to the Roman invaders and contrasts it with the Vatican which uses not catapults, but bores from within through the Spanish nobility; he reminds us, furthermore, that only when the temporal power of Rome disintegrated did it become eternal in its spiritual power. In "To the Neutral State" the poet denounces the king of Spain as successor to Pontius Pilate, for he surrenders Christ to the successor of Annas, the Pope; then he calls for a free Church in a free State, and warns that when there are two powers in one state, one of them is superfluous. In "To the Christian Mercury" he goes even farther and compares the king to the Mercury who served the gods as pander and was a spurious god himself.

One of the most often quoted of these sonnets is "The Atheist's Prayer" woven of sharp contrasts, and beginning

> Hear my plea Thou, God who does not exist
> and receive these my plaints into Thy nothingness,
> Thou who never leavest sorrying man
> without the solace of deception.
> (*Oye mi ruego Tú, Dios que no existes*
> *y en tu nada recoge estas mis quejas,*
> *Tú que a los pobres hombres nunca dejas*
> *sin consuelo de engaño.*)

The grandeur of God is such that it can only be an idea and all of reality is too narrow to embrace Him:

> I suffer because of Thee,
> nonexistent God, since if Thou existed
> I would also truly exist.
> (*Sufro yo a tu costa,*
> *Dios no existente, pues si Tú existieras*
> *existiría yo también de veras.*)

Indeed, that is why God can only be apprehended through offense to the intellect or the leap into infinity ("Reason and Faith"):

one must earn endless life
with reason, without reason, or against it.
(*hay que ganar la vida que no fina*
*con razón, sin razón o contra ella.*)

God, however, has given us reason and some, seduced by that
faculty, turn into libertines of ideas ("Don Juan of Ideas");
fortunate indeed are those who are free from that disease ("The
Disease of Thinking"). There is no consolation in the "abra-
cadabra" slogans of "fraternity" or "progress" since they are
inevitably followed by disenchantment ("Unmodern"); the only
consolation comes from hope that with death, the mind, "free
of the tombstone of thought, source of illusions," will sleep in God's
powerful hand ("In the Hand of God").

But if for one who thinks along these lines and divulges his
thought, there is danger of excommunication, there is also solace
in that private covenant between him and that "heretic" God whom
even His Fisherman in Rome does not understand ("My Heretic
God"). So long as the conventionalized religion marked by God's
middlemen does not destroy the poet's own desire for faith, and so
long as thought cannot replace the need for infinity, he can continue to battle in a way that may triumph in the beyond, and in
"Neither Martyr nor Executioner" the poet again seeks war in
peace and peace in war, the tranquillity in action that is God's
design.

### III   El Cristo de Velázquez (The Christ of Velázquez)

*The Christ of Velázquez,* 1920, is considered, by at least one
critic, the most important religious poem written in Spanish since
the Golden Age.[18] As Unamuno stands before the disturbing canvas on which the great Spanish realist depicted Christ nailed on
the Cross, a cloth carelessly tied about His loins, and one side of
His face covered by a thick veil of falling hair, he sings in resounding tones of the Incarnation, Death, and Resurrection of
Jesus, and derives from these beliefs his hope of escaping total
death. Free of the mesh of doctrine and philosophy, he is carried
away by pure love, by a fundamental devotion to Gospel whose
meanings he deepens, embroiders, and personalizes. Once Don
Quixote had accepted Dulcinea, he performed his deeds in her
name, and in this poem Christ becomes the center of all gravity,

struggle is suspended, and the poet can concentrate on adoration.

Divided into four parts and into chapters of unequal length, the poem has a total of 2538 hendecasyllables. By the beginning of 1914 Unamuno had already written 1500 lines which he polished, retouched, and expanded until 1920, when the completed poem was published. In *The Tragic Sense of Life* Unamuno had called attention to a basic difference between Protestant and Catholic artistic expression: ". . . in a Protestant theologian, Ernest Troeltsch, I have read that the greatest contribution of Protestantism to the conceptual order is in the art of music where Bach gave it its most artistic expression. That is how Protestantism is dissolved, into celestial music! We can say, on the other hand, that the loftiest Catholic—or at least Spanish—artistic expression, is in the more material, tangible, and permanent art—since sounds are carried off in air—of sculpture and painting, in the Christ of Velázquez, in that Christ who is always dying but never dies, in order to give us life!" [19] In a letter to the Portuguese poet Teixeira de Pascoaes a year or so later, he states clearly that in the poem he is preparing and which he called *Standing Before the Christ of Velázquez (Ante el Cristo de Velázquez)*, he is formulating the faith of his people which could not be contained in logic petrified in molds but only in a realistic Christology. [20]

It is interesting to speculate on why, of all the artistic representations of Christ, plentifully available in his country, Unamuno chose the one hanging in the Prado Museum. Referring to another, all too common graphic representation of Christ, one adopted by the king of Spain as an official symbol, Unamuno said: "Is there anything . . . blander and more softly sensual than the cult of the Sacred Heart of Jesus . . . to which we owe those horrible images with which they have infested our churches? Compare such a representation . . . with our old bloody and bloodless Spanish Christs, and above all with the stupendous one by Velázquez." [21] But the other "Spanish Christs" did not please him either. "The Christ of Cabrera" to which he had dedicated a poem in his *Poems* was too awkward, granitic, "terraceous," [22] while "The Supine Christ of Santa Clara" included in *Spanish Wanderings and Vistas* and which he had seen in 1913 in the church in Palencia— the scene of the legend of the nun "Margarita the Gate-Keeper" made famous in Spain by Zorrilla—was too much of a "wooden mannequin . . . covered with skin and paint." [23]

This Christ is not the Verb
incarnate in living flesh . . .
(*No es este Cristo el Verbo
que se encarna en carne vividera* . . .)

This Christ is one whose will is destroyed with matter; it is a
Christ as horizontal as the plains, an inert God who does not
vouchsafe salvation since "this Christ of my land is earth" (*este
Cristo de mi tierra es tierra*).

It was, Unamuno avers, a certain measure of remorse over
having composed this "ferocious" poem that prompted him to
undertake *The Christ of Velázquez*,[24] in which he humanizes Christ
as he had done with the mountains, hamlets, and churches of his
peninsula. The matrix of such an approach lies in the biblical prose
of Fray Luis de León's *On the Names of Christ* (*De los nombres
de Cristo*) which amplifies the meanings of the names given to
Christ in the Scriptures: "tender bud" (*pimpollo*), "path" (*camino*), "shepherd" (*pastor*), "mountain" (*montaña*), "Father of
the World to Come" (*Padre del siglo futuro*), "Arm of God"
(*Brazo de Dios*), and so on. Most of the cantos of Unamuno's
liturgical epic also bear headings to indicate points of departure:
"Moon," "Ecce Homo," "God-Darkness," "Blood," "Life is a
Dream," "Dawn," "Rose," and proceed on to the very features of
Christ visible to the eye on the Velázquez canvas: crown, head,
hair, brow, face, eyes, ears, nose, cheeks, arms, shoulders, hands,
index finger of the right hand, wound in the side, belly, knees, feet.
Woven into these dithyrambic glosses are quotations from and references to the Old and New Testaments, chapter and verse being
scrupulously indicated in the margins and then paraphrased. Thus,
richly orchestrated, the *Christ* is a major work of unflagging
vitality and resonances, a Cantata to the Son of God on the Cross,
made up of wave upon wave of Whitmanesque rhythms, or what
Unamuno himself called "a sort of rhythmoid, dense prose."[25]

Visionary images abound in such mounting profusion that silent
reading is made almost impossible (Unamuno did give public
readings of portions of the poem). These are verses to be de-
claimed to wind, thunder, and swirling waters. The poet is an
intoxicated evangelist whose oversized and rough-hewn imagination
appropriates to itself all the meanings of the Crucified One. The
story of the Passion is retold, not chronologically, but as each fact

and inference strengthens the possibility that death will die, for just as Unamuno had rejected all the paraphernalia erected by Cervantists around the figure of Don Quixote, he now disregards all argumentation and centers his attention on the Savior as his hope of redemption from finiteness.

The story of Christ is absolved from history and restored to eternal contemporaneity since, in Kierkegaardian terms, every implication of the Divine Message flows directly from the bearer of the message. Time and dogmatics have receded, leaving the poet and reader organically part of the Instant when Eternity became event. But if the difficulties of belief have been suspended, it does not mean that the poet is ready to submit to the authority of the Church.[26] It is instead a retreat to the *pistis* which the poet had much earlier defined as "true faith at one with hope . . . faith or confidence, religious faith, not theological . . . free of dogma."[27]

In short, the roaring rhythms of the *Cristo,* the heaping up of timeworn imagery in new juxtapositions, constitute another of Unamuno's attempts—this time, supremely successful—to break through the crust back to the core, to restore a sense of immediacy to the Creator-Creature relation. It is not the "unitive way"[28] that Unamuno attempts to achieve here, because complete fusion would signify the obliteration of self-consciousness; instead, he wants no reward but the strength to probe more deeply in order to hope more intensely, and the rhapsodic strength of the poem contains all the zeal and ardor and respect of the cry, "Lord, I believe; help Thou my unbelief!"

> Grant me,
> oh Lord, that when finally lost I am about
> to leave this dark night
> in which the dreaming heart is shrivelled,
> I may enter the clear day that has no end,
> my eyes fixed on Thy white body,
> Son of Man, complete Humanity,
> on the uncreated light that never dies;
> my eyes fixed on Thine eyes, oh Christ,
> my gaze submerged in Thee, oh Lord!
>
> (*¡Dame,*
> *Señor, que cuando al fin vaya perdido*
> *a salir de esta noche tenebrosa*

*en que soñando el corazón se acorcha,*
*me entre en el claro día que no acaba,*
*fijos mis ojos de tu blanco cuerpo,*
*Hijo del Hombre, Humanidad completa,*
*en la increada luz que nunca muere;*
*mis ojos fijos en tus ojos, Cristo,*
*mi mirada anegada en Ti, Señor!*)

IV   Rhythmic Vistas (Visiones rítmicas)

Of these poems, included in Unamuno's *Andanzas y visiones españolas* (*Spanish Travels and Vistas*), 1922, "In a Cemetery of a Small Spanish Town" ("En un cementerio de lugar castellano") and "On Gredos" ("En Gredos") are the two most imposing. In the second, a paean of praise to "holy Spain" written in August of 1911, the poet, on the Gredos Mountains, looks down upon eternal Spain, not of history but of life, the rocky heart of his country reaching high into the kingdom of God which is "the eternal freedom to be scaled." Even Charles V had realized that history is a fraudulent glory, a "shipwreck in a deep sea," and had turned his back in Yuste on such victories in order to prepare for the kingdom that is not of this world. With such thoughts the poet penetrates the essence of his Spain; here, being himself again, he is again Christian, Spanish Christian.

"In a Cemetery of a Small Spanish Town," written in 1913, has been called the counterpart of the "Cimetière Marin" of Paul Valéry, although its stark lines and themes contrast with the artistic and intellectual complexities of the French poem.[29] The sight of the ruined and abandoned graveyard near the Castle of Arévalo recalls to Unamuno the lines of Bécquer's dirge, "My God, How Lonely are the Dead!" ("¡*Dios mío, qué solos se quedan los muertos!*"), Gray's *Elegy,* and Rosalía de Castro's "The Cemeteries of Galicia" ("De Galicia os cimiterios"), but the composition is unmistakably Unamuno's for here again his thoughts wander to the intrahistory which contrasts with the "vain tumult" of history. Here again the deserted fields, the sheep, the larks, the hidden poppies, the immortal silence of the walled "island" or graveyard, are more meaningful than the noises made by those who are "free" on the world's side of the wall. For eternity withstands all comings and goings and is watched over from Heaven by Christ, the Sovereign Shepherd, counting the sheep of His flock. Eternity is fixed, given, sanctified, while history vainly swirls about it. The poem is indeed a long prayer, an elaboration of the sonnet, "In the Hand of God," a quiet surrender to the inevitable, worthy of its place among the best known of Unamuno's poems.

## V  Rimas de dentro (Rhymes from Within)

Closely related to "In a Cemetery of a Small Spanish Town" is the poem "Aldebarán," from *Rhymes from Within,* published in 1923, for it too encompasses the cardinal themes of Unamuno's work: God, the universe, the relation of life to Divinity, infinity, the awareness of personality, love, death, and immortality.[30] It is a series of questions addressed to the star, "a ruby shining in the divine forehead," concerning the earth, a "speck of dust." What is on the other side of space? Are all the worlds in space, each following its own path? Will not God gather all the stars one day into His sheepcote? If, as has been pointed out, this "Aldebarán" bears a certain resemblance to Fray Luis de León's "Serene Night" ("Noche Serena"), its interrogative movement is quite different from the Renaissance poet's strain after freedom from mortal coils, and is closer to Leopardi's "The Nocturnal Song of a Wandering Asian Shepherd" ("Canto Notturno di un pastore errante dell'Asia"). Although the red star Aldebaran has replaced Leopardi's moon, the central question posed in both poems is the same: the why and wherefore of existence. But whereas Leopardi arrives at the conclusion that both God and Nature are indifferent to man's travail, Unamuno finds no answer, and the questions he asks are the very substance of that uncertainty which supports the possibility of comfort. While Fray Luis de León swooned at the fearful symmetry of the stars and sighed over his estrangement from the perfection of the heavens, Unamuno wonders whether the star is alone and lost in a myriad of solitary planets, or is part of a larger pattern. Analogously, is the poet a part of a vaster design than his mind can encompass? And when Aldebaran dies, what will become of it, where will God dispose of the star, in what "rubbish heap of worlds?" And from the very silence that meets his questions, the poet derives a measure of hope:

> A pledge of eternity is your silence,
> Aldebaran!
> (*De eternidad es tu silencio prenda,*
> *¡Aldebarán!*)

## VI  Teresa

If "Aldebarán" may indeed be said to be made up of "deep, melodious organ sounds that would have gladdened the Psalmists,"[31] *Teresa,* 1924, subtitled "Rhymes of an Unknown Poet Presented by Miguel de Unamuno" ("Rimas de un poeta desconocido presentadas y presentado por Miguel de Unamuno"), gives off an anachronistic odor of albums and fans, tuberculosis, sighs, and tears. It is meant to be a poem on the metaphysics of love—Unamuno calls it *meterótica*—in which meditation on love leads to meditation on death. For Unamuno's purpose was to create another archetypal pair of ill-fated lovers, much on the pattern of Dante and Beatrice, Petrarch and Laura, Tasso and Leonora, or the lovers of Verona and Teruel, and to show that frustration attendant on the premature death of the tubercular lady leads the surviving partner to higher knowledge.

In subject and form it seems almost a deliberate challenge to the aesthetics of his time, a defiance of all the vanguard movements, especially the *ultraists,* with their arcane imagery, tight syntax, Freudian and surrealistic colorings. The influences on his sentimental, lachrymose poem are from the nineteenth century, by his own admission, from Querol, Campoamor, and especially Bécquer, with the medieval Ausias March and the twentieth-century Antonio Machado thrown in. The imagery is drawn from the thesaurus of romanticism while the slight story is in direct descent from the graveyard school of poetry. Even the convention of the author's having received these ninety-eight polymetric poems from an unknown but bereaved poet thrusts us back at least one century, and makes it a period piece out of its period, the reproduction of an antique.

The verses were presumably sent to Unamuno after Teresa's death by her lover Rafael, who shortly thereafter followed her to the grave to become one with her. In an indirect way, it might be said that the entire disjointed work is Unamuno's expansive tribute to the spiritual comforts afforded to man by his mate, but instead of singing the delights of married love *à la* Patmore, he extends himself to one of the possibilities he escaped—one of his ex-futures (a fact he partly and equivocally denies)—and sings the loss he might have sustained. A love such as Teresa's and Rafael's guarantees immortality since the depth of their feelings, as gushed forth in this poetic garland, denies finite boundaries and makes mortality unjust.

If the meters are traditional, the varied rhyme schemes are singsong, facile, jogging. The similes are too often embarrassing—skies dotted with flowers, furtive tears like pearls, eyes like suns, and Teresa's grave is covered by a mantle of green. When Rafael leaves Teresa's handkerchief, spotted with her blood, on Teresa's grave, he recites Bécquer's "My God, how lonely are the dead!" as "My God, how lonely are the living!" And recalling Bécquer's death, also from tuberculosis, the dying Rafael exclaims: "I am dying of a vulgar illness, oh Bécquer; my lungs are giving out" (*"Me muero de un mal cursi, Bécquer mío; se me agota el pulmón"*), and to rhyme with *acordeón* (for Eugenio d'Ors, Bécquer was an angel playing on an accordion) he refers to the frogs singing *clinclón, clinclón, clinclón.*

Banalities and bad taste are given free rein: when Rafael cuts his fingers peeling an apple, Teresa sucks the blood; when she goes off for a cure—heliotherapy it is called—Rafael admonishes her: "We must get you cured . . . do not go and catch another cold . . ." (*"Lo que nos hace falta es que te cures . . . no te me vuelvas a cojer un frío . . ."*); when she fails in her attempt and dies, Rafael burns the poems she inspired and scatters the ashes over her grave. And like Dante, Rafael's thoughts even wander temporarily to another lady—Teresa's sister—but it is a wholly innocent hiatus in his constancy.

Yet among all these saccharine expressions of heartbreak, among the pseudo-homey conversations redolent of Campoamor, Unamuno can sound some poignant notes. The prayer to the Virgin can stand by itself as a simple, tender expression of appeal:

> Thou who knowest of love and grief
>    hear my plea, oh Lady,
> And pray for us sinners
> now and in the hour of our death
>
> For her sake at the hour of death
>    at the last stage of life,
> when the vessel of my soul finally breaks,
>    grant that our Father give
>       eternal life
> with my grave and hers together.

*(Ya que sabes de amor y de dolores*
*óyeme bien, Señora,*
*Y ruega por nosotros pecadores*
*ahora y en la hora*
                   *de nuestra muerte*

*Haz por ella que en la hora del ocaso*
*en el último trance,*
*Cuando de mi alma al fin se rompa el vaso,*
*de nuestro Padre alcance*
                   *eterna vida*
*mi tierra con su tierra confundida.)*

Other brief passages save the poem from calamity: the rhapsodic thanks Rafael offers to God for his imminent death; the Petrarchan vision Rafael has of his dead Teresa, an angel spinning the "white sheets of our eternal marriage bed in heaven." Yet despite such saving graces, if the reader is not to wonder about the poetic aberrations that clog the work, he must in truth accept Unamuno's injunction written into the final "Epistle" ("Epístola") not to criticise, but to understand.

## VII   *Poems of Exile*

Of the 103 sonnets making up the collection *From Fuerteventura to Paris* (*De Fuerteventura a París*), published in Paris in 1925 during Unamuno's exile, sixty-six cover the time spent on the island mentioned in the title (the first two were composed in Salamanca before February 21, 1924) and the thirty-seven others cover the period in Paris. Into this sonnet-sequence—most of the sonnets are followed by prose commentary—as Unamuno told a friend in a letter that prefaces the collection, he poured all the agony he felt as a Spaniard and Christian.

Already in the first sonnet he excoriates the dictator Primo de Rivera as a Don Juan Tenorio playing at being a Don Quixote, and later goes on to call him a stupid fool whose Manifesto of September 13, 1923, revived the Inquisition and revealed the sensibility of a bull, a stud horse, a jackass, a sheep or billy goat, a graft-taking politician, a protector of whores, and a hirer of assassins. The king is not so much a Bourbon as an Austrian, a Hapsburg who reveals the taint of the last of that dynasty, the idiotic Carlos II. Along with the "epileptic pig" General Martínez Anido, these are the men who persecute the heretic, not so much because his doctrines imperil the salvation of his fellowmen, but because he will not conform to the spirit of Father Astete's catechism.

That Primo de Rivera should bear the same given name as the author of *Don Quixote* is an outrage to the Unamuno whose first name was also Miguel and who, as the St. Paul of the religion of quixotism, hurled the new gospel at his nation and at the world. But Spain, instead of being fortified by the lofty ideas he had taught them, had surrendered to the hands of "progressive paralytics . . . ill with that terrible disease which blows like a strong wind from the sea over a convulsed Europe." Instead of being inured against professional politicians, demagogues, and militarists, Spain is again in the clutches of its endemic moral cancer, the Cainite envy which is the evil passion incubated in monasteries and sacristies, or around the nauseating throne which is now no more than a snare.

As he wrote these vitriolic poems, Unamuno was thinking of that other irate exile, the Victor Hugo of the *Châtiments,* and especially of the great seventeenth-century Spanish satirist and poet, Quevedo, who had also suffered at the hands of corrupt leaders. But unfortunately, too many of Unamuno's sonnets overflow with more rage than art, and the prose explanations provided by the author are indeed indispenable for the topical allusions whose meanings fade with time. Yet when the stridency of political versifying is replaced by a lyricism of unadorned sadness, the sonnets may stand on their own merits. The poetry of personal depression, of nostalgia and *taedium vitae,* the hushed verses to the sea, to the night, the stars, the moon, sun, and clouds, to his memories of his wife—". . . Concha, my habit . . ." (". . . *Concha, mi costumbre . . .*")—the grateful memories of Fuerteventura and Salamanca, the sonnet on his forthcoming sixtieth birthday, these stand out as poetry rather than as invective or versified pamphleteering.

The *Ballads of Exile* (*Romancero del destierro*), published in Buenos Aires in 1928, and made up of thirty-seven poems of various meters plus eighteen ballads, are also inspired in the main by the sad political state of Spain. Of the first four, signed in

Paris (the rest are from Hendaye), the first is the most moving. Starting with the simple words, "If I fall here, on this green earth . . ." ("Si caigo aquí, sobre esta tierra verde . . ."), it is a solemn injunction to be buried in Spain, and captures the slow funereal note of grave command and prophecy, the tread of the processional to the last resting place. The next, composed the Saturday night before Pentecostal Sunday, May 31, 1925, is one of his most deservedly famous:

> It will come at night when all is asleep,
> it will come at night when the sick soul
>     is cloaked in life,
> it will come at night with quiet tread,
> it will come at night and place its finger
>     on the wound.
> (*Vendrá de noche cuando todo duerma,*
> *vendrá de noche cuando el alma enferma*
>     *se emboce en vida,*
> *vendrá de noche con su paso quedo,*
> *vendrá de noche y posará su dedo*
>     *sobre la herida.*)

Fear and resignation are appositive to the premonition of death, and are rendered in a series of two long lines and one short line as if in recoil, combinations which match the longing for surcease that is inextricable from the splinters of fear; relief is followed by tremor, expectation by doubt.

"The Mystery of St. Joachim, Grandfather of God" ("El misterio de San Joaquín, Abuelo de Dios") is at the same time a poetic elucidation of the dogma of the Immaculate Conception and a personal ecstatic rumination, while "Good-bye to Spain" ("Adiós, España") is a poem of dejection in which simplicity curbs shrill anger, a gasp of pain rather than jarring harangue. Such graveyard verse as "Orhoit Gutaz" (Basque for "Remember Us") and "The Cemetery of Hendaye" ("El Cementerio de Hendaya") are examples of the tardy romanticism which characterizes so much of Unamuno's verse and contain reverberations of Gray's "Elegy" and Hugo's "Oceano Nox." On the other hand, the poems of the sea are of admirable simplicity, surpassed only by the mystical lullaby he sings to his own soul:

Sleep, little child,
in sleep you will find health;
sleep, sleep a while . . .
for you may yet awaken . . .
(*Duérmete, niño chiquito,*
*durmiendo te curarás;*
*duérmete, duerme un poquito . . .*
*que acaso despertarás . . .*)

But principally the motifs of rancor and contempt make of his style a stiletto, as he himself boasts; he throws up to the king his mistakes, his evil counsellors, the venality of his "crusade" in Morocco, and reminds him that God is above life. Alfonso has made of his throne a toilet seat and of his crown a barber's basin; he is the king of horseraces and Mercedes cars, and his country is in the hands of acolytes, bordello braggarts, bootblacks, carousers, legionnaires, gangsters, and croupiers. Furious denunciations hurled at those who prostitute patriotism and religion for their own interests alternate with self-pity, weeping, and gnashing of teeth, and although here and there a musical chord is struck, these poems are in the main Jeremiads, outbursts justified by circumstances but not wrought into poetry.[32]

## VIII  Cancionero (Book of Songs)

Quite a number of Unamuno's uncollected poems were long unavailable until brought together and edited by Manuel García Blanco, and finally incorporated into Volume XIV of the *Complete Works* (*Obras Completas*) as *Scattered Poems* (*Poesías sueltas*). However, the most imposing of Unamuno's posthumous works is his *Book of Songs* published in its completeness in 1953 under the editorship of Federico de Onís. Written over a period of nine years from February 16, 1928, to December 28, 1936, three days before the author's death, these 1755 compositions of varying lengths were originally jotted down in little pocket-sized notebooks. Referring to the fertility of the book, Unamuno remarked that "it seems . . . that my soul wishes to empty itself of all that it has to say before entering the eternal silence of rest."[33]

The cornucopia of the *Book of Songs* pours forth its produce pell-mell in a sort of unordered *dictionnaire d'idées non reçues*.

Existence, Unamuno knew, was insistence, and the relationships he discerned between passing fancy and the central themes of life are endless. It would seem that he never allowed even the most evanescent thought or notion to pass without exploiting it for connections with his ideological ganglia; the adjectival becomes substantive, the conceptual somersaults and capers sound like the parodies of syllogisms, but the lacerated *sentidor* or "feeler" is never far from the recurrent play on the meanings of Don Quixote, the Bible, the history of Spain, exile, death, God, immortality, holy desire. At best, the gnomic sharpness of so many of these compositions reflects the coincidence of a nimble turn of mind with a perfect rhythm, yielding a flawless quatrain, sextet, octave. As the poet dissolves and rearranges fragments of intuition, knowledge, and feeling, he passes from anger to brusquerie, from relaxed tenderness to querulousness, and releases fortuitous thoughts and unsuspected prismatic nuances, or conjugates irreconcilables and underlines neglected implications. In this way he produces small gems of succinctness that leave trails of longing, sadness, surprise, and shock.

He may, in some instances, draw magic effects from the harsh syllables of proper geographical names, endow new meanings on the classics, or breathe freshness into the ancient ballad form. In his poems on exile or the fear of death, he can deftly fuse biblical and national myth; in an exquisite prayer to the Virgin, in a song of praise to St. John of the Cross, in the biblical dignity of a patriotic hymn, in a cradle song to the infant Jesus, he is capable of remarkable achievement. Even at such successful moments, it must be noted however, the banal hovers dangerously near, but they happily escape the fate of the foreshortened homilies, the bright sayings, and haphazard quips scattered throughout the book, since they combine high seriousness with a grace that saves the moralist turned poet from *sensiblerie* or pompousness.

In a word, the *Book of Songs* is a mine of slag to be worked patiently for nuggets of pure gold. As in the essays, we are dealing here with a writer shaken by many moods, some transcendental, some petty, and unwilling to sacrifice any flippancy or random notion for the total good. The poet's pen obediently follows the unpredictable course of a tormented, rebellious, grieving soul and will come up very often with a perfectly finished product, but equally often with a childish design—much like the paper animals he delighted in fashioning—too cryptic, casual or gratuitous to be either aesthetically or intellectually satisfying. Many of the poems are a ravel of conceits more like verbal doodles than anything else, contortions of thought that had long exhausted their potential, or infelicitous jingles touched off by a word or expression rather than by unfolding thought.

Even the antiliterary Unamuno, who referred to writing as the sad profession of abortion, understood the impurity of his work, and hoped that if anything gave his poems hardness and life, it would not be the purely poetic charms of language, but human passion and disquietude.[34] Asked why he did not cut the quantity of the poetry, Unamuno replied that they were all organs of the same body and that the good ones would make up for the bad, while the bad would not spoil the good. "Pruning can make an urban garden but it unmakes a mountain forest."[35] The comparisons are apt, for the *Book of Songs* is a sprawling, irregular book, devoid of overall design, clogged by profusion and overabundance, yet if technical carelessness and the unwillingness to be selective may produce the canard or even an occasional vulgarity, there is yet generous proof in the *Book of Songs* that the deepest meditations on life and death cannot avoid becoming poetry.

## IX   *Comments*

Both José María Valverde and Luis Felipe Vivanco agree that Unamuno is compensation for the great poet that Spain did not produce in the nineteenth century.[36] He finds his place, not with the modernists, their epigones, and other experimentalists of twentieth-century Spain, but with a Leopardi, a Carducci, a Whitman, an Antero de Quental, yet as Vivanco says, a belated poet is not necessarily an antiquated one.[37]

Unlike his contemporaries who held Verlaine and Mallarmé in highest esteem and considered them sources of inspiration, Unamuno thought of them as *poseurs* who could not manage to say what they thought because they thought incompletely and foggily.[38] Unable to perceive the similarity between "his" Leopardi's *noia* and Baudelaire's *spleen,* he was indifferent to the French poet's depth of suffering and perfection of form, and exclaimed on one occasion that nowhere does Baudelaire measure up to the exquisite refinement of Swinburne's "Dolores."[39] He was equally contemptuous of the "difficult" poetry written in his own tongue: to condemn

Góngora's ultrarefined lines, he used the poet's own words, "they catch much of the ocean and little water" (*mucho océano y pocas aguas prenden*),[40] and referred to the ethereal Juan Ramón Jiménez' "pure poetry" as "spiritual onanism."[41]

One is fully justified in maintaining that the only attitude Don Miguel had towards beauty was an ethical one,[42] for he himself categorically said, "I understand philosophy only as poetry, and poetry only as philosophy."[43] Writing was for him a sort of therapy or outlet for emotions too vehement to be recollected in tranquillity, while literature practiced as a deliberate, specialized craft suffered, in his eyes, from a devitalization of spirit: it was "literatism," a vice of the French, and in Spain he saw no place for it. Rubén Darío he accused of "Parisianism,"[44] or fascination with the glittering French cosmopolitanism, where versatility stood for depth, where *logique* and *esprit* meant frivolity and insincerity, where *joie de vivre* was a spurious replacement of the *espérance de survivre*.[45] True spiritual tensions, he held, shattered smooth surfaces; the aesthete, therefore, entangled in sensuous or intellectual gratifications, could not move on to absolutes.

Unamuno's objective in his poetry, as indeed in all his work, was to play the role of secular priest and to reach the widest audience possible. In this he coincided with the Tolstoy of *What is Art?* for both believed that art is essentially religious and that too much of the art of their times was perverted and upper-class, lacking in sincerity and motivated by vanity. Both the Russian and the Spaniard after him denounced art for pleasure's sake and literature accessible only to a select minority; art that did not justify itself in terms other than the purely artistic was relegated by both moralists to a subordinate and even undesirable status.

"What a pity," exclaims Camille Pitollet, "that the form of Unamuno's poetry does not correspond to the spirit behind it!"[46] The "philosophic vibration" of which Azorín speaks[47] finds its way too often into prolixity made of dry, hard, pedestrian materials. Unamuno's spirit found its most uninhibited expression in poetry, but his ear, unfortunately, was less than that of a poet.[48] Endeavoring to express his feelings and ideas *in statu nascente,* he rejected what he scornfully called the *hojarasca* (the dead leaves, trash, or rubbish), but in so doing, José María de Cossío has said, he neglected many flowers and instead shows us knotty formless roots.[49]

Strictness, balance, tone, and color are all elements foreign to Unamuno's verse; had he turned on his own poetry the jaundiced eye he reserved for the "aesthetes" of his time, he might have benefitted immeasurably. Had he drained off the smothering repetitions and hackneyed imagery; had he eliminated some of the grandiloquence and old-fashioned sonorities, he would have endowed his verse with greater tautness and firmer contour. A measure of that detachment and *sang-froid* he railed against would have enabled him to tighten his periods, curb his oratory, purge and sharpen his vision. Admittedly, his thoughts are frantic and supercharged, but poetic expression demands not only sincerity and range, but balance, euphony, wit, and shading. Raw material deposited in turgid iteration, may impress us by sheer mass, but unshaped, it can become tiresome and its resonances blurred and dim.

The poet Unamuno is therefore deficient in the artisanship and novelty so conspicuous in Darío or J. R. Jiménez; Antonio Machado's verse is more compressed and subtle, while the younger poets who wrote during Unamuno's lifetime make use of a far wider range of sophisticated techniques. The very weight, however, of Unamuno's verse output, the magnitude and intensity of his themes, the sheer humanity of the author's self-disclosure, make of him an extremely significant poet. And we might repeat what Dámaso Alonso points out, namely that despite Unamuno's basic lack of talent for form (*primaria incapacidad formal*) his poetry must be appreciated in its totality; as such it has a strength "without equal in contemporary literature, but to arrive at such a conclusion [one] must almost forget each of the particular examples." [50]

CHAPTER 7

# Evaluations

## I  *Unamuno and Ortega*

IT is instructive to compare Unamuno with Ortega y Gasset, the other thinker who, younger by nineteen years, shared with him the intellectual leadership of their country for approximately two decades. Both published a good portion of their work in newspapers and periodicals, both were teachers, Unamuno of disciplines which, outside the classroom, were of subordinate interest to him, Ortega of a discipline, philosophy, that filled his life. Formally trained in this area, Ortega could apply the powers of rigorous analysis to subjects ranging from history and sociology to literary and art criticism, confining himself always to the essay. Unamuno, a philosophical autodidact and undaunted by fears of inadequacy and slovenliness, ventured into all genres with equal aplomb. Unamuno's style is a complex of lyricism and rant, aphorism and mawkish prolixity, sharp intuition and ragged edges, while Ortega honed his style to a brilliant smoothness unmatched in modern Spanish letters.

The concept of vital reason, central to Ortega's thinking, and expounded fully in *The Theme of Our Time* (*El tema de nuestro tiempo*), should have proved congenial to Unamuno, since the contention that reason is "only a tiny island floating in the sea of primordial life," that thought is one of the many functions of existence, and that the primacy of culture is a "subversion of the part against the whole," is akin to much of Unamuno's own philosophy. On the other hand, Ortega's frank intellectualism, his outspoken admiration of German culture, his distance from mystical or theological preoccupations, his insistence on man's historical nature, were all anathema to Unamuno.

Already in 1907 Ortega referred to the " 'Africanist' deflection inaugurated by our master and hermit Don Miguel de Unamuno . . ."[1] and the following year spoke of the older man as the "demoniac mystic" who bludgeoned his countrymen with the oak-trunk of his personality, although he qualified his admiration by alluding to Unamuno's spirit as a dizzying current combining good sense with many useless, unhealthy things.[2] The quarrel between the two men broke out over a letter Unamuno wrote to Azorín to congratulate him on an article he had written in the newspaper *ABC* of September 12, 1909, defending his country against foreign detractors during the war Spain was waging in Africa. In this letter, unfortunately made public in *ABC* almost immediately, Unamuno referred to the simpletons (*papanatas*) fascinated by Europeans: "They say we do not have a scientific spirit. But ours is of a different sort. . . . Let the others invent, and we shall find out about it and apply it." Then he added: "If it were impossible for one nation to produce both a Descartes and a St. John of the Cross, I would choose the latter."[3]

Ortega felt the affront had been directed at him and answered with his article, "Unamuno and Europe, a Fable" ("Unamuno y Europa, Fábula"),[4] in which he took his opponent to task for breaking the rules of good manners and good sense, and compared him to those young men at country dances who always feel impelled at about midnight to bash in the oil lamp and precipitate a wild fight in darkness. At the end of the article, he suggests that the towers of Salamanca bear a reddish tinge because the stones blush at what Unamuno says. A little earlier the same year, 1909, as if refuting Unamuno's concept of a book as primarily the autobiography of its author, Ortega asserted that if we seek the author behind a great work, we find "rags of a soul without any charm, hanging from the nail of a body." Genius is the power to create a "new piece of universe, a progeny of objective problems, a bundle of solutions," and anyone who would attribute genius indifferently to both Newton and St. Teresa commits a crime against humanity: ". . . if the *Moradas* [St. Teresa's *Dwellings of the Soul*] are of as much value to the history of the planet Earth as the *Philosophiae naturalis principia mathematica,* then the aforementioned planet is hurtling into absurdity without norm or direction . . ."[5]

Some four years later, in answer to another article of Ortega y Gasset, Unamuno argued that there is a difference between wisdom, religious feeling, justice, prudence, and goodness on the one hand, and an acquaintance with Newton's binomial theory on the other. "I do not wish an Alonso Quijano swollen with vain knowledge that swells but does not comfort, as the Apostle said. And if the Spanish nation is, as those who have the philosophical audacity to affirm, the most abnormal nation in Europe . . . I would wish for it an abnormal Alonso Quijano also, but without eyeglasses, looking with naked eye upon his brothers about him and seeing himself in them, and without any need to study mathematics, let him punish Juan Haldudo and free the galley slaves, and let himself be laughed at by the idealists." [6]

When in 1914 Ortega went to Salamanca to enlist Unamuno's collaboration in the *League for Spanish Political Education* (*Liga de Educación Política Española*), Unamuno listened carefully and then exclaimed: "So, Ortega, you wish to be the father of the party and give me the role of the Holy Ghost. No, I am father, son, and Holy Ghost of my own party! If anyone joins it, I resign." [7] In his *Meditations on the Quixote* (*Meditaciones del Quijote*) of that same year, Ortega no doubt had Unamuno's earlier work on the "Spanish Christ" in mind when he referred to the grotesque errors made by authors who consider Don Quixote as if Cervantes had not existed and "invite us to an absurd existence, full of bizarre deeds." [8]

Despite occasional signs of mutual respect between the two writers, Unamuno never contributed to the prestigious *Revista de Occidente* founded by Ortega in 1924. Yet when Unamuno died, Ortega dedicated to him some of the most heartfelt words he had ever written. Unamuno, he said, had died of the "sickness of Spain" (*mal de España*), and was now with death, his perennial "friend-enemy," after making of his life an endless *meditatio mortis*. Ortega brackets Unamuno with Shaw as members of a generation of intellectuals convinced that humanity existed for no loftier end than to witness "their mountebank wit, their arias, their polemics," and that wherever Unamuno was, he placed himself in the spotlight and left others no alternative but to adopt a passive role. Yet, he confessed, Unamuno had been a giant, both in his positive and negative qualities, enormously dynamic and courageous, possessed of a resonance which, upon its cessation, was sending Spain into an era of "atrocious silence." [9]

## II  *Contradictions and Judgments*

Pedro Salinas says that Don Miguel was always seated at his desk as if at a gambling table, facing death the croupier and trying to break the bank with his cards.[10] The cards he used were the endless writings in which he assayed every combination of idea and fancy—from logic to poetry to outlandishness—to solve the mystery of the Sphinx. And as he changed positions, he treated his notions as he did clothing: "When they are worn out by time, I turn them around or give them to some needy person." [11]

By dissecting his own soul for all to see, he exposed the endless chain of contraries in which the human condition is enmeshed, and urged that the adoption of any position is the choice not to recognize the justice of other positions. If he snorted contemptuously at culture or hailed himself as the supreme Spaniard, he was nevertheless steeped in the crosscurrents of European learning. The man who expounded the concept of the flesh-and-blood individual clung fiercely to the diffuseness of intrahistory. The Unamuno who refused to surrender his separateness fervently loved the mystics whose ecstasy derived from self-detachment. Although he sought religion undistorted by dogma, he turned in wrath against anticlerical attitudes held by others; as he cried out against the stultifying effects of feeling hardened into code, he yet assumed the semiclerical garb. If he was plagued by the degeneration suffered by authenticity in communication, and suffered guilt over his own division into professor, official, journalist, public penitent, he admitted that truth can be disseminated mainly through organized channels. He alternated between whipping the masses into action and allaying their fears; he upbraided them for their addiction to routine and envied them the even rhythm of their trivial preoccupations. He regretted that the Spanish mystics had been prevented from effecting an indigenous reformation, yet anathematized all attempts to identify religion with nationalism. God was the absolutely different, yet he anthropomorphized Him as the projection of man into infinity. He was indeed the Bedouin of the spirit, and he quoted Whitman: "Do I contradict myself?/ Very well then, I contradict myself,/ (I am large, I contain multitudes)." [12]

As a consequence of Unamuno's own mobility, students of his work have disagreed on the question of his true belief, or, more specifically, whether he was a believer or atheist. Romero Flores calls Unamuno "one of the cases of deepest faith in all of Christendom," [13] Agustín Esclasans calls his religion "poetic, antiphilosophical and antitheological, a triumph of material faith over learned reason," [14] Julián Marías claims Unamuno's faith took the form of confidence in God, [15] a position with which Alain Guy agrees. [16] José Luis Aranguren argues that what Unamuno calls Catholic desperation is the laicizing of Protestant desperation in the line of decreasing faith going from Luther to Pascal to Kierkegaard to Unamuno and Heidegger. [17] Pedro Corominas wrote that *"Unamuno thought he believed, but he did not believe. His conviction was as sincere as it was false."* After the 1897 crisis his life was the inexhaustible echo of a will to believe that was actually sterile. [18] Following Corominas' lead, Sánchez Barbudo holds that Unamuno was an atheist who tried to hide the void by playing the role of *luchador,* or "struggler," with a fury that he turned into literature. Pascal and Kierkegaard accepted a Christianity they could not grasp rationally, but Unamuno did not start with the faith which he could doubt "from within" and harbored a basic atheism which he took great pains to disguise through a constant display of grief, an exhibitionism *à la* Chateaubriand. This was an attitude, Sánchez Barbudo holds, which Unamuno finally rejected in *St. Manuel Bueno, Martyr* when the author's alter ego, the priest, confessed to himself and to Lazarus that he did not believe. [19] Father Benítez, who carried on a lively debate with Sánchez Barbudo, disagrees and claims that Unamuno was a "heretic grafted on to a Catholic, or, if you like, a Catholic grafted on to a heretic," [20] while Armando Zubizarreta has attempted to refute both Corominas and Sánchez Barbudo and to prove Unamuno's complete sincerity in his desire to believe. [21] Henry Daniel-Rops declares that Unamuno was assuredly a Catholic in spirit, tradition, and essence, albeit not an obedient one, [22] while Vicente Marrero inclines to agree with the opposite camp that Unamuno sought earthly glory so vehemently because he did not believe. [23]

In dealing with so anarchic a thinker as Unamuno, and in the face of such a welter of disagreements, we would perhaps do well to repeat with Unamuno himself that he was so religious that he did not have to be a believer, while, in the case of other men, so long as their Christianity was not a part of their very marrow, they had no choice but to preserve its forms.[24]

### III   *Style: Power and Limitations*

If Unamuno the *fabbro* leaves us strangely unsatisfied, the gigantic personality woven into his work never fails to provoke and confound. In contrast to philosophers, novelists, and essayists who remain shadowy figures behind their creations, the outlines of the personalist Unamuno are discernible everywhere in his writings, accounting both for their dramatic cogency and their limitations.

As a philosopher he is lacking in composure and sobriety, as a novelist he is too indifferent to the creation of microcosm, as a poet he is too prosaic, but as *excitator*[25] he lays claim to being one of the most disturbing figures in modern literature. "The very maximum of what one human being can do for another in relation to that wherein each man has to do solely with himself, is to inspire him with concern and unrest," said Kierkegaard,[26] and Unamuno infects us with the agony generated by ideas too often frozen in abstraction, for we are not so much touched by the coin Unamuno hands us as by the heat it bears from his hand.[27] Curtius has summed it up aptly: "Spain has thinkers of keener ideas, poets of sweeter song, personalities with richer power of structure, and artists with a purer sense of form. Unamuno is nevertheless unique because of the dynamism of his personality." [28]

He could never regard literature as a craft, but rather as a receptacle that came into being, in a sort of creative evolution, to receive the natural overflow of his torment, and if, as Buffon had said, style is the man, Unamuno added that it must reflect man at first hand, with all his imperfections. Style is like a garment the author makes for himself as he wears it, whereas the "stylism" of the professional writer or scholar separates the personality from the person just as the stylized Divinity is separated from God.[29] Good taste, prudence, urbanity in literature meant for Unamuno a dimming out of the man behind the work, a modesty often used as a blind for superficiality, a consistency which reduced man's complexity to counterfeit orderliness. With his free associations, his careless ramblings, ideological and verbal dodges and somersaults, he sought to wrestle with the enigma of death before which all rules, canonical and aesthetic, were irrelevant and obstructing.

Although a professor of Greek, he had to admit that Greek language and literature had confirmed his anti-Hellenic spirit: "They say that Hellenic means to distinguish, to define, to separate; my way is to undefine, to confuse." [30] His own style was nearer to that of Seneca, Lucan, Prudentius, all of Spanish birth, passionate, violent, "passing from ellipsis to redundancy, sometimes falling victim to subtlety, oratorical and even declamatory . . . never Horatian." [31]

One of the most characteristic techniques of Unamuno is to play with a word, expression, idea, or congeries of ideas etymologically in order to rip ideological synapses asunder, to tear up conventional associations. Reinforced by the erudition of the professor of philology, he decomposes a word and recomposes it, thus releasing neglected shades of meaning and suggesting further developments. Concepts, too, can be moribund for being too familiar, and must be revitaminized through dislocation, interrogation, rearrangement. His favorite notions he treats like gems, holding them up as high as possible to enjoy every subtle refraction of light, coaxing from them every conceivable permutation of meaning. Thus, by treading on the callouses of common sense,[32] by refurbishing banalities, by the use of outrageous paradox to reveal a neglected possibility, and through the marriage of incompatibles, he strikes poetry out of new systems of configurations.

In the finest of Unamuno's work, therefore, the reader is treated to the rare privilege of being at the very center of the struggle taking place in a mind superbly stocked with clashing ideas and emotions. We co-witness the exhausting debate that has no end, and in which the protagonist will resort to hit-or-miss, and will not stop short of the orneriness of the jigsaw puzzle player who must force the piece that does not fit. As his contemporaries, the men of the Generation of 1898, were reworking style in the direction of muted impressionism, naked statement, or the musical values of symbolism, he preferred the hortatory tone of the preacher or the improvisations of the dazzling conversationalist, and his writings evince all the defects, as well as the incandescence, of such unorganized volubility.

Therefore, it is in his power to heighten "the relevance of the thinker to his thought," [33] that Unamuno's greatness lies, that the *curé manqué* becomes an *artiste malgré lui*. If he belabors a limited number of themes, they are in a major key, for he combines lyricized confession with universal resonance in his desire not to die, to "undie," in his defense of his strife with his own limitations. As a "self-thinker . . . thinking on himself, reflecting on himself . . ." [34] Unamuno offers knowledge of his own substance as a broad pattern of all human substance, and his egotism is Montaigne's. With the monumental erudition he scatters helter-skelter, and the endless, often recondite quotations he appropriates from a thousand sources, he is a man speaking to other men: "I wish only to be, reader, the mirror in which you see yourself. Is the mirror concave or convex and of such a concavity or convexity that you do not recognize yourself and it grieves you? Well, it is best that you see yourself in every light possible. It is the only way you will be able to know yourself truly." [35]

Often shrill in tone, peevish in attitude, self-righteous, verbose, and magniloquent, Unamuno is nonetheless one of the greatest confessionists in literature, a writer who strikes profound echoes in the conscience of his readers for as he reveals every facet of himself he reveals to them the ambiguities built into their own identities. If the reader holds Unamuno to strict account for his ideas, he will be repelled by the untidiness, the jumble, the repetitiveness, but if he judges the entire work for range, intensity, and the directness of the *pensée pensante,* he will be swept up by the exuberance of a mind pushing to the extreme and even beyond. If, in his attempt to urge men to extend their consciousness into embracing possibilities commonly considered untenable, Unamuno falls into histrionism and sheer absurdity, these are correlative to the gasping effects of reason trying to move into supra-reason, and Antonio Machado showed good judgment when he classified Unamuno with those men whose voices seem "crude and extemporaneous" but who, we feel, are in tune with "deeper, truer realities." [36]

As the continuator of Kierkegaard, Unamuno is "nearer to the existentialist or existential philosophies than to any others." [37] If there is a thread connecting the various existentialisms, it is the dread, guilt, and insecurity that characterize each man as he, concretely and alone, confronts his destiny. On the one side stand Kierkegaard and Dostoevski, the Dane staggering under the strain that boundless Divinity imposes on the finite mind, the Russian, desperate over the immeasurable distance separating the evil that is committed from the perfection that is conceivable. On the other side stand Nietzsche, Heidegger, Sartre, and Camus, all concerned with the direction to be taken by self-determining man who, dissociated from God, is alone with his conscience and awareness and must follow the embattled road over the absurdity of life environed by the gratuitousness of suffering and death. Both the religious and atheistic forms of existentialism, then, place man in a position of travail: in the first case, that he may be worthy of Divinity, and in the second, that he may evolve an ethos to negate meaninglessness and to achieve a new form of transcendence.

Unamuno partakes of one and the other, and yet adds a new major dimension. With Kierkegaard he shares the sentiment of each man's personal exertion to God; with Nietzsche he suggests a new level of heroism that incorporates despair and yet surpasses it; with Heidegger he shares the stress on man's being for death. The omnipresence of the famous injunction from *Obermann* relates him, at least tangentially, to the concept of commitment celebrated by Sartre and Camus. But Unamuno shares neither Kierkegaard's certainty of the existence of God, nor Heidegger's and Sartre's apparent indifference to the other-worldly. An absolutist without an absolute, he exhorts men to change and yet turns in disgust from any specifics; he is both attracted and repelled by the static and the dynamic, by the need for action and the futility of action. In his incessant alertness, he longs for peace and denounces the comforts of peace as treason, and if he coined the broad-spectrum term "the tragic sense of life," he nonetheless understood the importance of cultivating the common sense of life. If he admired his uncomplicated creations—Marina, Rosa, Pedro Antonio, Josefa Ignacia, and Blasillo—he argued that those who avoid taking sides in the battle of life have no metaphysical status.

It has therefore been argued, very justifiably, that Unamuno is at least two men in alternance: the agonist and the contemplative. "The agonist may be important for the history of modern thought but both were equally important for *him* when he was able to look upon himself as divided in two, as from the standpoint of a third person."[38] Unamuno was torn betwen the "rigorous" view vital to sanctity and the "relaxed" view vital to sanity.[39] He indicts implicit faith as odious and extols it as devoutly to be wished, and tells us of the two types of dangerous men: those who, caring only for the next world, neglect this one, and those who, caring only for this world, neglect the next,[40] proving once again Jasper's assertion that after Kierkegaard and Nietzsche, philosophy "can no longer bring its thought into a single, complete system to be brought out as a presentation derived from its principles."[41] What Kierkegaard, Nietzsche, and Unamuno have in common is a scorn for those who will not let go of the moorings of safety to step out into an heroic, unresolved venture, in Kierkegaard's case, towards the full challenge of New Testament Christianity, in Nietzsche's case towards a courage that defies timorousness disguised as virtue, in Unamuno's case towards a hope in a Supremacy that cannot be contained in any ossified tradition.

Unamuno is the *Gegendenker* with no paradigm of belief, fertile in indicating directions that turn out to be as contradictory as only man, in his fullness, can be. Conceptually, Unamuno wedded the Catholic tradition he inherited to nineteenth-century Protestant theology in an uneasy, morganatic alliance, while as Kierkegaard's disciple he is the ultimate development of the *total* thinker for whom philosophy exists in terms of thought and need, outline and feeling. Since the questions of axioms and rules, principles and laws, theories and equations are, for the man of flesh and blood encumbrances or a blocking off of the fullest vision, Unamuno urged himself beyond proof to possibility and beyond definition to desire. He strained beyond philosophy to the object for which philosophy exists: man, but man as a complex of knowledge and dream, fact and fantasy, a creature who yearns for more than he can embrace.

With Kierkegaard and Nietzsche, moreover, Unamuno forms what might be called the trio of dramatic poet-philosophers who in their unprofessional scorn for pettifogging research and approved method, act out their thoughts in the grand romantic manner with frenzied gesture, defiant pose, and tortuous style. The calm, deliberate manner must give way to the ejaculatory expression, since dispassionateness has little place in the total personality-idea equation. In each case, the propositions expounded retain the quiver and rhythm of a subjective feeling too precious to be set aside, and in the case of Unamuno's work specifically, as in the case of highly charged lyric poetry, only partial meanings may be transliterated out of texts that are, in effect, confessions compounded of quotations, commentary, impulse, and free associations. Therefore, just as the fullest meaning of a poem is inherent in its very structure, so, in the main, must Unamuno's convictions be identified with the degree to which his effusions move us. His peculiar version of the monologue—or auto-dialogue—will not be inhibited by self-contradiction, posturing, or daydreaming. As derivative as he may be in certain areas, Unamuno earns the cachet of originality in his *sui generis* accommodation of what he borrows, in what he rediscovers or re-knows (*re-conocer*), in his revivification of important commonplaces, in his breaking up of comfortable relationships through the prisms of his own spirit, in his pointing out the further powers of interiorization. As a poet-philosopher, in short, Unamuno avails himself of the poet's privilege to use a statement for its dramatic fitness rather than its accepted connotations, and is uncannily able to potentiate absurdity with a measure of logic.

Since Unamuno's preoccupations were of the longest range and highest reach, he could accept no given conclusions and labored against stiff-necked righteousness in pedagogy, science, politics, and above all, religion. He fought against the substitution of symbols for being; his aim was to show how pure conceptual reasoning is a Procrustean bed; he vindicated the dignity of life's schisms as against categories and objectification. While he voiced the unhappiness of the religiously oriented man no longer able to accept the formalities of dogma and ritual, he was aware that as religion is updated, it acquires a social hue that weakens the nexus between God and His every creature. Consequently, although it is just to say that we cannot live "by Unamunos alone,"[42] it is equally important to stress that all the certainties of "ideocrat" and "theocrat" sound sanctimonious alongside the essential humility of Unamuno's assertions that he could not truly understand what is most vital. And if his complexities and qualifications are often bewildering, he is nonetheless one of the great religious "disturbers" of our times, since he makes us feel, as few others have been able to do, that the meaning of life may depend, in the last analysis, on the degree of finality that death brings.

# Notes and References

## Preface

1. Marcel Gabriel, "Kierkegaard en ma pensée," *Kierkegaard vivant* (*Colloque organisé par l'Unesco à Paris du 21 au 23 avril 1964*), (Paris, 1966), p. 79.
2. Pío Baroja, *Obras completas*, VII (Madrid, 1949), 499.
3. Ramón J. Sender, *Unamuno, Valle-Inclán, Baroja y Santayana—Ensayos críticos* (Mexico, 1955), p. 11.
4. Antonio Machado, *Juan de Mairena* (Buenos Aires, 1957), II, 74.
5. Hermann Keyserling, *Europe*, tr. Maurice Samuel (New York, 1928), p. 87.
6. Ernst Robert Curtius, *Kritische Essays zur Europäischen Literatur* (Bern, 1950), pp. 224-46.
7. Miguel Cruz Hernández, "La misión socrática de Don Miguel de Unamuno," *Cuadernos de la Cátedra Miguel de Unamuno*, II (1952), 46.
8. José Ortega y Gasset, "En la muerte de Unamuno," *Obras completas*, V (Madrid, 1958), 265.

## Chapter One

1. *Time*, LXII (Oct. 26, 1953), 50; *Life*, XXXV (Dec. 21, 1953), 31-32. Also Lawrence Fernsworth, *Spain's Struggle for Freedom* (Boston, 1957), pp. 269-70, based on Jean Creach's "Scandale à Salamanque ou L'Espagne renie Unamuno," *Le Monde*, Dixième Année (Oct. 20, 1953), p. 5.
2. "Crónica unamuniana (1956-1957)," *Cuadernos de la Cátedra Miguel de Unamuno*, VIII (1958), 100-105.
3. The pastoral letter of the Bishop of the Canary Islands, issued Sept. 19, 1953, bears that title.
4. Miguel de Unamuno, "Sobre la erudición y la crítica," *Obras completas*, ed. Manuel García Blanco (Madrid, 1959-1964), III, 914.

The *Obras completas* will hereafter be referred to as *OC*.

5. Juan Arzadun, "Miguel de Unamuno, íntimo," *Sur*, CXIX (Septiembre de 1944), 107-08.

6. Juan Arzadun, "Cartas de Miguel de Unamuno," *Sur*, CXIX (Septiembre de 1944), 37.

7. Sergio Fernández Larraín, *Cartas inéditas de Miguel de Unamuno* (Santiago de Chile, 1965), p. 394.

8. César Real de la Riva, *Salamanca y su universidad* (Salamanca, 1949), p. 23. In my account of the history of Salamanca, I have leaned heavily on this pamphlet and Manuel García Blanco, *Salamanca y la literatura* (Salamanca, 1949).

9. César Real de la Riva, *op. cit.*, p. 25.

10. Miguel de Unamuno, "Lo que ha de ser un Rector en España," *OC*, VII, 870.

11. Juan Arzadun, "Cartas de Miguel de Unamuno," *Sur*, CXX (Oct., 1944), 57-58.

12. Peter G. Earle, *Unamuno and English Literature* (New York, 1960), p. 143.

13. "De la enseñanza superior en España," *OC*, III, 92.

14. "Sobre la erudición y la crítica," *OC*, III, 917.

15. Yvonne Turin, *Miguel de Unamuno universitaire* (Paris, 1962), p. 61.

16. "Conferencia leída en el Ateneo de Madrid el 25 de noviembre de 1914," *OC*, VIII, 869.

17. Juan Arzadun, "Cartas de Miguel de Unamuno," *Sur*, CXIX (Sept., 1944), 44.

18. Yvonne Turin, *op. cit.*, p. 70.

19. "La educación. Prólogo a la obra de Bunge, del mismo título," *OC*, III, 515.

20. Letter of Oct. 19, 1900, to Pedro Jiménez Ilundain, in Hernán Benítez, *El drama religioso de Unamuno* (Buenos Aires, 1949), p. 320.

21. "Soledad," *OC*, III, 895.

22. "La civilización pantalónica," *OC*, V, 1081.

23. *Contra esto y aquello* is the title of a book of essays (1912), *OC*, V, 747-949.

24. José A. Balseiro, *Blasco Ibáñez, Unamuno, Valle-Inclán, Baroja. Cuatro individualistas de España* (New York, 1949), p. 88.

25. Antonio Machado, *Abel Martín, Cancionero de Juan de Mairena, Prosas varias* (Buenos Aires, 1958), p. 140.

## Chapter Two

1. Juan López-Morillas, *El Krausismo español* (Mexico-Buenos Aires, 1956), p. 71.

2. *Ibid.*, p. 81.

3. José Alberich, "Sobre el positivismo de Unamuno," *Cuadernos de la Cátedra Miguel de Unamuno,* IX (1959), 61-75.

4. Hernán Benítez, *El drama religioso de Unamuno* (Buenos Aires, 1949), p. 379.

5. For Unamuno's work as translator, see Manuel García Blanco, "Unamuno, traductor y amigo de José Lázaro," *Revista de Occidente,* XIX (Oct., 1964), 97-120.

6. "El pórtico del templo," *OC,* IV, 503-16.

7. Armando Zubizarreta, "Una desconocida 'Filosofía lógica' de Unamuno," in *Tras las huellas de Unamuno* (Madrid, 1960), pp. 30-31.

8. "Ver con los ojos," *OC,* IX, 115-23.

9. Benítez, *op. cit.,* p. 260.

10. Charles Moeller, "Miguel de Unamuno et l'espoir désespéré," in *Littérature du XXe siècle et Christianisme,* IV (Tournai, 1960), 82-83.

11. Juan Arzadun, "Cartas de Miguel de Unamuno," *Sur,* CXIX (Sept., 1944), p. 56. Quoted from letter of Oct. 30, 1897.

12. *Cartas inéditas de Miguel de Unamuno,* ed. Sergio Fernández Larraín (Santiago de Chile, 1965), p. 323.

13. "Nicodemo el fariseo," *OC,* III, 121-53.

14. Moeller, *op. cit.,* 105-6.

15. *Cartas inéditas de Miguel de Unamuno,* ed. Fernández Larraín, p. 215.

16. Benítez, *op. cit.,* p. 256.

17. Adolf Harnack, *Outlines of the History of Dogma,* tr. Edwin Knox Mitchell, introd. Philip Rieff (Boston, 1957), p. 413.

18. *Ibid.,* p. 434.

19. Adolf Harnack, *What is Christianity?,* tr. Thomas Bailey Saunders, introd. Rudolf Bultmann (New York, 1957), p. 295.

20. *Ibid.,* p. 271.

21. "La Fe," *OC,* XVI, 99-113.

22. "¡Pistis y no gnosis!" *OC,* IV, 1019-25.

23. *Epistolario a Clarín,* ed. Adolfo Alas (Madrid, 1941), p. 101.

24. *Miguel de Unamuno, Ensayos,* ed. Bernardo G. de Candamo (Madrid, 1942), II, 56.

25. "La ideocracia," *OC,* III, 434.

26. Benítez, *op. cit.,* p. 434.

27. "Ibsen y Kierkegaard," *OC,* IV, 426-32.

28. *The Living Thoughts of Kierkegaard,* presented by W. H. Auden (Bloomington, 1952), p. 130.

29. *The Journals of Kierkegaard (1834-1854),* ed. and trans. by Alexander Dru (London, 1958), p. 213.

30. *Ibid.,* p. 215.

31. *Kierkegaard's Concluding Unscientific Postscript,* tr. by David F. Swenson and Walter Lowrie (Princeton, 1944), p. 207.

32. William Barrett, *The Irrational Man* (New York, 1958), p. 157.

33. Walter Lowrie, *Kierkegaard* (New York, 1962), I, 8.

34. William James, *The Will to Believe* (New York, 1956), p. 31.

35. *Ibid.,* p. 25.

36. *Ibid.,* p. 56.

37. *Ibid.,* p. 25.

38. Included in a letter to Federico Urales, in the latter's *Evolución de la filosofía en España* (Barcelona, 1934), II, 206. See also Unamuno, "Maese Pedro. Notas sobre Carlyle," *OC,* III, 522-32.

39. Carlos Clavería, "Unamuno y Carlyle," *Temas de Unamuno* (Madrid, 1953), p. 23.

40. "Epílogo al libro de W. E. Retama, *Vida y escritos del doctor José Rizal,"* *OC,* XVI, 780.

41. *Ibid.,* 781.

42. 'Conferencia dada en el teatro de La Zarzuela, de Madrid, el 25 de febrero de 1906," *OC,* VII, 676.

43. Paul Tillich, *The Protestant Era* (Chicago, 1957), p. 185.

44. "La patria y el ejército," *OC,* III, 984.

45. "Sobre la consecuencia, la sinceridad," *OC,* III, 1043.

46. "Mi religión," *OC,* XVI, 117-24.

47. "¡Plenitud de plenitudes y todo plenitud!" *OC,* III, 768.

48. Benítez, *op. cit.,* pp. 293-94.

49. Antonio Machado, *Juan de Mairena* (Buenos Aires, 1957), II, 118.

50. José Ortega y Gasset, *Obras completas,* V (Madrid, 1958), 264-65.

51. José Ferrater Mora, *Unamuno: A Philosophy of Tragedy,* tr. Philip Silver (Berkeley and Los Angeles, 1962), pp. 34-35.

52. "Religión y patria," *OC,* III, 633.

53. Paul Tillich, *The Religious Situation* (New York, 1956), p. 165.

54. *Del sentimiento trágico de la vida en los hombres y en los pueblos, OC,* XVI, 245.

55. "Egologías y consistiduras," *OC,* XI, 1074.

56. Kierkegaard, *Either/Or,* tr. Walter Lowrie with revisions by Howard A. Johnson( Princeton, 1946), II, 80.

57. Alfred North Whitehead, *Science and the Modern World* (New York, 1948), p. 191.

58. Kierkegaard, *Either/Or,* II, 279.

59. Kierkegaard, *Concluding Unscientific Postscript* (Princeton, 1944), p. 207.

60. "La feliz ignorancia," *OC,* V, 869.

61. *Concluding Unscientific Postscript,* p. 398.
62. *Ibid.,* p. 463.
63. Karl Jaspers, *Reason and Existenz* (Noonday Press, 1955), p. 73.
64. Gabriel Marcel, *The Philosophy of Existentialism* (New York, 1961), p. 18.
65. *Ibid,* p. 44.
66. Martin Heidegger, *An Introduction to Metaphysics,* tr. Ralph Manheim (New Haven, 1959), pp. 186-87.
67. *Ibid.,* p. 188.
68. *Ibid.,* p. 197.
69. James Collins, *The Existentialists, A Critical Study* (Chicago, 1952), p. 204.
70. Karl Jaspers, *The Way to Wisdom, An Introduction to Philosophy,* tr. Ralph Manheim (New Haven, 1960), p. 20.
71. *Ibid.,* p. 47.
72. Arland Ussher, *Journey Through Dread* (New York, 1955), p. 17, note 1.
73. "Intelectualidad y espiritualidad," *OC,* III, 712.
74. "¡Plenitud de plenitudes y todo plenitud!" *OC,* III, 765.
75. Werner Heisenberg, "L'Image de la Nature selon la physique contemporaine," tr. A. E. Leroy, *La Nouvelle Revue Française,* VII (1959), 88.
76. Quoted in Bill Becker, "Pioneer of the Atom," *The New York Times Magazine* (October 20, 1957), p. 52.
77. J. W. N. Sullivan, *The Limitations of Science* (New York, 1949), pp. 141, 143.
78. *Ibid.,* p. 171.
79. José Ortega y Gasset, *El hombre y la gente, Obras completas,* VII (Madrid, 1961), 133.

## Chapter Three

1. Ramón Menéndez Pidal, *Los españoles en su historia* (Buenos Aires, 1959), p. 225.
2. *Epistolario a Clarín,* ed. Adolfo Alas (Madrid, 1941), p. 53.
3. Juan Arzadun, "Cartas de Miguel de Unamuno," *Sur,* CXIX (Sept., 1944), pp. 55, 56.
4. *El porvenir de España, OC,* IV, 992.
5. *La vida de Don Quijote y Sancho, OC,* IV, Part II, Chapter LXXI.
6. Pedro Laín Entralgo, *La generación del Noventa y Ocho* (Buenos Aires-Mexico, 1947), p. 187.

7. "Diario de un azulado," *OC*, X, 475.

8. Hernán Benítez, *El drama religioso de Unamuno* (Buenos Aires, 1949), p. 119.

9. *El porvenir de España, OC,* IV, 990.

10. Angel Ganivet, *Idearium español* (Madrid, 1962), p. 128.

11. Friedrich Nietzsche, *The Use and Abuse of History,* in *The Search for Being,* ed. Wilde and Kimmel (New York, 1962), p. 130.

12. Pedro Laín Entralgo, *op. cit.,* p. 175.

13. "Paleontología" (Sonnet XXXI), *Rosario de sonetos líricos, OC,* XIII, 538.

14. "Excursión," *Por Tierras de Portugal y de España, OC,* I, 504.

15. "La civilización es civismo," *OC,* IV, 451.

16. Quoted by Jacques Chevalier, "Hommage à Unamuno," *Cuadernos de la Cátedra Miguel de Unamuno,* I (1948), 21.

17. "La vida es sueño," *OC,* III, 407-17.

18. "La dignidad humana," *OC,* III, 447.

19. "¡Adentro!" *OC,* III, 418-27.

20. Nemesio González Caminero, *Unamuno* (Comillas, 1948), p. 150.

21. "Soledad," *OC,* III, 881-901.

22. *En torno al casticismo, OC,* III, 188.

23. "Sobre la europeización," *OC,* III, 1119.

24. *Ibid.,* 1114.

25. Letter of May 7, 1912, to José María Palacio, in Manuel García Blanco, *De la correspondencia de Miguel de Unamuno* (New York, 1957), pp. 9-10; reproduced in Manuel García Blanco, *En torno a Unamuno* (Madrid, 1965), p. 224.

26. "¡Muera Don Quijote!" *OC,* V, 712-16. Also "¡Viva Alonso el Bueno!" *op. cit.,* 717-20.

27. "De la enseñanza superior en España," *OC,* III, 110.

28. José Ortega y Gasset, *Goethe desde dentro, Obras completas,* IV (Madrid, 1957), 419.

29. "Sobre la lectura e interpretación del 'Quijote,' " *OC,* III, 852-53.

30. Nicolas Berdyaev, *Dostoevsky* (New York, 1957), p. 175.

31. Antonio Machado, *Juan de Mairena* (Buenos Aires, 1957), II, 125-26.

32. Vicente Marrero, *El Cristo de Unamuno* (Madrid, 1960), p. 189.

33. *Ibid.,* p. 181.

34. "Epílogo" to *Amor y pedagogía, OC,* II, 579.

35. Kierkegaard, *Fear and Trembling* (New York, 1954), pp. 64-77.

## Chapter Four

1. "La envidia hispánica," *OC*, IV, 423.
2. "Glosas a la vida," *OC*, IV, 455-59.
3. "Cientificismo," *OC*, IV, 527.
4. Kierkegaard, *The Point of View for My Work as an Author* (New York, 1962), p. 110.
5. "Algo sobre parlamentarismo," *OC*, V, 405.
6. *Ibid.*, 407.
7. *Ibid.*, 407-8.
8. *La vida de Don Quijote y Sancho, OC*, IV, 263.
9. "El problema religioso en el Japón," *OC*, V, 327-28.
10. Kierkegaard, *op. cit.*, p. 108.
11. "Política y cultura," *OC*, IV, 443.
12. Sergio Fernández Larraín, *Cartas inéditas de Miguel de Unamuno* (Santiago de Chile, 1965), *passim*.
13. "La supuesta anormalidad española," *OC*, IV, 1101.
14. "Prólogo a la edición española de la *Historia ilustrada de la guerra*, de G. Hanotaux," *OC*, VII, 339.
15. *Ibid.*, 341.
16. *Ibid.*, 348.
17. "Algo sobre parlamentarismo," *OC*, V, 411.
18. "Sobre el paganismo de Goethe," *OC*, VIII, 1117.
19. "Discurso en la comida anual de la revista madrileña *España*, celebrada en el Hotel Palace el 28 de enero de 1917," *OC*, VII, 942-57.
20. "De vuelta de Italia en guerra," *OC*, X, 379-89.
21. "Confesión de culpa," *OC*, X, 393-96.
22. "El jubileo de la Gloriosa," *OC*, X, 410-14.
23. "De las tristezas españolas: la acedia," *OC*, IV, 1129-35.
24. "La estrella ajenjo," *OC*, IV, 1165-68.
25. "Mi visita a Palacio," *OC*, X, 494-98. See also Conde de Romanones, *Notas de una vida (1912-1931)* (Madrid, 1947), pp. 194-95.
26. *Nosotros,* XLV (Diciembre de 1923), 520-21. This letter is reproduced in Francisco Madrid, *Genio e ingenio de Don Miguel de Unamuno* (Buenos Aires, 1943), pp. 70-71.
27. Jean Cassou, "Unamuno, déporté," *Mercure de France,* CLXXI (1924), 250.
28. *La agonía del cristianismo, OC*, XVI, 461-62. The essays that reflect his attitudes towards France are contained in *En el destierro, OC*, X.
29. Francisco Madrid, *op. cit.*, p. 80.

30. Antonio Sánchez Barbudo, "The Faith of Unamuno. The Unpublished Diary," *Unamuno Centennial Studies* (Department of Romance Languages, The University of Texas, 1966), p. 157.

31. *Cómo se hace una novela, OC*, X, 884.

32. *Dos artículos y dos discursos* (Madrid, 1930), p. 146.

33. *Cómo se hace una novela, op. cit.*, 923.

34. Included in *Dos artículos y dos discursos* (Madrid, 1930).

35. Francisco Madrid, *op. cit.*, p. 116.

36. "Conferencia dada en el teatro de La Zarzuela, de Madrid, el 25 de febrero de 1906," *OC*, VII, 678.

37. "Renán sobre la política," *OC*, VIII, 981.

38. "Cartas al amigo, XI," *OC*, XI, 1017.

39. Kierkegaard, *The Point of View for My Work as an Author* (New York, 1962), p. 113.

40. "El hombre interior," *OC*, XVI, 887.

41. "El hijo del hombre y el señorito," *Cuenca Ibérica* (Mexico, 1943), p. 165.

42. "La ciudad de Henoc," *OC*, XVI, 874.

43. "Delirium furibundum," *OC*, VIII, 724-25.

44. "Maestros y curas," *La enormidad de España* (Mexico, 1945), p. 73.

45. *Dos artículos y dos discursos*, p. 207.

46. Francisco Madrid, *op. cit.*, pp. 177-78.

47. Mathilde Pomès, "Unamuno et Valéry," *Cuadernos de la Cátedra Miguel de Unamuno*, I (1948), 67.

48. "Salud mental del pueblo," *OC*, IX, 1058.

49. "Schura Waldajewa," *OC*, XVI, 947.

50. "Visiones y palillos," *La enormidad de España*, p. 164.

51. "Lo religioso, lo irreligioso y lo antirreligioso," *ibid.*, p. 82.

52. "La universidad hace 20 años," *OC*, X, 988.

53. "El liberalismo español," *OC*, VIII, 705.

54. "Don Marcelino y la esfinge," *OC*, V, 507-8.

55. "Discurso en las Cortes de la República el día 25 de septiembre de 1931," *OC*, VII, 1001.

56. "Sed de, reposo," *OC*, XVI, 898-901.

57. "Lo religioso, lo irreligioso y lo antirreligioso," *La enormidad de España*, p. 81.

58. "Caciquismo, fulanismo y otros 'ismos,'" *OC*, X, 927-30.

59. "La enormidad de España," *OC*, V, 74.

60. Francisco Madrid, *op. cit.*, p. 119.

61. *Ibid.*, pp. 195-96.

62. "La clase y el fajo," *De esto y de aquello*, ed. Manuel García Blanco, IV (Buenos Aires, 1954), 277-80.

63. "Doce cartas a González Trilla (Notas de Hernán Benítez)," *Revista de la Universidad de Buenos Aires*, XVI (1950), 549.

64. Francisco Madrid, *op. cit.*, p. 239.

65. "Engaitamientos," *OC*, XI, 1099.

66. "La educación. Prólogo a la obra de Bunge, del mismo título," *OC*, III, 506.

67. "Hinchar cocos," *OC*, XVI, 943.

68. Francisco Madrid, *op. cit.*, p. 199.

69. Kierkegaard, *The Present Age*, tr. by Alexander Dru and Walter Lowrie (Oxford, 1940), p. 56.

70. *Cancionero, OC*, XV, p. 286.

71. *Cómo se hace una novela, OC*, X, 875-76.

72. "El liberalismo español," *OC*, VIII, 703.

73. "Cartas a Bogdan Raditsa," *Cuadernos*, XXXIV (1959), 54. Letter of November 19, 1928.

74. *Dos artículos y dos discursos*, p. 229.

75. "Nueva vuelta a Portugal," *OC*, I, 1122-23.

76. "Junto al cabo de la Roca," *OC*, I, 1119.

77. "Cruce de miradas," *OC*, X, 1022.

78. "Svástika," *OC*, XI, 1088-91.

79. Francisco Madrid, *op. cit.*, p. 171. Also "De nuevo la raza," *OC*, VI, 908-11.

80. Francisco Madrid, *op. cit.*, pp. 229-30.

81. Francisco Bravo, *José Antonio, el Hombre, el Jefe, el Camarada* (Madrid, 1939), pp. 86-92.

82. "Otra vez con la juventud," *OC*, X, 1028-31.

83. "¿Fajismo incipiente?," *La enormidad de España*, p. 253.

84. "Un español de cemento," *OC*, V, 66-67.

85. "En retiro de remanso serrano," *Inquietudes y meditaciones* (Madrid, 1957), p. 270.

86. Paul Tillich, *The Protestant Era* (Chicago, 1957), p. xii.

87. *Soren Kierkegaard. The Last Years. Journals 1853-1855*, ed. and trans. Ronald Gregor Smith (New York and Evanston, 1965), pp. 216-17.

88. "Literatura al día," *OC*, V, 842.

89. Hernán Benítez, *El drama religioso de Unamuno* (Buenos Aires, 1949), pp. 277-78.

90. *Ibid.*, p. 449.

91. "Realismos," *OC*, X, 1001-2.

92. Sergio Fernández Larraín, *Cartas inéditas de Miguel de Unamuno* (Santiago de Chile, 1965), p. 402.

93. "Después de una conversación," *OC*, X, 117-18.

94. "Letter to a Belgian Socialist," written on August 10, 1936, in

*Spanish Liberals Speak about the Counter-Revolution in Spain* (Spanish Relief Committee, San Francisco, 1937), pp. 23-25.

95. José Balseiro, *Blasco Ibáñez, Unamuno, Valle-Inclán, Baroja. Cuatro individualistas de España* (Chapel Hill, 1949), pp. 112-13.

96. Luis Portillo, "Unamuno's Last Lecture," printed in *Horizon* and reproduced in *The Golden Horizon*, ed. Cyril Connolly (London, 1953), pp. 397-403. See also André Malraux, *L'Espoir* (Paris, 1937), pp. 272-75; Guillermo de Torre, *Tríptico del sacrificio* (Buenos Aires, 1948), pp. 13-14. Hugh Thomas, *The Spanish Civil War* (New York, 1961), has reproduced Portillo's account on pp. 353-55. Emilio Salcedo, in *Vida de Don Miguel* (Salamanca-Madrid-Barcelona, 1964), pp. 407-11, gives a modified account of what happened. Since Portillo's article, there have been many versions.

97. The account is from the chapter "Le Desperado," in Jérôme et Jean Tharaud, *Cruelle Espagne* (Paris, 1937), pp. 233-54. Fragments translated from the original article published in *Candide* (Paris, December 10, 1936), will be found in *Repertorio Americano* of San José de Costa Rica, XXXIII (1937), 12-13. It is also discussed by Eduardo Ortega y Gasset, *Monodiálogos de Don Miguel de Unamuno* (New York, 1958), pp. 244-51.

98. Francisco Madrid, *op. cit.*, p. 252.

99. *Cancionero, OC,* XV, 811.

100. "Prólogo" of José María Ramos Loscertales, "Cuando Miguel de Unamuno murió," to Bartolomé Aragón Gómez, *Síntesis de Economía Corporativa* (Salamanca, 1937), pp. 13-16. The information about Unamuno's burning slipper is given in Ramón Gómez de la Serna, *Retratos contemporáneos* (Buenos Aires, 1944), p. 427. See also Francisco Madrid, *op. cit.*, pp. 252-53.

101. Ramos Loscertales, *op. cit.*, p. 16.

102. Quoted in Unamuno, *OC,* VII, 106.

103. José Ortega y Gasset, "En la muerte de Unamuno," *Obras completas,* V (Madrid, 1958), 266.

104. "Socialism of the Gallows," in *Resistance, Rebellion and Death,* ed. Justin O'Brien (New York, 1961), pp. 170-71.

105. "Disolución de problemas," *OC,* IX, 947.

106. "La Fe de Renán," *OC,* VIII, 1000.

107. *La agonía del cristianismo, OC,* XVI, 462-63.

108. Kierkegaard, *The Point of View for My Work as an Author,* p. 107.

109. André Gide, *Dostoevsky* (Norfolk, Conn., 1961), p. 42.

110. H. Richard Niebuhr, *Christ and Culture* (New York, 1956), p. 68.

111. *Ibid.,* p. 73.

112. Quoted in Vicente Marrero, *El Cristo de Unamuno* (Madrid, 1960), p. 58.

*Chapter Five*

1. "La regeneración del teatro español," *OC,* III, 336-37.

2. "Ibsen y Kierkegaard," *OC,* IV, 426-32.

3. *Soledad, OC,* XII, 611. Although *OC,* XII, contains all the plays of Unamuno, a separate volume, published outside the *Obras completas* as *Teatro completo* (Madrid: Aguilar, 1959) has the added advantage of including all the tales related to the plays, and essays on the dramatic art.

4. "Prólogo" to *Tres novelas ejemplares y un prólogo, OC,* IX, 421.

5. See "Sobre la lujuria," "Sobre la pornografía," "Sobre Don Juan Tenorio," *OC,* III, 468-74, 475-81, 482-90, respectively.

6. Gonzalo Torrente Ballester, *Teatro español contemporáneo* (Madrid, 1957), p. 175.

7. For a definitive listing of Unamuno's short stories, see Eleanor Krane Paucker, *Los cuentos de Unamuno, clave de su obra* (Madrid, 1965); also her definitive edition of his stories in *Miguel de Unamuno. Cuentos,* 2 vols. (Madrid, 1961).

8. Carlos Clavería, "Unamuno y la 'Enfermedad de Flaubert,' " *Temas de Unamuno* (Madrid, 1953), pp. 59-91.

9. "Cientificismo," *OC,* V, 525.

10. "La sociedad galdosiana," *OC,* V, 467; "Galdós en 1901" and "Nuestra impresión de Galdós," *OC,* V, 468-70, 471-74, respectively. Also, "Discurso en al Ateneo de Salamanca en la velada en honor de Don Benito Pérez Galdós con ocasión de su muerte, Noviembre de 1920," *OC,* VII, 958-61. An early scholarly article on Unamuno-Galdós, still of use, is H. Chonon Berkowitz, "Unamuno's Relations with Galdós," *Hispanic Review,* VIII (1940) 321-38.

11. "A lo que salga," *OC,* III, 789-805; "Escritor ovíparo," *OC,* X, 106-9.

12. "Solitaña," *OC,* I, 113-24.

13. "El hombre de la mosca y del colchón," *OC,* V, 985.

14. Juan Arzadun, "Cartas de Miguel de Unamuno," *Sur,* CXIX (Sept., 1944), 51-52. For an excellent discussion of Tolstoy's influence on Unamuno's novel and his thought in general, see C. Marcilly, "Unamuno et Tolstoi," *Bulletin Hispanique,* LXVII (1965), 274-313.

15. Isaiah Berlin, *The Hedgehog and the Fox* (New York, 1957), p. 28.

16. Joseph E. Gillet, "The Autonomous Character in Spanish and

European Literature," *Hispanic Review,* XXIV (1956), 182. Also Ruth House Webber, "Kierkegaard and the Elaboration of Unamuno's *Niebla,*" *Hispanic Review,* XXXII (1964), 118-34.

17. Carlos Clavería, "Sobre el tema de Caín en la obra de Unamuno," *Temas de Unamuno* (Madrid, 1953), p. 104.

18. *Del sentimiento trágico de la vida, OC,* XVI, 182.

19. "La envidia hispánica," *OC,* IV, 419.

20. "Sobre la soberbia," *OC,* III, 806.

21. William James, *The Will to Believe* (New York, 1956), p. 23.

22. "A una aspirante a escritora," *OC,* IV, 718. Also "Nuestras mujeres," *op. cit.,* 702-10.

23. *Vida de Don Quijote y Sancho, OC,* IV, 144.

24. "Las tijeras," *OC,* II, 768-73.

25. "A lo que salga," *OC,* III, 796.

26. "San Pío X," *Visiones y comentarios* (Buenos Aires-Mexico), p. 128.

27. Kierkegaard, *Fear and Trembling* (New York, 1954), p. 30.

28. "Prólogo a la edición española," *La agonía del cristianismo, OC,* XVI, 457.

29. "San Pío X," *op. cit.,* p. 129.

30. "De la correspondencia de un luchador," *OC,* IV, 395.

31. "Francisco de Iturribarría," *OC,* X, 638.

32. John V. Falconieri, "The Sources of Unamuno's *San Manuel Bueno, mártir,*" *Romance Notes,* V, Number 1 (Autumn, 1963), 18-22.

33. *The Myth of Sisyphus and Other Essays,* tr. Justin O'Brien (New York, 1959), p. 83.

34. *La Peste* (Paris, 1947), p. 210.

35. "La España que permanece," *De esto y de aquello,* ed. Manuel García Blanco, III (Buenos Aires, 1953), 574.

36. Kierkegaard, *Concluding Unscientific Postscript,* tr. David F. Swenson and Walter Lowrie (Princeton, 1944), p. 319.

37. "Prólogo" to *Andanzas y visiones españolas, OC,* I, 601.

38. Julián Marías, *Filosofía existencial y existencialismo en España* (Madrid, 1955), p. 163.

39. Germaine Brée and Margaret Guiton, *An Age of Fiction* (New Brunswick, 1957), p. 136.

40. Gonzalo Torrente Ballester, *Panorama de la literatura española contemporánea* (Madrid, 1956), p. 165.

41. "Prólogo a la segunda edición," *Abel Sánchez, OC,* II, 1003.

42. Miguel Cruz Hernández, "La misión socrática de Don Miguel de Unamuno," *Cuadernos de la Cátedra Miguel de Unamuno,* III (1952), 51.

## Chapter Six

1. "Tres cartas de Unamuno a Federico de Onís," *La Torre*, Año IX, XXXV-XXXVI (1961), 59.

2. "Unamuno, poeta," *Teresa, OC,* XIV, 257.

3. José Ferrater Mora, *Unamuno, a Philosophy of Tragedy,* tr. Philip Silver (Berkeley and Los Angeles, 1962), p. 93.

4. Marjorie Grene, *Heidegger* (London, 1957), pp. 106-11.

5. Martin Heidegger, *Introduction to Metaphysics,* tr. Ralph Manheim (New Haven, 1959), p. 145.

6. Antonio Machado, *Juan de Mairena* (Buenos Aires, 1957), I, 162-63.

7. *Unamuno y Maragall, Epistolario y escritos complementarios* (Barcelona, 1951), p. 26.

8. Marjorie Grene, *op. cit.,* p. 109.

9. Gerardo Diego, *Poesía española, Antología (contemporánea)* (Madrid, 1934), p. 56.

10. Antonio Machado, *Juan de Mairena,* II, 142.

11. Unamuno, *Recuerdos de niñez y de mocedad, OC,* I, 302.

12. Guillermo Díaz Plaja, *Modernismo frente a Noventa y Ocho* (Madrid, 1951), p. 156.

13. Manuel García Blanco, *Don Miguel de Unamuno y sus poesías* (Salamanca, 1954), p. 46.

14. "Prólogo al libro *Alma América . Poemas indoespañoles, de José Santos Chocano,"* *OC,* VII, 192.

15. Manuel García Blanco, *Don Miguel de Unamuno y sus poesías* (Salamanca, 1954), p. 167.

16. "La literatura portuguesa contemporánea," *OC,* I, 362.

17. "Religión y patria," *OC,* III, 658.

18. José María Cossío, *Miguel de Unamuno. Antología poética* (Buenos Aires-Mexico, 1946), p. 11.

19. *Del sentimiento trágico de la vida, OC,* XVI, 197. In Spanish, *música celestial* is colloquial for "nonsense."

20. *Epistolário Ibérico. Cartas de Pascoaes e Unamuno* (Nova Lisboa, 1957), p. 50.

21. "El Unamuno censurado," *La Torre,* Año IX, XXXV-XXXVI (1961), 32.

22. Vicente Marrero, *El Cristo de Unamuno* (Madrid, 1960), p. 84.

23. "En Palencia," *OC,* I, 824.

24. *Ibid.,* 825.

25. "Prólogo al libro *Los poemas de la serenidad,* de Ernesto A. Guzmán," *OC,* VII, 301.

26. José Miguel de Azaola, "Las cinco batallas de Unamuno contra la muerte," *Cuadernos de la Cátedra Miguel de Unamuno,* II (1951), 105.

27. "La Fe," *OC,* XVI, 101.

28. Concha Zardoya, *Poesía española contemporánea* (Madrid, 1961), p. 166.

29. *The Poem Itself,* ed. Stanley Burnshaw (New York, 1960), p. 69. I lean heavily on the excellent *explication de texte* made of this poem by Juan Marichal.

30. Julián Marías, *Miguel de Unamuno* (Buenos Aires-Mexico, 1950), pp. 129-30.

31. Rubén Darío, *op. cit.,* 263.

32. The reader should be advised that *De Fuerteventura a París* and *Romancero del destierro* contained in *OC,* XIV, are not complete. The original editions are: *De Fuerteventura a París. Diario íntimo de confinamiento y destierro vertido en sonetos* (Paris: Excelsior, 1925) and *Romancero del destierro* (Buenos Aires: Editorial Alba, 1928).

33. Manuel García Blanco, *op. cit.,* p. 344.

34. *Ibid.,* p. 343.

35. *Ibid.*

36. L. F. Vivanco, *Introducción a la poesía española moderna* (Madrid, 1957), p. 20.

37. *Ibid.,* p. 21.

38. *Obras completas de Rubén Darío, Epistolario,* ed. Alberto Ghiraldo (Madrid, n. d.), I, 166-67.

39. "Lujuria de dolor," *OC,* XI, 442.

40. *Cómo se hace una novela, OC,* X, 886-87. The words are from *Soledades,* II, line 75.

41. Benjamín Carrión, *San Miguel de Unamuno* (Quito, 1954), p. 15.

42. Federico Sopeña, *Música y antimúsica en Unamuno* (Madrid, 1965), p. 19.

43. Manuel García Blanco, "El poeta uruguayo Zorrilla de San Martín," *América y Unamuno* (Madrid, 1964), p. 82.

44. Of the many essays written on Unamuno's opinions of Rubén Darío, the following are recommended: Manuel García Blanco, "Rubén Darío y Unamuno," *ibid.,* pp. 53-74; Antonio Oliver Belmás, *Este otro Rubén Darío* (Barcelona, 1960), pp. 156-67; Philip Metzidakis, "Unamuno frente a la poesía de Rubén Darío," *Revista Iberoamericana,* XXV (1960), 229-49; José Luis Cano, "Unamuno y Rubén Darío," *Poesía española del siglo XX* (Madrid, 1960), pp. 15-27. In his article, "¡Hay que ser justo y bueno, Rubén!" *OC,* VIII, 518-23, Unamuno makes public admission of his unfairness towards the Nicaraguan poet.

45. Hernán Benítez, *El drama religioso de Unamuno* (Buenos Aires, 1949), p. 378.

46. Camille Pitollet, "Notas unamunescas," *Cuadernos de la Cátedra Miguel de Unamuno,* IV (1953), 24.

47. Azorín (José Martínez Ruiz), *Madrid* (Buenos Aires, 1952), p. 31.

48. José María Valverde, "Notas sobre la poesía de Unamuno," *Primeras Jornadas de Lengua y Literatura Hispanoamericana,* Filosofía y Letras, Tomo X, núm. 2 (Salamanca, 1956), 239.

49. José María Cossío, *op. cit.,* p. 16.

50. Dámaso Alonso, *Poetas españoles contemporáneos* (Madrid, 1952), p. 394.

## Chapter Seven

1. José Ortega y Gasset, "Sobre los estudios clásicos," *Obras completas,* I (Madrid, 1957), 64.

2. José Ortega y Gasset, "Sobre una apología de la inexactitud," *ibid.,* 118.

3. Emilio Salcedo, "Unamuno y Ortega y Gasset; diálogo entre dos españoles," *Cuadernos de la Cátedra Miguel de Unamuno,* VII (1956), 104.

Aside from Salcedo's excellent article on the subject of Unamuno and Ortega, the following are also recommended: Nemesio González Caminero, "Unamuno y Ortega," *Unamuno* (Comillas, 1948), pp. 363-85; by the same author, "Circunstancia y personalidad de Unamuno y Ortega," *Gregorianum,* XLI, 2 (1960), 201-39; Julián Marías, *Ortega, I, Circunstancia y vocación* (Madrid, 1960), pp. 149-62; José Luis Abellán, *Ortega y Gasset en la filosofía española* (Madrid, 1966), pp. 89-106.

4. José Ortega y Gasset, "Unamuno y Europa, Fábula," *Obras completas,* I (Madrid, 1957), 128-32.

5. José Ortega y Gasset, "Renán," *ibid.,* 443-44.

6. "La supuesta anormalidad española," *OC,* IV, 1104.

7. Salcedo, *op. cit.,* 109-10.

8. José Ortega y Gasset, *Meditaciones del Quijote, Obras completas,* I (Madrid, 1957), 326-27.

9. José Ortega y Gasset, "En la muerte de Unamuno," *Obras completas,* V (Madrid, 1958), 264-66.

10. Pedro Salinas, *Ensayos de literatura hispánica* (Madrid, 1958), p. 316.

11. Juan Arzadun, "Miguel de Unamuno, íntimo," *Sur,* CXIX (Sept., 1944), p. 110.

12. "Sobre la consecuencia, la sinceridad," *OC,* III, 1055.

220 MIGUEL DE UNAMUNO

13. H. R. Romero Flores, *Unamuno* (Madrid, 1941), p. 38. Quoted in Vicente Marrero, *El Cristo de Unamuno* (Madrid, 1960), p. 263. I lean heavily on Marrero's listing of critical opinions.

14. Agustín Esclasans, *Miguel de Unamuno* (Buenos Aires, 1947), p. 147.

15. Julián Marías, *Miguel de Unamuno* (Buenos Aires-Mexico, 1950), p. 156.

16. Alain Guy, "Miguel de Unamuno, pèlerin de l'Absolu," *Cuadernos de la Cátedra Miguel de Unamuno*, I (1948), 74-102.

17. José Luis L. Aranguren, *Catolicismo y protestantismo como formas de existencia* (Madrid, 1963), pp. 198-99.

18. Joan Corominas, "Correspondance entre Miguel de Unamuno et Père Corominas," *Bulletin Hispanique*, LXII (1960), 72. Corominas's own italics. The actual article from which this quotation is taken is "La fin tragique de Miguel de Unamuno," pp. 68-76, included in the first reference above, and was translated into French from the original Catalan published in the *Revista de Catalunya*, LXXXIII (1938), 155-70. The original article was first translated into Castilian as "El trágico fin de Miguel de Unamuno," *Atenea*, LIII (1938), 101-14; it was retranslated into French because, as Joan Corominas, son of the writer, says, it is full of errors. See also, the first part of the "Correspondance," *Bulletin Hispanique*, LXI (1959), 386-436.

19. A. Sánchez Barbudo, *Estudios sobre Unamuno y Machado* (Madrid, 1959).

20. Antonio Sánchez Barbudo and Hernán Benítez, "La fe religiosa de Unamuno y su crisis de 1897," *Revista de la Universidad de Buenos Aires*, XVIII (1951), 442.

21. Armando F. Zubizarreta, "Miguel de Unamuno y Pedro Corominas," *Tras las huellas de Unamuno* (Madrid, 1960), pp. 153-95.

22. Henry Daniel-Rops, *Carte d'Europe* (Paris, 1928), p. 153.

23. Marrero, *op. cit.*, p. 248.

24. *Epistolario a Clarín*, ed. Adolfo Alas (Madrid, 1941), p. 54.

25. Ernst Robert Curtius, "Unamuno," *Kritische Essays zur Europäischen Literatur* (Bern, 1950), pp. 245-46.

26. Kierkegaard, *Concluding Unscientific Postscript*, tr. David F. Swenson and Walter Lowrie (Princeton, 1944), p. 346.

27. "A mis lectores," *OC*, IV, 579.

28. Curtius, *op. cit.*, p. 245.

29. *Alrededor del estilo*, *OC*, XI, 796.

30. *Niebla*, *OC*, II, 787.

31. "España y los españoles," *OC*, IV, 1081.

32. Amando Lázaro Ros, "Unamuno, filósofo existencialista," appended to Marjorie Grene, *El sentimiento trágico de la existencia (Existencialismo y existencialistas)*, tr. Amando Lázaro Ros (Madrid,

1952), p. 221. The original book by Marjorie Grene is *Dreadful Freedom. A Critique of Existentialism.*

33. James Brown, *Subject and Object in Modern Theology* (New York, 1955), p. 14.

34. "Francisco de Iturribarría," *OC*, X, 637.

35. "El dolor de pensar," *OC*, X, 318.

36. *De la correspondencia de Miguel de Unamuno*, ed. García Blanco (New York, 1957), p. 12. Also in García Blanco, *En torno a Unamuno* (Madrid, 1965), p. 230.

37. José Ferrater Mora, *Unamuno, A Philosophy of Tragedy,* tr. Philip Silver (Berkeley and Los Angeles, 1962), p. vii.

38. Carlos Blanco Aguinaga, *El Unamuno contemplativo* (Mexico, 1959), p. 288.

39. Charles Williams, *The Descent of the Dove* (New York, 1956), p. 31.

40. *San Manuel Bueno, mártir, OC,* XVI, 620.

41. Karl Jaspers, *Reason and Existenz* (New York, 1955), pp. 128-29.

42. Juan Marichal, *La voluntad de estilo* (Barcelona, 1957), p. 257.

# Selected Bibliography

A. Bibliographies

ONÍS, FEDERICO DE. "Bibliografía de Miguel de Unamuno." *La Torre* (*Revista General de la Universidad de Puerto Rico*), Año IX, núms. XXXV-XXXVI (1961), 601-36.

FOSTER, DAVID WM. "Adiciones y suplemento a la bibliografía de Unamuno," *ibid.*, Año XII, núm. XLVIII (1964), 165-72.

GARCÍA BLANCO, MANUEL. "Crónica unamuniana," *Cuadernos de la Cátedra Miguel de Unamuno* (Universidad de Salamanca), I-XIX. Volume XVII has no such section, and in XVIII and XIX it is called "Bibliografía unamuniana." The best ongoing bibliography available.

B. Primary Sources

*Obras completas* (Madrid: Vergara Editorial, por concesión especial de Afrodisio Aguado, 1959-1964). Sixteen volumes edited with prologues and notes by Manuel García Blanco. This edition is being reprinted in another format by Editorial Escelicer of Madrid in ten volumes. The *Obras completas* are, however, lacking some of the articles which may be found in posthumous collections whose titles are contained in the Chronology at the beginning of this volume, and in excerpts in Elías Díaz, *Unamuno, pensamiento político* (Madrid: Tecnos, 1965). In Rafael Pérez de la Dehesa, *Política y sociedad en el primer Unamuno* (Madrid: Ciencia Nueva, 1966), pp. 177-95, there is a title listing of 178 of Unamuno's uncollected articles. The articles contributed by Unamuno during his exile to *España con honra* and *Hojas libres* have not been collected.

C. Correspondence

Of Unamuno's voluminous correspondence, little of which is contained in the *Obras completas* (except for some excerpts and letters written by him concerning his *Cancionero* or *Book of Songs* in Volume XV, 821-934), the following letters are recommended as indispensable to an understanding of the author.

NOSOTROS (Buenos Aires), XLV (1923), 520-21. The letter which was the immediate cause of Unamuno's exile. Reproduced in Francisco Madrid, *Genio e ingenio de Miguel de Unamuno* (Buenos Aires: Aniceto López, 1943), pp. 70-71. Also *Living Age* (Boston), CCCXXI (1924), 681-82.

URALES, FRANCISCO. *La evolución de la filosofía en España* (Barcelona: Ediciones de la Revista Blanca, 1934), II, 203-13. A very revealing letter from Unamuno to Urales.

EPISTOLARIO A CLARÍN, ed. Adolfo Alas (Madrid: Ediciones Escorial, 1941).

CANDAMO, BERNARDO G. DE, ed. "Unamuno en sus cartas (Antología epistolar comentada)," *Miguel de Unamuno. Ensayos* (Madrid: Aguilar, 1942), II, 9-68.

SUR (Buenos Aires), CXVII (July, 1944), 7-11; CXIX (Sept., 1944), 33-61; CXX (October, 1944), 55-70. The first item contains two letters to Elvira Rezzo de Henriksen, the other two some important letters to Juan Arzadun.

GHIRALDO, ALBERTO, ed. *El archivo de Rubén Darío* (Buenos Aires: Losada, 1943), pp. 29-46. Letters to Rubén Darío.

BENÍTEZ, HERNÁN. *El drama religioso de Unamuno* (Buenos Aires: Universidad de Buenos Aires, 1949). Pp. 195-458 contain "Cartas a Pedro Jiménez Ilundain."

————, ed. "Doce cartas a González Trilla," *Revista de la Universidad de Buenos Aires*, XVI (1950), 535-51.

UNAMUNO Y MARAGALL, EPISTOLARIO Y ESCRITOS COMPLEMENTARIOS (Barcelona: Edimar, 1951).

"LETTRES À JEAN CASSOU," *Cahiers du Sud* (Marseille), XLI (1954), 390-98.

EPISTOLÁRIO IBÉRICO. CARTAS DE PASCOAES E UNAMUNO (Nova Lisboa: Cámara Municipal de Nova Lisboa, 1957).

"CARTAS A BOGDAN RADITSA," *Cuadernos* (Paris), XXXIV (1959), 51-56.

COROMINÁS, JOAN. "Correspondance entre Miguel de Unamuno et Père Corominas," *Bulletin Hispanique* (Bordeaux), LXI (1959), 386-436; LXII (1960), 42-77.

"EL UNAMUNO CENSURADO," *La Torre* (*Revista General de la Universidad de Puerto Rico*), Año IX, núms. XXXV-XXXVI (1961), 21-54. Also "Tres cartas a Federico de Onís," *ibid.*, 56-62.

BADANELLI, PEDRO, ed. *13 Cartas inéditas de Miguel de Unamuno a Alberto Nin Frías* (Buenos Aires: Editorial "La Mandrágora," 1962).

"EPISTOLARIO ENTRE UNAMUNO Y ORTEGA," *Revista de Occidente*, Año II, 2 ép., No. XIX (1964), 3-28.

NUEZ, SEBASTIÁN DE LA. *Unamuno en Canarias* (Santa Cruz de Tenerife: Universidad de La Laguna, 1964), pp. 283-91. Letters to Ramón Castañeyra.

————, ed. "Cartas de Unamuno a Galdós," *Papeles de Son Armadans* (Madrid-Palma de Mallorca), Año X, Tomo XXXVII, Núm. CX (May, 1965), 144-78.

GARCÍA BLANCO, MANUEL, ed. "Unas cartas de Unamuno y de Pérez de Ayala," *Papeles de Son Armadans* (Madrid-Palma de Mallorca), Año X, Tomo XXXVIII, Núm. CXIV (Sept., 1965), 236-54.

FERNÁNDEZ LARRAÍN, SERGIO, ed. *Cartas inéditas de Miguel de Unamuno* (Santiago de Chile: Zig-Zag, 1965). Extremely informative letters to Pedro de Mugica.

TARÍN-IGLESIAS, JOSÉ. *Unamuno y sus amigos catalanes* (Barcelona: Editorial Peñíscola, 1966), pp. 111-93. Letters to Santiago Valenti Camps.

D. Translations

*Abel Sánchez and Other Stories,* tr. Anthony Kerrigan (Chicago: Henry Regnery, 1956).

*The Agony of Christianity,* tr. Kurt F. Reinhart (New York: Frederick Ungar, 1960).

*The Christ of Velazquez,* tr. Eleanor L. Turnbull (Baltimore: Johns Hopkins Press, 1951).

*Essays and Soliloquies,* tr. J. E. Crawford Flitch (New York, A. A. Knopf, 1925).

*Mist: A Tragi-Comic Novel,* tr. Warner Fite (New York, A. A. Knopf, 1928).

*Our Lord Don Quixote (The Life of Don Quixote and Sancho with Sixteen Essays),* tr. Anthony Kerrigan (Princeton: Princeton University Press for Bollingen Foundation, 1967). First volume in a series of seven, called *Selected Works of Miguel de Unamuno,* ed. Anthony Kerrigan and Martin Nozick.

*Perplexities and Paradoxes,* tr. Stuart Gross (New York: Philosophical Library, 1945).

*Poems by Miguel de Unamuno,* tr. Eleanor L. Turnbull (Baltimore: Johns Hopkins Press, 1952).

*The Tragic Sense of Life,* ed. J. E. Crawford Flitch (New York: Dover Publications, 1954).

*Three Exemplary Novels and a Prologue,* tr. Angel Flores (New York: Grove Press, 1956).

E. Secondary Sources

ABELLÁN, JOSE. *Unamuno a la luz de la psicología* (Madrid: Tecnos, 1964). Unamuno's egocentrism is the psychological "error" that counteracts the philosophical import of his work.

ALBERICH, JOSÉ. "Sobre el positivismo de Unamuno," *Cuadernos de la Cátedra Miguel de Unamuno,* IX (1959), 61-75. Very good for the impact of Spencer and Darwin on Unamuno.

ALBORNOZ, AURORA DE. *La presencia de Miguel de Unamuno en Antonio Machado* (Madrid: Gredos, 1968). Exhaustive study of every facet of the relations between both writers.

ARANGUREN, JOSÉ LUIS L. *Catolicismo y protestantismo como formas de existencia* (Madrid: Revista de Occidente, 1963). Stimulating, professional treatment of Unamuno's "religious disposition" on pp. 193-211.

AZAOLA, JOSÉ MIGUEL. "Las cinco batallas de Unamuno contra la muerte," *Cuadernos de la Cátedra Miguel de Unamuno*, II (1951), 33-109. How Unamuno tried to overcome death.

BALSEIRO, JOSÉ A. *Blasco Ibáñez, Unamuno, Valle-Inclán, Baroja. Cuatro individualistas de España* (Chapel Hill: U. of North Carolina Press, 1949). Chapter on Unamuno good for information.

BASDEKIS, DEMETRIOS. *Unamuno and Spanish Literature* (Berkeley and Los Angeles: U. of Calif. Press, 1967).

BENÍTEZ, HERNÁN. *El drama religioso de Unamuno* (Buenos Aires: Universidad de Buenos Aires, 1949). Contains indispensable letters to Pedro Jiménez Ilundain.

BLANCO AGUINAGA, CARLOS. *El Unamuno contemplativo* (Mexico: Publicaciones de la Nueva Revista de Filología Hispánica, 1959). The other, "non-agonic" Unamuno.

————. "El socialismo de Unamuno: 1894-1897," *Revista de Occidente*, XLI (1966), 166-84. Unamuno's Marxist period, with some indications of Hegel's influence.

————. "De nuevo: El socialismo de Unamuno (1894-1897)," *Cuadernos de la Cátedra Miguel de Unamuno*, XVIII (1968), 5-48. More on Unamuno's socialism.

CLAVERÍA, CARLOS. *Temas de Unamuno* (Madrid: Gredos, 1953). Very important essays on Unamuno and Carlyle, Flaubert, the Cain and Abel theme.

COLLADO, JESUS ANTONIO. *Kierkegaard y Unamuno. La existencia religiosa* (Madrid: Gredos, 1962). Most comprehensive treatment of parallels and relations.

CUADERNOS DE LA CÁTEDRA MIGUEL DE UNAMUNO. Nineteen issues thus far, starting with 1948, published by the University of Salamanca. The best way to keep abreast of the continuing Unamuno bibliography.

DÍAZ, ELÍAS. *Revisión de Unamuno* (Madrid: Tecnos, 1968). Excellent treatment of Unamuno's political thought, showing him to be essentially an "elitist."

EARLE, PETER G. *Unamuno and English Literature* (New York: Hispanic Institute, 1960).

FERNÁNDEZ, PELAYO H. *El problema de la personalidad en Unamuno y San Manuel Bueno* (Madrid: Mayfe, 1966). Keen analysis of Unamunian question of the "self," and of the symbols of his last novel.

————. *Miguel de Unamuno y William James, un paralelo pragmático* (Salamanca, 1961).

FERNÁNDEZ TURIENZO, F. *Unamuno, ansia de Dios y creación literaria* (Madrid: Ediciones Alcalá, 1966). Good on the metaphysics of *The Tragic Sense of Life.*

FERRATER MORA, JOSÉ. *Unamuno, a Philosophy of Tragedy,* tr. Philip Silver (Berkeley and Los Angeles: U. of Calif. Press, 1962). Revised edition of *Unamuno: Bosquejo de una filosofía,* and an excellent introduction to the entire matter.

GARCÍA BLANCO, MANUEL. "Unamuno, traductor y amigo de José Lázaro," *Revista de Occidente,* XIX (1964), 97-120. Very important for Unamuno's translations.

————. *Don Miguel de Unamuno y sus poesías* (Salamanca, 1954). An uncritical mine of information on Unamuno's poetry.

————. *América y Unamuno* (Madrid: Gredos, 1964). Essays on Unamuno and American writers.

————. *En torno a Unamuno* (Madrid: Taurus, 1965). A collection of dispersed essays full of indispensable data.

GARCÍA MOREJÓN, JULIO. *Unamuno y Portugal* (Madrid: Ediciones Cultura Hispánica, 1964). Extremely important study of Unamuno's relation with the neighboring country he loved.

GONZÁLEZ CAMINERO, NEMESIO. *Unamuno* (Comillas, Santander: Universidad Pontificia, 1948). Fair discussion of Unamuno's thought by a Jesuit.

GRANJEL, LUIS S. *Retrato de Unamuno* (Madrid: Guadarrama, 1957). Extremely readable and sensible.

GULLÓN, RICARDO. *Autobiografías de Unamuno* (Madrid: Gredos, 1964). Unhurried, close reading of all of Unamuno's fiction, sometimes making much of little.

HUARTE MORTON, FERNANDO. "El ideario lingüístico de Miguel de Unamuno," *Cuadernos de la Cátedra Miguel de Unamuno,* V (1954), 5-183. Unamuno and language.

ILIE, PAUL. *Unamuno. An Existential View of Self and Society* (Madison: The Univ. of Wisconsin Press, 1967). Valuable discussions of Unamuno and Nietzsche and of Unamuno's treatment of Old Testament myths.

LAÍN ENTRALGO, PEDRO. *La generación del Noventa y Ocho.* (Buenos Aires-Mexico: Espasa-Calpe Argentina, 1947). Still a basic book on Unamuno and his generation.

LIVINGSTONE, LEON. "Unamuno and the Aesthetic of the Novel," *Hispania,* XXIV (1941), 442-50. Very good, succinct discussion.

LÓPEZ-MORILLAS, JUAN. "Unamuno and Pascal: Notes on the Concept of Agony," *PMLA,* LXV (1950), 998-1010. Included in

*Intelectuales y espirituales* (Madrid: Revista de Occidente, 1961), pp. 41-69.

MADRID, FRANCISCO. *Genio e ingenio de Miguel de Unamuno* (Buenos Aires: Aniceto López, 1943). Full of revealing information not available elsewhere.

MARÍAS, JULIÁN. *Miguel de Unamuno* (Buenos Aires-Mexico: Espasa-Calpe Argentina, 1950). Still one of the most solid studies.

————. *Filosofía actual y existencialismo en España* (Madrid: Revista de Occidente, 1955). Contains essays on Unamuno's thought and fiction.

MARICHAL, JUAN. *La voluntad de estilo* (Barcelona: Seix Barral, 1957). Chapts. X and XI concern themselves with Unamuno and Spain, and Unamuno's originality in confessional literature.

MARRERO, VICENTE. *El Cristo de Unamuno* (Madrid: Rialp, 1960). On Unamuno's Christology, by a traditionalist author.

MEYER, FRANÇOIS. *L'ontologie de Miguel de Unamuno* (Paris: Presses Universitaires, 1955).

MOELLER, CHARLES. "Miguel de Unamuno et l'espoir désespéré," *Littérature du XXe siècle et Christianisme* (Tournai: Casterman, 1960), IV, 45-146. Valuable for quotations from the unpublished *Diario*.

————. *Textos inéditos de Unamuno,* tr. Alberto Colas (Cartagena: Athenas Ediciones, 1965). Further commentary on quotations from the *Diario*.

ORTEGA Y GASSET, EDUARDO. *Monodiálogos de Don Miguel de Unamuno* (New York: Ibérica Publishing Co., 1958). Remembrances of Unamuno in exile, to be used with caution.

ORTEGA Y GASSET, JOSÉ. "Unamuno y Europa, Fábula," *Obras Completas* (Madrid: Revista de Occidente), I (1957), 128-32. Interesting for Ortega's criticism of Unamuno.

————. "En la muerte de Unamuno," *ibid.,* V (1958), 264-66. Ortega's eulogy on Unamuno's death.

OTERO, C. P. "Unamuno and Cervantes," *Unamuno, Creator and Creation,* ed. José Rubia Barcia and M. A. Zeitlin (Berkeley and Los Angeles: Univ. of Calif. Press, 1967), pp. 171-87. A refreshingly independent denunciation of Unamuno's intellectual sins.

PARÍS, CARLOS. *Unamuno. Estructura de su mundo intelectual* (Barcelona: Ediciones Península, 1968). Wordy, but good on the comparison between Unamuno and Teilhard de Chardin.

PAUCKER, ELEANOR KRANE. *Los cuentos de Unamuno, clave de su obra* (Madrid: Minotauro, 1965). A complete account of the short stories.

PÉREZ DE LA DEHESA, RAFAEL. *Política y sociedad en el primer Una-*

*muno* (Madrid: Ciencia Nueva, 1966). A sober study of Unamuno's connections with socialist thought.

PORTILLO, LUIS. "Unamuno's Last Lecture," *The Golden Horizon,* ed. Cyril Connolly (London: Weidenfeld and Nicolson, 1953), pp. 397-403. An account of the October 12, 1936 occurrence.

REGALADO GARCÍA, ANTONIO. *El siervo y el señor* (Madrid: Gredos, 1968). Unamuno as atheist, conservative, rationalist.

RUDD, MARGARET R. *The Lone Heretic. A Biography of Miguel de Unamuno y Jugo* (Austin: U. of Texas Press, 1963). The only biography in English, to be used with extreme caution.

SALCEDO, EMILIO. "Unamuno y Ortega y Gasset; diálogo entre dos españoles," *Cuadernos de la Cátedra Miguel de Unamuno,* VII (1956), 97-130. The most comprehensive account of the relations between the two thinkers.

———. *Vida de Don Miguel* (Madrid, Barcelona: Ediciones Anaya, 1964). The most complete, reliable biography thus far.

SÁNCHEZ BARBUDO, ANTONIO, and BENÍTEZ, HERNÁN. "La fe religiosa de Unamuno y su crisis de 1897: Dúplica a Hernán Benítez por Antonio Sánchez Barbudo y Tríplica a Antonio Sánchez Barbudo por Hernán Benítez," *Revista de la Universidad de Buenos Aires,* XVIII (1951), 381-443. Polemic over Sánchez Barbudo's opinion of Unamuno as an atheist.

———. *Estudios sobre Unamuno y Machado* (Madrid: Guadarrama, 1959). Admirable essays on Unamuno, open to rebuttal, but indispensable.

———. "The Faith of Unamuno. The Unpublished Diary," *Unamuno, Centennial Studies,* ed. Ramón Martínez-López (Department of Romance Languages, The University of Texas, 1966), pp. 130-65. A first-rate analysis of Unamuno's moods at the time of the writing of the *Diario.*

SENDER, RAMÓN J. *Unamuno, Valle-Inclán, Baroja y Santayana* (Mexico: Colección Studium, 1955). Interesting disparagement of Unamuno.

SERRANO PONCELA, S. *El pensamiento de Unamuno* (Mexico: Fondo de Cultura Económica, 1953). Excellent review of Unamuno's thought.

SOBEJANO, GONZALO. *Nietzsche en España* (Madrid: Gredos, 1967), pp. 276-318. The author proves that Unamuno knew Nietzsche better than he cared to confess, and admirably demonstrates the affinities between both men.

TURIN, YVONNE. *Miguel de Unamuno universitaire* (Paris: S.E.V. P.E.N., 1962). Unamuno on and in the university.

ZARDOYA, CONCHA. "La 'Humanación' en la poesía de Unamuno," *Poesía española contemporánea* (Madrid: Guadarrama, 1961), pp. 91-178. Themes and techniques in Unamuno's poetry.

ZAVALA, IRIS M. *Unamuno y su teatro de conciencia* (Salamanca, 1963). Uncritical but minute analysis of all the plays.

ZUBIZARRETA, ARMANDO F. *Tras las huellas de Unamuno* (Madrid: Taurus, 1960). Collection of essays, mainly concerned with the early Unamuno, and his religious crisis.

————. *Unamuno en su "Nivola"* (Madrid: Taurus, 1960). Mainly on *Cómo se hace una novela,* but generally valuable.

# *Index*